D1576169

Ann Rule worked the late-night shift at a suicide hotline with a handsome, whip-smart psychology major who became her close friend. Soon the world would know him: Ted Bundy, one of the most savage serial killers of our time. . . .

THE STRANGER BESIDE ME
Now in an updated edition!

"Shattering . . . written with compassion but also with professional objectivity."
—*Seattle Times*

"Overwhelming!"
—*The Houston Post*

"Ann Rule has an extraordinary angle [on] the most fascinating killer in modern American history. . . . As dramatic and chilling as a bedroom window shattering at midnight."
—*The New York Times*

HEART FULL OF LIES

"A convincing portrait of a meticulous criminal mind."
—*The Washington Post*

"Fascinating. . . . The sheer weight of [Rule's] investigative technique places her at the forefront of true-crime writers."
—*Booklist*

EVERY BREATH YOU TAKE

"Affecting, tense, and smart true crime."
—*The Washington Post Book World*

"Absolutely riveting . . . psychologically perceptive."
—*Booklist*

Books by Ann Rule

In the Still of the Night
Too Late to Say Goodbye
Green River, Running Red
Every Breath You Take
Heart Full of Lies
. . . And Never Let Her Go
Bitter Harvest
Dead by Sunset
Everything She Ever Wanted
If You Really Loved Me
The Stranger Beside Me
Possession
Small Sacrifices

Ann Rule's Crime Files

Vol. 15: Don't Look Behind You and Other True Cases
Vol. 14: But I Trusted You and Other True Cases
Vol. 13: Mortal Danger and Other True Cases
Vol. 12: Smoke, Mirrors, and Murder and Other
True Cases
Vol. 11: No Regrets and Other True Cases
Vol. 10: Worth More Dead and Other True Cases
Vol. 9: Kiss Me, Kill Me and Other True Cases
Vol. 8: Last Dance, Last Chance and Other True Cases
Vol. 7: Empty Promises and Other True Cases
Vol. 6: A Rage to Kill and Other True Cases
Vol. 5: The End of the Dream and Other True Cases
Vol. 4: In the Name of Love and Other True Cases
Vol. 3: A Fever in the Heart and Other True Cases
Vol. 2: You Belong to Me and Other True Cases
Vol. 1: A Rose for Her Grave and Other True Cases

Without Pity: Ann Rule's Most Dangerous Killers

The 1-5 Killer
The Want-Ad Killer
Lust Killer

ANN RULE

FATAL FRIENDS, DEADLY NEIGHBORS

AND OTHER TRUE CASES

ANN RULE'S CRIME FILES: Vol. 16

POCKET BOOKS

New York   London   Toronto   Sydney   New Delhi

Pocket Books
A Division of Simon & Schuster, Inc.
1230 Avenue of the Americas
New York, NY 10020

The names of some individuals have been changed. Such names are indicated by an asterisk (*) the first time each appears in the narrative.

POCKET and colophon are registered trademarks of Simon & Schuster, Inc.

Manufactured in the United States of America

ISBN 978-1-62090-922-5

*For Susan, Charlie, Braden, Max, Becky,
Opal, Burle, Marci, Nadine, Sonia, Dina, Sue Ann,
Kit, Rose, Jeffery, and Wendy.*

*In the hope that losing you and your innocence
will teach us to save others.*

Contents

ix

CONTENTS

Introduction

Most murder victims know their killers. Some were afraid of the stalkers who would one day rob them of their very lives; some had no idea of the danger that waited quietly for them. Stranger-to-stranger homicides are committed by serial killers and rapists, or during the process of other crimes such as armed robbery or violent home invasions.

Still, the last face the majority of murder victims see is that of someone they know—intimately or casually. And so superior detectives look first for connections, the interweaving of lives that may have led to homicide. Those who are naïve and inexperienced prefer to believe that they can discern some hidden menace in those who intersect their paths.

I used to think that. Now, I look back and see how smug I was when I believed I was foolproof. I had many courses in abnormal and criminal psychology at the University of Washington. After I graduated, I worked at Hillcrest, the Oregon State girls' reformatory, was a Seattle police officer, and studied for weeks in basic homicide investigation school. I have both attended and lectured at scores of law enforcement seminars, and I've pored over what seems like miles of police reports to research thirty-three books and over a thousand articles on criminal cases. After so many years of writing about true crimes, I still haven't been able to grow a thick enough emotional hide so that tragic stories don't affect me. And I'm glad that I haven't; black humor abounds in the homicide units I visit when I'm researching a book—but I know the detectives there joke to keep from crying. The sadder the case, the more they joke.

It never means they don't care. And I have never reached a place where I don't care deeply for the people I write about. But I am also an avid student of human behavior, always wondering how and why lives interconnect in scenarios that end in violence.

Despite all that, as the years have passed, I have come to realize how limited my own powers of perception are when it comes to *really* knowing what someone else may be thinking . . . or hiding.

In this book, the sixteenth in my Crime Files series, I relate some of the weirdest and the most chilling cases I have ever come across. Some are recent, even current. There are others that I first came across three decades ago. The first two investigations are novella length.

The first case is "Fire and Ice: The Powell Family Tragedy." This began with the baffling disappearance of Susan Powell from her Utah home in December 2009. A blizzard raged outside on the last night anyone saw Susan.

The main "person of interest" in this case was her own husband, the father of their two small boys.

Months ago, I promised Susan Powell's parents that I would write her story, and I am honoring that promise. None of us knew then how horrifically the Powell story would play out in 2012. Had I known, I probably would not have attempted it.

The second case—"Two Strange Deaths in Coronado"—is only a year and a half old, and it raises the question of why the San Diego County Sheriff's Office closed their July 2011 death investigation after only seven weeks. There are myriad theories on how and why Maxfield Shacknai, six, and Rebecca Zahau, thirty-two, perished in a billionaire's mansion in Coronado, California, within forty-eight hours. Are any of these possibilities the true story?

I don't have all the answers. I cannot tell you exactly what happened over the course of a few black days in sunny Coronado. I can only share with you what I have managed to glean. This case made sweeping headlines and was the subject of numerous newspaper articles and television and radio reports, as well as a surge of gossip in the popular resort area where it took place.

And then, almost as suddenly as it happened, Max's and Becky's deaths faded to newspapers' inside pages and from the top of the news, only to be quickly replaced by other mysteries, leaving family members of the deceased with an overwhelming sense of emptiness.

I am still wondering what could possibly have happened to two very unlikely victims. And I am not the only one still pursuing answers in a baffling case that cries out for a final chapter.

"Double Death for the Kind Philanthropists" explores the deaths of two lifetime philanthropists. It is such a sad case for almost everyone involved that it still haunts me.

"Fire!" tells the story of a real-life towering inferno, the end result of a dangerous arsonist's fantasies. No one was safe in the many-storied hotel, and the casualty count could have been disastrous. When the smoke and flames were finally extinguished, the prime suspect was *most* unlikely.

In the case I've titled "An Obsession with Blondes," I cover a serial rapist's lust and deception as he carefully targeted his victims. He found them in seemingly safe venues, but he took them to locations where they were ultimately vulnerable. Luckily, an astute Oregon detective proved to be an adversary he could not overcome.

"The Last Valentine's Day" recounts an inexplicable tragedy that took place back in the seventies and was eventually stored away in cold-case files as unsolved, and probably unsolvable.

Until recently.

After a very long time, one of several suspects I wrote about at the time of the crime finally emerged as the real killer of a trusting sixteen-year-old girl.

"The Man Who Loved Too Much" describes a murder case that embodies the familiar—and selfish—threat, "If I can't have you, then no one can!" Those words can be an idle warning, but too often they are voiced by someone who means every word. Human beings are not possessions to be caught in an inescapable net. In this case, what once was love gradually became desperate entrapment for a frightened woman named Sue Ann.

"Terror on a Mountain Trail" pits a highly trained and powerful military man against two vulnerable women. A member of the U.S. Army's elite 75th Ranger Regiment, the stalker may have killed more women, including an airline ticket clerk who left her job one day and has never been seen again. As I traced this Ranger's life since, I was surprised at what I found—and concerned for all women who fail to realize the perils of being alone where human predators watch them.

"No One Knows Where Wendy Is" is about every parent's worst nightmare. All too often, people who seem to be safe, kind, and trustworthy are anything but. After *Small Sacrifices,* I vowed that I would never again write about the death of children, but there are some cases where I *need* to write cautionary tales that may save other children. Wendy's story is one. Susan Powell's sons' fate is another.

Over time, many of the unsolved cases that I believed would never come to a satisfactory conclusion *have* been closed successfully. Often, the person or persons arrested were the last individuals I—and the initial investigators—suspected. After the fact, they make complete sense as all the gears mesh and physical evidence provides proof. It wasn't nearly this easy from the other side.

The emergence of DNA testing and advanced forensic science in general are primarily responsible for these latter-day arrests and convictions. We can also thank the cold-case squads that have been added to major crime units in larger police departments throughout America.

One of the earliest theorems in the art of solving homicide cases is that the chance of a successful conclusion diminishes in direct proportion to the passage of time. If a murder isn't solved in the first forty-eight hours, chances are that it never will be. That is still true today, but detectives who investigate murder have more of a head start now.

Sherlock Holmes—if he were real and not fictional— would be amazed by the new tools that can track and trap killers. Still, I don't count out the homicide detectives whom I wrote about back in the day when I had to use my male pen name: *Andy Stack.* I was supporting my five small children by writing for magazines such as *True Detective* and for several Sunday newspaper syndicates. These publications fascinated crime buffs long before infamous murders were instantly covered on the Internet. But no one believed a woman could possibly know much about solving crimes, so I had to choose a male pen name. I became "Andy" for many years.

Police work is tough on the body and tougher on emotions, and many of those great detectives who were so kind in the beginning as they helped me find cases to write are gone now—retired or deceased. Without almost-miraculous forensic science updates, they solved crimes just as horrifying and seemingly impenetrable as those in today's media. They knew how to gather and preserve evidence, and they also "hit the bricks" or went out "heel and toeing" as they canvassed neighborhoods looking for witnesses and clues. Moreover, they had the native-born intelligence and empathy—even psychic sense—that all first-rate detectives use to winnow out suspects.

In the seventies and eighties, most police departments had an 85 percent homicides-solved rate. What we now call "cold cases" were referred to as "losers," an appellation homicide investigators dreaded.

It takes a special kind of police officer to become a detective; it always has.

Over the years, the killers themselves haven't changed all that much; they remain convinced that they won't be caught—ever. Sometimes their consciences bother them—if, indeed, they have consciences. More often, they barely think of the lives they end. Even when—*especially* when—their victims knew and trusted them.

If it wasn't so trite, I might have called this book "Too Close for Comfort," because it is full of violent crimes committed by people whose faces and voices were familiar to the victims. They all shared their lives in certain ways, sometimes for years and occasionally for only a brief period when fate placed both murderer and victim at the same crossroads in time and space.

FIRE AND ICE

THE POWELL FAMILY TRAGEDY

Chapter One

One of the questions I am asked frequently is "Don't you have nightmares about the cases you cover?" Usually, I don't. There is nothing as cathartic for me as emptying my brain of the awful details I learn about murders and pouring them onto a blank screen. Yes, I have had nightmares over the last forty years—but only a handful.

The twisted maze of horrendous events that began on December 6, 2009, in West Valley City, Utah, however, has given me dark images as I slept. I will never forget writing about what has been deemed "pure evil."

Only in retrospect can I see where many of the tragic aspects of this story could have been and should have been prevented. If only they had been.

Of the nine cases in this book, I have put off writing this one until the very last. I know why. I didn't want to think about it day after day, as I knew I would have to once I began to dig into the mental cesspools of two depraved minds.

*   *   *

Loving parents treasure their babies and watch over them as they grow. The irony of parenthood is that as much as we want to protect our children from any kind of harm, we have to prepare them to leave us and enter a world where there are dangers we can neither perceive or prevent. It can be so worrisome the first time children walk to school by themselves, or have a sleepover at a friend's house. And, before we know it, they are old enough to date and to drive a car, or ride in a car with drivers we don't really trust.

But we bite our tongues and give them wings to fly by themselves. When grown children fall in love and choose someone to marry, we hope that person will be good to them. Sometimes we can see trouble ahead, but the more we find fault in whom they've picked, the more likely they are to cling to them. Our eyes are not blinded by infatuation or love, and we can see personality traits that give us cause to worry when we know in our bones that our beloved children may end up with broken hearts and broken marriages. But, again, we keep our mouths shut and hope for the best.

Chuck and Judy Cox, who currently live in Puyallup, Washington, married for love, and they raised their four daughters in a happy and safe home. Mary was their first-born in 1977, then Denise in 1979, Susan in 1981, and finally, Marie in 1984. Although many men might have been disappointed that they had no sons, Chuck was quite happy with his quartet of daughters. From the moment they were born, he was a protective father, doing his best to look after his girls.

The Coxes are devout members of the Mormon faith. They met in eastern Washington, at Medical Lake, and Chuck soon decided the pretty young woman with long dark hair was the one for him, and it's obvious that he sees Judy today as he did then. He finds her as lovely as she was when she was a teenager, and she clearly cares for him the same way. As often happens, Chuck is the extrovert and Judy is the quiet one. Their likenesses and differences have bonded to make their marriage very successful over the years. At this point in their lives, they should be enjoying the retirement years most couples look forward to.

Instead, they have lived with terror and despair.

Chuck Cox is a pilot and a flight instructor, and Judy has made a home for him and their girls in many places around America: Denver; Minot, North Dakota; Holloman Air Force Base in Alamagordo, New Mexico; and Anchorage, Alaska. When he was in the air force, Chuck was an air traffic controller—a "Tower Flower," as he puts it—and he scanned the boards constantly when he was on duty to be sure that all the planes he was responsible for were "laddered," and that no two planes were ever on the same altitude and flight path at the same time.

It is a high-stress job, of course, but Chuck was good at it. He learned to live with having the responsibility for so many lives in the air, and he never lost his cool. Back in civilian life, he had to choose whether to be a full-time pilot or a civilian air traffic controller. He chose the latter and worked at Portland International Airport and Troutdale Airport in Oregon. After that he was an Aviation Safety Inspector in Renton, Washington.

Cox investigated crashes and near-crashes, and all of his jobs involved one aspect of flying or another. He recalls examining the circumstances of a particular collision in Moses Lake, Washington, where navy jet pilots in training routinely practiced low-level, high-speed flying maneuvers.

"A navy A3 jet flying low and at high speed collided with a crop duster. The A3's right engine impacted the biplane's left wing, and the propeller of the crop duster scratched and punctured the external fuel tank on the navy plane," Chuck explained. "Both of the military pilots ejected safely, and the crop duster plummeted to the ground, which was freshly plowed and soft. A local man heard the crash and he was able to pull the biplane pilot out and call for help.

"While I was investigating the accident, some military investigators claimed, 'That agriculture plane hit our jet.'

"I asked them how a hundred-mile-an-hour crop duster could catch up with and hit a five-hundred-mile-an-hour jet. They didn't have an explanation for that. I was just happy that all three pilots lived!"

Chuck Cox was always able to keep a level head when he had to, something that is a prerequisite for both a pilot and an air traffic controller. Those jobs, however, involved people he didn't know well—or at all. They didn't deal with the people he loved and devoted his life to.

Cox speaks his mind, and he can be stern when he needs to be. Lesser men would have broken long ago—but not Chuck Cox. When he commits to a cause, he is a bull-dog and nothing can shake him. His cause now is one that no one on earth would envy.

Before Chuck Cox retired in February 2011, both he and Judy looked forward to a serene life. His father suffered from heart disease, but with a pacemaker, he was expected to live at least ten years. Chuck and Judy and his parents considered creating one household to reduce living costs so both families would be able to travel while they were still young enough to do so. Sadly, events involving Susan Cox Powell, Chuck and Judy's daughter, would put unbelievable stress on both couples and end their hopes for rewarding retirements.

"My dad died suddenly in January 2011," Chuck said. "I think what happened to Susan put so much worry on his heart that it killed him. There were so many things that we all needed to say in response to attacks on us—but we couldn't. We had to remain silent."

Since the Christmas season of 2009, the Cox family has lived with huge anxiety about Susan, their third daughter. Chuck and Judy have no idea if Susan is alive or dead. She vanished from the Utah home she shared with her husband, Josh, and their two little boys—Charlie and Braden. She had allegedly left home in a blizzard on a frigid Sunday night. There was no word at all from her, no sightings, nothing. She was simply gone.

The circumstances of her vanishing defy any rational explanation. For her family, dealing with them was excruciating. Susan's parents and sisters wanted to believe that she was alive and would come home again, but as the days and weeks passed, they sought for her in vain. Her case was so bizarre that the search for her spread across America. Dozens of publications, including *People* magazine, covered the story, which was picked up by the Associated Press. Surely, the Coxes thought, if Susan was able to she would have come forward. In a way, it's harder for families not to know where someone they love is than it is to accept their death and begin to recover.

Judy, Chuck, and Susan's sisters were in limbo.

Josh Powell was quite sure that his wife was safe and well, and he reassured those who were baffled and grieving. Indeed, Josh explained that he hadn't wanted to raise an alarm when Susan left their home on the night of December 6, 2009, because he didn't want to upset anyone prematurely.

He was positive she was okay, even though she had seemingly disappeared into the whirlwind of snow and ice. Josh appeared to be embarrassed as he confessed that he believed Susan had run off with another man, leaving him alone to care for Charlie and Braden, who were only four and two.

Although the Josh Powells sometimes seemed an unlikely couple, and had their share of problems, most of which they kept between themselves, the idea that Susan would have an affair with another man and desert her family to be with him was mind-boggling.

Susan was a devout member of the Church of Latter-day Saints and she adored her little boys. She believed in her religion's tenets that marriage was for life—and beyond—and she had fought to save her own union. To everyone who knew her, the thought that she would abandon her children for a sinful affair was unbelievable.

Susan Cox was a bubbly, happy little girl and she remained that way into adulthood.

She was a romantic who wanted to make the world better—or, in her case, "prettier." When the Coxes were living in Alaska, and she was four or five, she once used crayons to draw a flower on a newly painted wall. She explained why to her perturbed parents: "I wanted to make it prettier."

Hearing that, they couldn't punish her. Chuck cleaned the wall and Susan helped.

In high school, one of her teachers asked her what her philosophy of life was.

"What do you mean?" Susan asked.

"What do you want to do with your life?" the teacher explained. "How do you look at the world?"

"I want people to be pretty," she said. "So they will be happy."

After graduation, she attended the Gene Juarez Academy of Beauty in Seattle, preparing for a career in that field. Her dream was to have her own beauty salon one day.

Susan herself was attractive—in a young Debbie Reynolds sort of way. She had bright blue eyes, wavy brown hair, and dimples. Dozens of photographs of her have been published and it's hard to find one in which she isn't smiling.

Conversely, there are few pictures of Josh Powell where he *is* smiling. Once Susan's goal was to make Josh happy, to help him forget his abusive childhood.

She was sure she could do that.

Like many young Mormon singles in their late teens and twenties, she and her sisters often went to an LDS Stake Center at Twelfth and Pearl streets in Tacoma to interact with their peers in the single adult ward who were eighteen to thirty.

"It was a marriage pool," Chuck Cox explains. "She met Josh Powell there. She was nineteen and he was twenty-six. We felt he was hunting for someone who believed that the husband was the head of the house. Susan was in love—you know, like the songs 'I Am Sixteen Going on Seventeen' or 'They Tried to Tell Us We're Too Young.' She was in love with Josh Powell, and no one could change her mind."

On the surface, Josh didn't seem that bad a choice for Susan. He gave the impression that he believed in all the Mormon tenets, and Susan saw him as a very mature "older" man.

While she was very well liked by the group at the Stake Center, Susan was aware that Josh lacked social skills: He had trouble fitting in. That didn't make her like him less; she actually felt a little sorry for him and tried to draw him into her circle of friends. It wasn't that Josh was shy; it was more that he talked too much about himself and his many accomplishments, and didn't seem very interested in other people. His affect was awkward, even a little peculiar. At first, of course, Susan didn't find him odd.

Chuck and Judy couldn't understand Susan's fascination with Josh, and sometimes they argued about it, although they tried not to—aware that the more they criticized Josh, the more their daughter would be attracted to him. She was a teenager and parents' opinions aren't usually appreciated at that stage of life.

"I asked her once 'Why Josh?' " Judy Cox recalls, of when Susan started dating him seriously. "And she wouldn't answer me. I think she wanted to help him."

Although judging others' attractiveness is a most subjective position, most people would not describe Josh Powell as prepossessing. Rather than being a handsome, dynamic man, Josh looked like he was no older than sixteen or seventeen. At five feet, ten inches, he was slender and somewhat weak appearing. He had bright blue eyes and rosy cheeks, and scarcely any beard. Even though he was seven years older than Susan, he looked younger.

Maybe he seemed so full of himself because beneath the surface he felt he didn't really measure up.

Everything about Josh seemed weak. No one realized then that he was a "control freak."

But he was.

To her family's continuing bewilderment, Susan Cox saw something in Josh that others didn't see. He had originally tried to date Susan's oldest sister, Mary, who didn't care for him at all. On the night of one of Mary's dances—where she had a date with someone else—Josh came over to the Coxes' home to ask her for a date, unaware that this was totally inappropriate. He hung around her house, waiting for her until she came home. It was an awkward situation.

Mary didn't want to go out with him, and she was alarmed when his attention turned to Susan. She kept warning Susan about Josh and advised her not to date him; there was just something about him that Mary neither liked nor trusted.

Josh Powell often exaggerated or told outright lies. Susan was so thrilled with her new romance that it never occurred to her to check out some of the things he said. He told Susan and her parents that he had a degree in business administration from the University of Washington. But he complained about his professors, saying that he knew more than any of them did.

Years later, when Nate Carlisle, a Salt Lake City reporter, attempted to verify Josh's degree from the University of Washington, he found there was no record of it. Josh countered by saying he was on a "special list." That was a lie, but he would never admit it.

Susan wanted to marry and have a family; her parents had been young when they wed and she had never known anything but a happy home. She was in love with love. When she looked at Josh, she was impressed that he had a job, his own apartment, and his own car. She either didn't know that he'd lived with his father, Steven Powell, until he was twenty-six—just before they started dating—or it didn't seem important.

To her, Josh seemed stable and ready to settle down.

"Josh wasn't stable," Chuck Cox says. "After ten minutes, anyone could see there was something wrong with him. He talked *all* the time."

And it was mostly about himself. He was a braggart, and Susan's parents didn't agree with her that all he needed was love. And then he proposed to her.

"I tried to tell her that you don't marry a 'project.' "

Judy Cox and Susan's friends threw a bridal shower for her. There weren't many there—only her friends Rachel, Terry, Jody, and Josh's sisters Alina and Jennifer. All of a sudden, another person walked into the room. They were all shocked to see that it was Josh. He was wearing a skirt, and lots of makeup, all dressed up as a female.

"He wanted to attend the girls' bridal shower, and be in the spotlight," Judy recalls. "It was really odd and embarrassing, and we told him he had to leave.

"When he did, I said to Susan, 'You're not going to *marry* him, are you?' And Susan was upset."

Judy remembers seeing "blackness" as the wedding approached and having a "very bad feeling."

Susan married Josh Powell on April 6, 2001. She chose the Portland LDS temple, in Clackamas County, Oregon. She looked lovely and was thrilled with her beautiful wedding gown. It was white satin with a deep round neckline, fitted bodice, and full skirt. Josh wore a tuxedo and had a white rose in his lapel. Both of them looked very happy.

Outside the temple, plum and cherry trees were in full bloom. A sudden wind scattered the white petals over the grassy lawn as Susan posed in her wedding dress.

Susan's and Josh's families hadn't met each other before the wedding rehearsal. While Chuck and Judy Cox

ANN RULE

were picking up the wedding expenses at a cost of several thousand dollars, they were shocked to hear Josh's father, Steve Powell, grousing over the cost of the wedding party's post-rehearsal meal at the Old Country Buffet, something just over a hundred dollars.

Although Steve and Josh's mother, Terry, were divorced, they attended the wedding and the wedding reception. Judy and her family had provided the flowers, decorations, wedding cake, and a lavish spread of food. The wedding guests ate heartily, but the cake was only half-gone and there was quite a lot of food left over, too. Even so, Judy Cox was shocked when her daughter's new mother-in-law asked if she could pack everything in her car to take back to Spokane for the wedding reception she planned for Josh and Susan on the east side of Washington.

"I couldn't believe it," Judy recalled. "She wanted it all—from the cake to the decorations to the flowers. I told her no. And she couldn't understand why!"

The couple had a short honeymoon—one night in the Columbia Gorge Hotel.

Like so many women before her who believe marriage will change a man, Susan felt sure that she could make Josh happy, and that her family would see in Josh what she did.

Josh had held a job for several years. He worked for his father. Steve Powell's titular employer was the Washington State Department of Corrections, but he actually had nothing to do with the prisoners themselves. He was an "account executive" for the company that sold the furniture that convicts built under the Correctional Industries (CI) program. Their consumers were schools from kindergarten to twelfth grade and nonprofit companies.

Josh was an installer, which meant, basically, that he put legs on school chairs, tables, and desks. He chose the hours that he wanted to work, had complete control of his own time, and worked when he wanted to.

"Two weeks after their wedding," Chuck Cox remembers, "Josh came to me, wanting to borrow money. I suggested that he either take on more installations or get a better job."

Josh didn't follow his father-in-law's advice. Instead of working harder, he asked the furniture company to pay him mileage. But he went further. He insisted that, legally, they *had* to pay him for his travel costs from job to job. Instead, they fired him.

"He called them two weeks later," Chuck says, "to ask them if they missed him! They told him they didn't, and they were doing just fine without him."

It is an understatement to say that Josh Powell lacked tact; he had a severe deficit in getting along with people, particularly anyone he worked for. He didn't appear to have trouble *getting* a job; his problem was keeping it. He was hired next by the Home Depot. Within a short time, he told his boss he had hurt his back on the job and couldn't lift heavy items—a big part of his job description—and he also couldn't resist pointing out things that the Home Depot was doing wrong. Once again, he was fired.

Susan was the one who worked steadily. She was a hairstylist for Super Cuts, and then Regis, and she really liked her job, but she wasn't making enough to keep them afloat financially.

Josh took a job as a car salesman. He lasted a week before, once again, he was let go.

He and Susan could no longer afford to keep their apartment and they had to move in with Josh's dad, Steven Powell, for three weeks. Steve had been divorced from his children's mother, Terry, since the early nineties. Terry and her daughter, Jennifer, were living then in Spokane, but Steve's other children all lived with him: Josh's sister, Alina, and his two brothers, John and Michael.

There really wasn't enough room in Steve Powell's house for two more people, but he hung a sheet in the dining room to mark off a makeshift room for the recently married couple.

It was an untenable situation for Susan. They had no privacy and the Powells' living setup was so different from the Coxes' home. Almost from the beginning, her father-in-law made her nervous. He stared at her and made remarks that seemed much too personal to her, and were full of sexual innuendo.

Susan was relieved when Josh's next job was at an assisted living facility for the elderly. Both Josh and Susan were in training to be assistant managers. Providentially, the position came with an apartment and three meals a day. The couple qualified because they had no children and no pets. Susan longed to have children but their financial situation was too precarious to think about it for a while. And she was only nineteen; there was time.

At last, she and Josh had some privacy and she was

happy to get away from her father-in-law's creepiness. After their training, Susan and Josh were assigned to a home for the elderly in Yakima, Washington. Susan hoped that the assisted living field might be a niche where Josh would fit in. She got high praise from the company but he didn't. Two months later he was out of a job again, and they had to move.

Susan grew alarmed as she realized that her bridegroom simply could not get along with people, especially anyone in authority. He complained and criticized his bosses until he was let go. His résumé was a mishmash of short-term positions.

Josh clearly needed to be in control, and he felt most of his jobs were beneath a man with his intelligence and education. A lot of men in their twenties go through the same thing, but they learn to bite their tongues and learn as much as they can on a job in the hope that they can move up.

Every place they moved in Washington State, Susan got along fine. People liked her, and she was able to keep her job with Regis. But she had had to resign when she and Josh were sent to their new—if short-lived—positions in Yakima. It was Josh's third try—and the company owners finally deemed him "untrainable."

Then they had to move to Oregon for training seminars on his next job. "He insisted that Susan stop cutting hair and follow him wherever he moved," her father said. "But Josh went to the Oregon seminar and began to tear down management in front of those attending. And of course he got fired again."

Even if Josh Powell had taken only a few courses in business administration at the University of Washington, it was obvious that nothing had sunk in. He was at an entry level in all of his short-lived jobs, but he could not keep his mouth shut. His own ego was his stumbling block, and he acted as if he were smarter than anyone.

Chapter Two

In 2004, Susan Powell was pregnant with their first son, Charlie. This gave her even more reason to want her marriage to succeed. Josh and Susan decided to make a fresh start in Utah. Although Susan didn't go into details with her family, they knew that she felt uncomfortable around her father-in-law and believed he intruded on her marriage too much. She hoped that moving out of state would lessen his impact on their lives. Susan and Josh hoped to find job opportunities in the Salt Lake City area and get themselves on a solid financial program.

Chuck and Judy Cox worried about Susan, who was more than eight months pregnant and living far away in Utah.

"We didn't know if she could count on him when she went into labor or after the baby came home," Judy recalls. "So we made a trip down there in January."

Charles Braden Powell was born on January 19, 2005. Susan's parents' instinct that she might need them was right on target. When she went into labor, Josh inexplicably said he couldn't drive her to the hospital because

ANN RULE

he had something important to do. He asked Chuck and Judy to take her. They were happy to do that but hoped her husband would at least show up for his first child's birth.

When Josh did show up at the hospital two and a half hours later, he brought his laptop computer with him. What had been more important than being with his wife as she labored to deliver? Josh explained that he had to back up the hard drive on his computer!

Indeed, he sat in a corner of the labor room and worked at his computer, barely noticing what his wife was going through. Chuck Cox watched, silently fuming.

"When she was in transition and really in pain, I went over to Josh and told him to put his computer down. Susan needed him to hold her hand and comfort her. He kept delaying, I finally said, 'Put your computer down, *now!*' "

Josh finally complied when Susan was only a few pushes away from delivering, and she gave birth to Charlie in a few minutes. "See," she told her father. "Josh was here when I needed him!"

Chuck didn't have the heart to tell her what really happened.

Susan was thrilled to be a mother, and Josh appeared to be genuinely pleased with baby Charlie. He held the infant proudly, but he refused to let either Judy or Chuck hold him.

"Charlie was his possession—he *belonged* to Josh," Judy said. "And he shut us out completely."

*   *   *

At first, Susan and Josh's move seemed to be a good idea. They had bought a nice home in the 6200 block of West 3945 South in West Valley City. A close southwest suburb of Salt Lake City, West Valley City has a population of something over 130,000 and is the second-largest city in Utah. There were plenty of job opportunities there in 2004.

Susan and Josh made friends with their neighbors, Kiirsi and John Hellewell, who were members of the Mormon church, and they connected with other members of the closest LDS stake.

The Powells and Hellewells spent a lot of social time together, sharing picnics, barbecues, and movies. Kiirsi and Susan were soon best friends, and Kiirsi's husband accepted Josh, saying, "If you're friends with Susan, Josh is part of the deal."

Both Josh and Susan were hired by a brokerage firm, Fidelity Investments. She quickly became a trusted employee popular with her coworkers. But, once again, Josh Powell became too verbal in his opinions about the faults of his new employer. Once again, he was fired.

It was only his first job in Utah, and Susan tried to believe it was just a wrong fit, and that Josh would soon find another position.

While Susan stayed on with Fidelity, Josh decided that he'd be better off working for himself and chose a career in real estate, where he thought he had what it took to be a success. Using money that Susan had managed to save for opening a beauty parlor in their home, Josh bought signs, lockboxes, and other paraphernalia Realtors need. The housing market was going great at the time. People were remodeling and flipping houses, and buyers were actually bidding against one another for homes, standing in line to make the best offer.

Josh sold a few houses, and he was enthusiastic about his success. He wanted Susan to get her real estate license, too, and join him in his business. As she usually did, she agreed to do that and got her license. She also went to work for Wells Fargo to ensure that they would have a steady, predictable income and medical insurance.

At Josh's suggestion, they took out life insurance policies—five hundred thousand dollars on each of their lives. If one of them should pass away, the other would have resources to pay for child care and other expenses.

Susan was pregnant again, and very happy about it. She called her mother in mid-2006 and impishly told Judy, "Seven. *Lucky seven!* Guess what's happening?"

Judy had six grandchildren at the time, and she quickly figured out that Susan and Josh were going to present her and Chuck with a seventh one.

Susan gave birth to Braden Timothy Powell on January 2, 2007. That was the second time that she and Josh had lost out on an income tax exemption by days, but it didn't matter. Charlie had dark hair and blue eyes, and it looked like Braden would be blond like his mother, with the same blue eyes that both she and Josh had.

One of Susan's friends would comment later that Josh's eyes had been as blue as Charlie's, but they began to change. Sometimes they were almost black.

Again Susan and Josh were happy with their new baby. Both the little boys seemed very intelligent and they were ahead of most babies in talking, walking, and showing other signs of maturation. Josh was often mean and demanding in the way he treated Susan, but he showed affection for his sons.

With his few house sales accomplished, Josh had dreams of glory about becoming one of the most successful Realtors in the Salt Lake City area. Without much planning, he bought a huge ad in the DEX Yellow Pages for ten thousand dollars, assuring Susan that it would bring a flock of house hunters to them. When she demurred, he explained that he didn't have to pay for the ad for a few months, not until after his ad was actually published. Josh figured he could well afford the ten thousand dollars by then.

When the new edition of the DEX directory came out, however, Josh was livid. Some of the phone numbers for his business were wrong, and he hated the pictures that appeared in the ad. He was right to be upset; house hunters who called the wrong numbers wouldn't reach him, and probably wouldn't bother trying to find his office. The directory printers had made a major error.

Josh went to Chuck Cox and asked him what he should do.

"I told him the first thing he should do was to be sure he had the phone directory company's admission of their mistake *in writing* so he would have proof," Chuck said. "That letter would be 'gold,' I said."

With the wrong phone numbers in print, Chuck felt that

Josh would be off the hook for the money he owed on the ad. He knew Josh couldn't afford such an expensive ad in the first place for what was only a fledgling company. Josh got a letter from the customer service manager, who was fired. The company started the collection process and Josh buckled.

"He didn't take my advice," Chuck recalls. "He filed for bankruptcy instead!"

It turned out that Josh and Susan had other debts that Josh couldn't pay. They had bought their house in West Valley City when they first arrived in Utah. They could make the mortgage payments at that time because they both had jobs. But, of course, Josh's steady employment ended shortly after that. Susan was the main breadwinner.

Josh had run up all the credit cards they had to the maximum limit, and those creditors were hounding them for payment, too.

Although Susan was embarrassed to ask her parents for more help, she had no choice but to stand behind Josh when he asked them for a loan.

"We gave them five thousand dollars," Chuck says, "so they wouldn't lose the house and they could pay their overdue mortgage debt. Susan promised to pay us back, and after Braden was born, she went right back to work at Wells Fargo. She was making payments to us as soon as she could."

Josh took a job as an assistant to an accountant, but he never varied from his usual path. He complained to Susan that he was much smarter than his boss, and he soon made that clear to his employer, too. He lost his job.

It was not a good time to be jobless. By 2009, the bottom had fallen out of the economy, scaring off house hunters who discovered that loans were drying up. Many recent home buyers found themselves upside down with their mortgages. Josh didn't sell any more houses.

Charlie and Braden were very young—only four and two. Susan would have loved to work part-time and be able to stay home with her children. Her goal was still to have a beauty parlor in their home, but she didn't manage to save any money. With a business in her home, she could make money and be with the boys, too.

As always, Susan was the main wage earner in the family. Even so, she had to use the money Josh doled out, and then explain everything she bought to him. She wasn't even allowed to withdraw money from the bank; Josh kept changing the PIN number so she wouldn't have access to it.

To be sure Susan didn't "overspend," Josh instructed her to go through weekly supermarket ads and check off the cheapest items offered. Then he told her what groceries she could buy, and he entered a list of those items on a spreadsheet in his computer. When she returned home, he scanned all her receipts into his computer to be sure she hadn't spent more than he'd allowed. If she went even pennies over the list he'd authorized, he would rail at her.

Trying to stay on such a frugal budget, Susan found it almost impossible to feed her family properly. She planted a ten-by-forty-foot garden. She grew everything from green beans and carrots to watermelons and pumpkins. By cooking fresh produce from her garden in the summer and foods she canned in the winter, she hoped that Charlie and Braden would have enough to eat.

Susan made everything from scratch when she cooked. For her, pumpkin pie meant growing the pumpkin, roasting it, scooping out the seeds, and also making the crust.

Susan was a vegetarian, and luckily her little boys liked carrots better than candy. She froze and canned the bounty from her garden and their fruit trees.

Josh was even more tightfisted when it came to other purchases. When Susan spent six dollars on shoes for Charlie, Josh was furious with her. She wasn't allowed to buy socks; Josh told her to knit them. But he complained if she spent too much money on yarn, especially when she knit baby bonnets, booties, and sweaters for her friends, one of her biggest pleasures.

When their day-care mom saw that Charlie and Braden often came to her without socks, she bought each of them a dozen pair. Susan was a little embarrassed but grateful.

Susan had to ask Josh's permission to drive their blue minivan, so she usually bicycled to where she had to go. And she rode a bike without gears to help on hill climbs. Most of the roads she traveled had no real shoulders so it was dangerous for her, but she rode on the pavement on busy streets.

No one but her best friend, Kiirsi, and a few others knew how Susan was struggling. Susan finally told her sister Denise how stingy Josh was, and Denise was appalled. None of the Cox family *really* knew how bad things were; Susan was too proud to tell them, and she didn't want them to resent Josh if somehow they managed to pull their marriage together.

Josh spent hours on the phone almost every day talking with his father, but he resented it when Susan took or made calls to Denise. Susan and Denise, the two middle daughters in their family, had always been close. They'd shared confidences, fun, and had even managed to breed parakeets and fish when they were in their teens.

"Those two once had *twenty-seven* parakeets," Judy Cox marveled.

One of the times Susan really grew impatient with Josh was when he disapproved of her phone conversations with Denise.

"You talk to your father for hours, and he fills you full of how hateful Mormons are," she argued. "And then you won't let me talk to my sister? That isn't fair."

Jennifer Graves, Josh's older sister, saw what was going on, and while she loved her brother, she felt sorry for Susan. Jennifer saw that Josh was "regressing," going downhill as the years passed. With every year, he was more of a failure at every job he had and in turn he seemed to control Susan more.

Personal power meant everything to Josh Powell, and the less he had, the more demanding he became. His appearance had changed so much in the seven years since he and Susan were married. He had bags under his eyes, and his face had a pinched look about it. Josh affected a wispy beard and mustache, and he usually had a frown on his face. The fresh-faced, teenager-like man that Susan had married had disappeared.

Chapter Three

The summer of 2008 was especially bad. Susan didn't mind working while Josh stayed home with their little boys, but she knew they needed to see a marriage counselor. Her husband was so "angry, irrational, and unpredictable" that after one prolonged fight, Susan threatened to call the police. He was beginning to frighten her. But when she said they *had* to get counseling, he adamantly refused, using one excuse after another.

At first he complained that there was no point in counseling, because he knew what they would say.

"Then do it [what they say]," Susan retorted.

Next he said counseling would be too expensive. When Susan said Wells Fargo would pay for counseling, Josh claimed that their private lives would become public—everyone would know—and they wouldn't be able to get any more life insurance or health insurance with that on their record.

Susan made an appointment with her bishop. She was living a life of despair, trying to save her marriage, even though most women would ask, *Why?* She was almost in tears when she arrived for her appointment.

The bishop opened their session with a prayer, and Susan realized she was rambling as she told him about the emotional chaos in her home. To her surprise, he agreed with her on all points.

"Josh has mental issues," she emailed a friend, "and isn't dealing with reality. My bishop agrees I'm a stressed, overworked, neglected/abused mother down to her last straw.

"And then my bishop said, 'What can I do to help?' "

Susan wanted counseling so much—not together with Josh at first—but for herself and Josh separately. She believed Wells Fargo would cover most of that under her health insurance. The bishop assured her that the church would pay the twenty-dollar-a-session copay that was Josh's current reason to refuse counseling.

For a time, she had hope. It was nearly the Fourth of July in 2008. When Josh asked her why she'd gone to see the bishop, she told him she'd asked for help on groceries and bills and Josh was okay with that.

Susan was working full-time, bicycling to work and back. It took her forty minutes in the morning and fifty minutes after work because the last mile was all uphill. Josh was still unwilling to go to counseling. Instead, she told friends that he gave her a list of things that would have to change in their marriage "so *he* won't be stressed . . . and everything will magically be all right."

Josh accused her of spending ninety dollars on groceries instead of the thirty she'd really spent. Her garden had yet to come to fruition, and Josh complained that watermelon at twenty-five cents a pound was too expensive, but then he spent more for one that was smaller.

"You have utter contempt for me because I don't have a job!" Josh shouted at Susan. He accused her of thinking he wasn't a man.

She denied it, but it did no good.

Josh no longer went to church. "We were with our friends while they were doing family scriptures and he looked bored, uninterested, and like he was finding reasons to leave the room," Susan wrote.

Kiirsi Hellewell recalled how Josh would make it almost impossible for Susan to go to church. "He'd belittle her, and tell her she shouldn't pay tithes or go to church. He would fight her over everything she did as far as her faith. When she was trying to get the kids up and ready for church by herself, Josh would say things like 'You want to go to boring, boring church with Mommy—or do you want to stay home and have cake with Daddy?'"

He often criticized her to the little boys, and young Charlie sometimes shouted at her, "Can't you see I'm busy—trying to work?" Words he echoed from hearing his father's complaints.

Susan's life was getting harder and harder.

"I don't know how you can help, except talk with me," she emailed a close friend. "And be another individual that would know about the situation if questioned b/c things went crazy later. Sad that I'm this paranoid.

"My huge problem is I don't know what to believe or what to do. I don't want to divorce or separate or take the kids somewhere and [he'd view] that as an act of war . . .

My current tactic is to pretty much not make waves and try to ignore the problems. I read mystery books checked out at the library and [try to] be a good mom for the boys. I came home from work on Sat. and felt so depressed that I couldn't make a decent dinner for my boys."

Susan was concerned that Charlie and Braden weren't getting enough protein. Hot dogs were the only meat products she could afford, although she sometimes had eggs on hand. Beans and rice took several steps to prepare—culling, soaking, and a long time cooking. Often she was just too tired to do all that.

She was frustrated that Josh didn't stick to the food budget he demanded of her and then made impulse purchases like "cheap donuts and individual yogurt servings." Susan would have suffered his wrath if she dared to buy something like that. She wouldn't have anyway—but that money could have gone to buy meat for the boys. She did her best to give the boys a proper diet with what she had in her cupboards.

"I just kept trying to disguise their food with sour cream and catsup, etc.," she emailed. "And I finally laid [*sic*] down on my bed and went to sleep around 7 P.M. I had only gotten 4 hours sleep the night before so I'm sure Josh just thought I was tired . . . I took another nap (out of depression) the next day, but I'm sure he has no clue/doesn't care."

In retrospect, it's easy to ask why Susan didn't just leave Josh. How could she stay in such a punishing relationship? She would have been welcomed by her own family in Washington State. But unless a woman has been there—and so many women have—it's difficult to explain.

Although Susan avoided Steve Powell, even he seemed sympathetic on one of their visits to Puyallup, telling her that his whole family knew how badly Josh treated her. That was unexpected support from a surprising source, but it didn't make Susan less wary of Steven. When she and Josh had moved from Washington State, his father's attention and inappropriate touching were among *her* main reasons for wanting to get away. He sometimes touched her breasts and then acted as if it was accidental.

She was still nervous when she had to visit him and Josh's siblings on holidays, or when Steve came to West Valley City for a visit. Her father-in-law seemed to dangle Josh like a puppet on a string. Every time now when Josh ended a phone conversation with his dad, it seemed that she and Josh had a fight.

Susan felt safe enough to confide information about Steve Powell's "weirdness" to Kiirsi Hellewell. "A few months after they moved here," Kiirsi remembered, "Susan told me the *real* reason they moved to Utah was to get away from her father-in-law. I just kind of stared at her, thinking I know people have troubles with their in-laws sometimes, [but wondering] why such a look of disgust and almost hatred [came over] her face—considering she was such a kind and loving person.

"She told me that he 'hit on her,' that he tried to kiss her, and that she caught him watching her get dressed one day."

Kiirsi sensed that Steve Powell was actually obsessed

with Susan. "Susan couldn't stand him. She described him as the 'devil.' "

Given a choice, Susan said she didn't even want to be in the same state with Steve Powell.

Susan was figuratively "between a rock and a hard place."

Divorce is a rarity in LDS mores, far more than most other religions. A family, once bonded, is supposed to last for life and all eternity. And Susan struggled mightily with the thought of divorcing Josh. Even though her bishop had seemed shocked to learn of the way she was being abused and overpowered by Josh and offered help from the church, Susan didn't think he would go so far as to advise her to break up her marriage. Her LDS stake had helped her with money for counseling, and with groceries, yes—but divorce? She thought, *Never!*

But she was torn more than anyone but a few close friends realized.

"We saw how controlling Josh was and the horrible way he was treating her," Kiirsi said. "She just kept saying, 'I don't want to live my life being miserable, but I want to make sure I have done *everything* I absolutely can to save my marriage before I walk away. But if it comes to that point and I know I do have to leave, [then] I have a clean conscience and [will know] I did everything I could to try and make it work.' "

Still, it was more than Susan's religious convictions that kept her with Josh. She lived in the grip of terror. He had promised her there would be hell to pay if she attempted to leave him or take his boys away.

"Every moment I step back and take stock of what I'm dealing with it feels like a never ending cycle," she emailed, "but I'm too afraid of the consequences, losing my kids, him kidnapping [them], divorce, or actions worse on his part if I take a stand on one of his ultimatums . . . or [like] cutting off his access to my paycheck."

Susan told her friends that she had written a will and hidden it in her desk.

Just in case.

Later, they would look for it.

And then, almost suddenly, things simmered down in the bizarre relationship that was Susan and Josh Powell's marriage. July 2008 had been the worst month. Had Susan left Josh then, no one knows what might have happened. But she still clung to her marriage, to the memory of the man she'd wed seven years before.

The romantic feelings that had marked their first year or so together had dried up. It was very rare for Josh to approach her for physical contact—much less sexual intercourse. Susan tried to look attractive and she had kept her figure. She was still very pretty. Josh was angry when she bought makeup or hair products, but she was able to buy a few things to enhance her looks. It didn't matter; Josh was unceasingly cold and disinterested in her sexually.

She believed that he was emotionally ill, that somehow he could change if he had psychiatric treatment or took the right kind of medications. There were people in Josh's family who suffered from bipolar and other mental disorders.

Maybe that was what was wrong with Josh. Maybe he was clinically depressed and couldn't help the way he acted.

She vowed to try once more, and she emailed her friends about that.

"I want him in counseling, on meds. I want my husband, friend, lover BACK. No more crazy, outrageous, outlandish beliefs/opinions.

"I know everyone else will support me in whatever decisions I make, even if that means I crash anyone's house in the middle of the night with my boys in tow. Hope *that* never happens! Or stay with him. But, believe me, my bottom line is HE WILL DO COUNSELING . . . I'm sure if he fixes himself, everyone else will see a much closer version of the guy I married. And it will be easy enough to forget the hell and turmoil he's put me through."

At one time over that bleak summer, a friend had told Susan, "If you can't have faith, have hope at least."

And Susan emailed the quote back to her, adding, "I WANT to have hope . . ."

Susan Powell didn't lack emotional support from her family, her friends, her church, and the worst of her troubles with Josh seemed to smooth over for the rest of 2008. He agreed to limited counseling for about four months, although Susan couldn't see much progress; Josh wouldn't admit to any fault on his part.

She worked full-time and Josh stayed home and looked after Charlie and Braden. He was good with the boys. Susan clung to that. Josh loved his kids, and maybe that would be the impetus for him to work on their marriage.

Chapter Four

In December 2008, Josh made some peculiar comments to their friends and to other men at an office Christmas party that Susan's company hosted. But no one took him seriously. He was an odd duck and most of the people the Powells knew in West Valley City and Salt Lake City had come to expect him to be a little socially unacceptable. They liked Susan a lot, and chatting with Josh just came along with their affection for Susan.

Josh Powell was the second child to be born to Steven Craig Powell and Terrica Martin Powell. All families are different, but the Powells' home was perhaps more bizarre than most. They were Mormons, too, but Steve was becoming more and more critical of those beliefs.

Josh's great-grandfather Samuel Lester Powell Sr. apparently embraced one branch of Mormonism that approved of multiple marriage. Born in Alberta, Canada, in 1904, he married two women—both around 1925. One was Ella Christina Reeves, who had two children before she married Samuel, and the other was Ouita A. Laughlin. The women were very close in age; both of them were born in the late spring of 1904. Ouita gave birth to Samuel Lester Powell Jr. in 1926. It may have been that Samuel Sr. was only giving Ella and her children a home, taking her under his wing as a platonic "wife." Brigham Young had provided rooms and "protection" in his huge home for spinsters whom no men had chosen.

The old man, the first Samuel, passed away in 1982 in Idaho Falls, Idaho, as did Ouita. Ella died in July 1989.

Samuel L. Powell Jr. was Steven's father. All of that connected family lived in Idaho.

Steven Craig Powell, Josh's father, was born in 1949, and his mother is listed on the family tree as Mabel J. Roach. Steven has always claimed that he was an abused child whose mother abandoned him often, leaving him with grandparents. According to him, his grandmother was cruel, telling him his mother was never coming back for him. Is this Steven's imagination?

It may be true. Or it may not. Steven was raised around Puyallup, Washington, in Pierce County, and later moved to Spokane.

Who initiated the family tree page on Ancestry.com is unknown, but it was probably Josh because his name and those of Susan, Charlie, and Braden are the last entered.

Steven Powell and Terrica Martin Powell had five children within the first several years of their marriage. Steven usually had a job, but they moved around Spokane County often. Once he began work selling prison-produced furniture, he stayed with the job for three decades.

Steven and Terrica spent quite some time near Spokane, and after they divorced in 1992, Steven eventually moved back to Puyallup. He was about eight years older than Terrica, and he was definitely the head of their household. Indeed, their marriage was almost a prototype for Josh and Susan's union some three decades later.

Terrica "Terry" Powell was petite and plump, very soft-spoken—although, as she did at Josh and Susan's wedding reception, she could ask for outrageous things. Her empathy—even sensitivity—was sometimes lacking. She was also a member of the Church of Latter-day Saints, but Steven had dropped away. Where he had once embraced Mormonism, he came to deny it and urged his children to do the same.

They had been married almost twenty years when Terry filed for divorce in Spokane County. She believed that Steven had emotional problems and felt he needed "serious medical help."

Jennifer, their older daughter, who was in high school at the time, recalls how cruelly her father treated her mother. "He was extremely controlling, verbally abusive. He was always putting her down, saying things, like petty things. I mean, she couldn't even cook a meal without getting insulted. She kept a reasonably clean house, you know, [but] with five kids, it's hard to keep things in perfect order."

Worse than her husband's constant criticism, however, was Terry's concern about the influence Steven had over their children. Some of his ideas and the books he brought home seemed focused on the dark side. One book was *The*

Occult: A History, by Colin Wilson. Wilson, a British author, usually writes about grotesque homicide cases. The blurb on the cover of the book was written by the author: "One day I believe man will have a sixth sense—a sense of the purpose of life, quite direct and un-inferred. This is Faculty X. And the paradox is that we already possess it to a large degree, but are unconscious of possessing it. It lies at the heart of all so-called 'occult' experience. It is with such experience that this book is concerned."

Occult is usually defined as relating to magic, witchcraft, or supernatural phenomena, something Terry found disturbing. Another of the books Steven Powell presented to their children was *The Symbolism of Evil.*

Steven had become very secretive, and Terry wondered what he kept under lock and key, forbidden to her.

Steven Powell was an angry man, particularly enraged at the LDS philosophies. He worked hard to influence his children to agree with him.

In November 1992, when Jennifer had graduated from high school and Josh was sixteen or seventeen, with John, Michael, and Alina younger, Terry filed for divorce and asked the Superior Court of Spokane to grant her an immediate restraining order to keep her estranged husband away from herself and her children. That presented a problem. Steven moved to an apartment, and he egged their children on to disobey her—even to threaten her.

Jennifer, the oldest, aligned herself with her mother, but the boys followed Steven's lead in disrespecting Terry. Alina was too young to be a threat.

In her affidavit, Terry began with her concern about

Steven's parenting. "The Respondent [Steven Powell] is continuing to involve the children in these proceedings, including our youngest son, Michael," Terry wrote. "Michael was at his shoulder reading Steven's response as he typed it. Steven took him out of school early the day before to talk to his attorney. I find this totally inappropriate and unbelievable that an attorney would involve a ten-year-old boy in these proceedings when there are prior restraining provisions to the contrary. I have attached to my affidavit a copy of a letter Michael was typing . . . Obviously, Steven is involving him in the details of these proceedings."

Terry claimed that at their father's urging, John and Josh were coaching Michael to ignore her as she tried to care for him. Michael was enjoying all the attention as his parents and siblings fought over him, and he'd begun shouting the same ugly lies at Terry that Steven did.

"Steven and the boys—John and Joshua—are continuing to harass me," Terry wrote in her affidavit.

"On Tuesday evening November 3, 1992, Steven was at a class. John and Joshua prevented me from putting Michael to bed. It was after 9:30 P.M. and I had already told Michael several times to get into bed. He and the big boys were in our bedroom, watching the election proceedings."

Terry wrote that she worried, too, that Steven had taken Michael into his bed to sleep, which seemed odd.

She described one night when, as she tried in vain to put her youngest son to bed in his own room, Josh and John ordered Terry to leave the room.

"John said to Josh, 'Kick her! Kick her!' " And she

wrote that she was afraid her sons were going to physically attack her. She turned the television off, but John immediately turned it back on and grabbed her wrist to stop her from turning it off. And then he stood in her way, blocking her from the set.

"Finally," Terry continued, "I walked around the bed and picked Michael up around his chest to take him to his own room and put him to bed. John came over and took him away."

Fearful that her smallest boy might get hurt if she tugged him away, she gave up.

Terry had complained to Steven about what had happened when he got home. He seemed unconcerned, and she told Josh that she was ashamed the way he and John were treating her.

"I told them they should show [me] a little respect, and Josh said, 'You have to earn respect, Mom. What have you done to earn my respect?' "

Terry didn't know what to do. Initially she had thought it might be okay for Josh and John to live with Steven after their divorce. But now she wondered if that was a good decision. She had found a story that one of her sons had written. It was called "Revealing Darkness" and it was horrifying. One of her sons—a boy in his teens—had written page after page of sadomasochistic fantasy, including rape, cannibalism, boiling a woman in a huge pot of scalding water and then stuffing her like a turkey and baking her. It would be ill-advised to go into any more details of his gruesome imagination.

He had also drawn pornographic and devil images.

There were several sketches of what looked like the Angel of Death, or perhaps a hooded monk with a scepter. There were photographs of nude *Playboy* models, with his disturbing comments. And there was a half man, half salamander with a *T* over its genitals.

How could this be? Terry wondered, appalled.

Something was wrong in the house that Steven Powell had created. If Steven didn't let Terry have custody of her older boys, she petitioned that they be placed in a normal, safe foster home. Indeed, she wasn't sure she could manage them; they were big and physically threatened her.

"I love my children very much," she explained. "[But] I am asking that minor children, Michael and Alina, remain with me and I am requesting that Joshua and John be placed with a third party until further hearing in this matter. I feel that it is very detrimental for all of us to remain in the same house with the Respondent. I feel he is not well, and it is obvious he is having severe adverse affects [*sic*] upon our children."

Steven and Terry's divorce took three years of fighting back and forth. Steven had moved into his own apartment, and he took his older sons—Josh and John—with him. Michael, eleven, Alina, seven, and Jennifer, eighteen, stayed in the family home in Veradale, Washington, near Spokane.

"My dad got Josh and John riled up," Jennifer recalled. "They were angry . . . vocal and hostile toward my mom."

Terry and Jennifer were truly afraid of the teenagers, fearful of what they might do to them.

"We had the doors locked against them coming in,"

Jennifer said. "And they actually climbed up onto the roof—and that was a pretty tall house—like three stories. They climbed up onto the roof and were trying like—I don't know—[to] damage the roof or something to get in. We were afraid and we called the police on them."

In the end, Steven got custody of their minor children. Even Alina, who was still in grade school. She would never move from her father's home and soon became his fierce defender.

Steven Powell's sons—particularly Josh—suffered emotional and physical abuse at the hands of their father. He was a fierce disciplinarian. Three of Steven's children were bed wetters, a problem that continued until they were eleven or twelve. When they wet their beds, Steven made them get in a bathtub that was filled with ice water. They had to stay there for at least half an hour, and usually more. Not surprisingly, their father's "reprogramming" didn't work; it only exacerbated the problem.

Josh was both dependent on his father's approval and afraid of him. As a teenager, he left Steven's house on May 6, 1992. He wrote a note to his father:

Dad,

We talked the other day about stuff [sic] *of me moving out and either living with someone else or in my car. You said that I'd probably be more unhappy, but I'm going to find out.*

Tonight I wanted to go to "Youth," but you grounded me. After some thought I decided to go anyway.

I would come home but you'd just yell, and that's the last thing I need right now, after a crappy week. I have to say it was definately [sic] worth it. I feel alot [sic] better now. I didn't have time to prepare so my room is a mess. I'll have to box up all my stuff later. Michael or John might as well have my room like we talked about. Things are a bit complicated now, so please try not to make it harder. I think it's going to work out. Maybe we can be better friends this way. Josh

PS I just didn't want you guys to stay up all night worrying.

As emotionally abusive as he was to his wife, Steven Powell rarely dated after they separated. He did fancy himself a lady's man and was especially attracted to women in their twenties.

Steven had an alter ego—Steven Chantry—who wrote poems and songs that he recorded in a soft, pleasant voice. Many of his lyrics were interesting, but most of the tunes were the same, and they were usually dedicated to an impossible love object. Steven had aspirations to be a famous recording artist. He often used his "career" as a conversational approach to young women.

To an outsider, Steven Powell, who was forty-six at the time, didn't appear to be an abusive woman hater. He was about five feet, ten inches tall, and he had fairly handsome, somewhat delicate features. His dark hair, which he styled in a pompadour, was beginning to turn gray at the temples. His normal expression was mild, as if he could be no danger to anyone.

But Steven Powell controlled his offspring firmly, seeming to be in no hurry to have them become independent. John and Alina never moved out of Steven's house; Michael joined the army for four years and seemed to be leaving the nest. But when he was mustered out, he moved back home and it appeared that nothing had changed. Eventually, Michael did move to Minnesota to attend college.

Josh, of course, stayed with his father until he was twenty-six. It isn't difficult to feel sorry for the teenager that Josh Powell was in 1992. His father played him like a yo-yo, and although Josh showed some bravado in his note, one can also see that he wanted Steven Powell to tell him to come home.

Josh's social ineptness and, again, false bravado, show in another letter he wrote during the same period. It was addressed to a girl, Cynthia,* and he heavily edited it, with whole sentences scratched out. He may never have actually sent it; "VOID" is scribbled in black ink across the first page.

Cynthia,
It's illegal for me to be here right now. It always was. Before I wasn't too worried because it's un-

---

* The names of some individuals have been changed. Such names are indicated by an asterisk (*) the first time each appears in the narrative.

likely that the wrong people would find out. The people who know me like me [most of them] and no one cares that I'm here.

If Jack* sees me and turns me in I could be arrested. Do you think I care about that? And about you?

Lynn* may think I'm ignoring her, and you may think I don't care about her, but I have spent more time with Lynn this past couple of months than I've spent with anyone. If you want examples, I went to her house for several hours just the other day. Lynn and I spending quality time together—untill [sic] *she invited us over to Scott's* house. After that she hardly payed* [sic] *attention to me because she was talking to Scott. That doesn't bother me. I hardly noticed it at the time.*

Lynn and I are good friends and I don't think that'll change.

For me high school is just a place to make and see friends, and that is what it's always been. [crossed out] When it comes to friends I make a special effort to see you through. *People just happen to introduce me to their friends and* [crossed out] alot of times I forget their names. Sometimes forget even having met them. *Then I always try to remember them and say hi when I see them.*

Josh next mentioned a girl who "has no friends" and said he always tried to be "nice" to her, but he scratched that out so thoroughly that it is difficult to read that paragraph.

47

"I like knowing alot of people," he continued. "So if that was a problem, you should have told me without getting mad.

"Friday night you were too busy with everyone else . . . so when I saw one of my friends I decided to go say hi. I thought I would see you third quarter . . ."

It is poignantly clear that the teenage Josh Powell really didn't have any friends and was probably making up the story about being "illegal" to sound more interesting.

He found living in his car was impossible, and he didn't have anyone he could move in with, so he returned to his father's house. How privy he was to Steven Powell's secrets may never be known. Certainly, no one outside the family and his ex-wife had any idea about the depth of Steven's hidden obsessions about sex and younger women.

When he was in his teens, Josh had made a halfhearted attempt to commit suicide, and he once actually pulled a knife on his mother. He had also killed family pets. There is no record of his getting counseling or being treated by a psychologist or psychiatrist after those incidents.

It was almost ten years before Josh Powell met Susan Cox. He was so damaged by then that disaster loomed ahead like an oncoming train. Josh Powell would one day become one of the most hated men in America, and yet one wonders exactly what drove him to it.

Chapter Five

In December 2009, Susan was still living with Josh and their sons in West Valley City. She had told friends that she "wouldn't take this crap" from Josh any longer, and if things didn't change for the better by their ninth anniversary, on April 6, 2010, she was going to leave him. Susan wasn't a meek goody-goody, and she used words like *crap* when they were called for. She wanted a life. She wanted Charlie and Braden to have a life. And she was almost at the very straggly ends of her rope.

Susan Powell wasn't as brave as she sounded, however, she was afraid. She had hidden a letter in a safe deposit box, along with her will. She wrote that she might suffer an accidental death, and asked that someone check into it. She told no one out loud about this fear.

She wasn't exactly asking for help; Susan wanted justice, even as she realized that might be all she would ever get. She had exhausted almost every avenue of help she considered. She had prayed, sought counseling, tried to go along with Josh's rules, tried to be a good mother no matter what blockades he put up in her way, and then prayed again.

Even her own parents and sisters had no idea how bad things were for Susan. If they had, they would have stepped in and, somehow, done their best to get her and the boys safely away from Josh.

And then, in the late fall of 2009, it seemed that things were getting better in Susan's situation. Josh had a new job—this time as a temp doing books and computer work for a trucking firm. He was called to work for them now and again, and he could do many of his computer tasks at home. His new employer apparently liked his performance, so much so that he was hired as a full-time employee.

"We were pleased and relieved," Chuck recalls. "Christmas was coming, they both had jobs, and it looked as though it might be all right after all."

Susan wasn't so optimistic. Although she made preparations for Christmas, she still marked April 6, 2010, in her mental calendar. Her closest friends were forewarned of her anxiety. Josh had had myriad jobs before, jobs that gave her hope—but he always ended up being fired. And his behavior toward her hadn't improved all that much. She would stay five more months. It seemed to her that it would be a miracle if her husband actually changed, and she hoped for that, but she was fully prepared to leave him in April if she had to.

December 6, 2009, was a Sunday, a bitterly cold day in the Salt Lake City area, with icy, windblown rain and half a foot of snow piling up on the ground. The minimum temperature was 10 degrees. It wouldn't get any higher than 25 degrees. In the desert areas of Utah, the wind roared across the plains and whistled down the thousands of mine shafts there. It was not a day when anyone would choose to go out into the weather—not unless they had to.

When Susan's friend JoVonna Owings dropped in, she invited her to stay for a late brunch, and Josh seemed okay with that. In fact, he seemed more convivial than usual. Although he *never* cooked, he announced that he would make pancakes for them. He made a big deal of how he served the hotcakes, designating each stack to a particular person. He carefully set Susan's plate in front of her.

It turned out to be a pleasant meal, although Susan began to feel ill and very tired soon after. At about five, her stomach was upset and she vomited, apologizing to her friend as she explained that she had to lie down for a while. JoVonna told her not to worry about it and left. Josh said he was going to take the boys—Charlie, four, and Braden, two—out sledding for a while.

One of their neighbors saw Josh's blue Chrysler minivan pull back into his driveway between eight and eight thirty. As most of those living on their street did in deference to the cold, Josh pulled his vehicle into the garage.

That night was uneventful as families went to bed; most of the parents had to start the workweek in the morning.

One neighbor, however, was awake into the early morning hours. She was sick with something like the flu and she was too uncomfortable to sleep.

At about 2 A.M., the woman heard someone arguing

loudly outside. She listened because it sounded serious, but she didn't know what to do. A man was yelling, "Get in the car! Get in the car!"

Then she heard a woman shouting, "No! No! You're going to hurt me if I do!"

Apparently the woman had finally gotten into the car, but within a minute, the neighbor woman heard the vehicle come to a brake-screeching stop.

Then the argument and shouting began again.

"Get back in the car, right now," the man ordered.

Evidently, the woman did what he said because the argument stopped. The witness peeked through her window and saw a light-colored minivan racing away.

She didn't call the police, thinking she had probably just overheard a family argument, and she didn't want to be a busybody. Still, the incident troubled her and she didn't sleep much that night, wondering if she should have done something more.

Neither Susan nor Josh arrived at work the next morning, nor did they call in sick that Monday of December 7, 2009. Even if Susan's nausea had been the precursor of the flu or serious stomach trouble, she would have phoned her supervisors at Wells Fargo. Or she would have asked Josh to call. It wasn't in her nature to simply fail to show up at her job without any explanation. Even more disturbing, the Powells didn't call the day-care mom, who expected Charlie and Braden, to let her know that the boys wouldn't be coming.

Since Josh often worked at home, it wasn't particularly unusual for him to be away from the trucking company's offices, so no one there was concerned about his absence.

No one saw any of the Powell family around their house that Monday. Their day-care provider tried to call them, but no one answered. Alarmed, she called Josh's mother, Terry Powell, and his sister Jennifer Graves—both of whom lived nearby—to tell them how concerned she was. They too tried to get in touch with Josh and Susan, with no success. Neither of the missing pair answered their cell phones.

Susan had told many women in her circle about her fears, and that may have been why the babysitter called Josh's family—*and* why Terry called the West Valley City Police Department with a "check on the welfare" request at 10 A.M. Although an adult has to be missing for at least forty-eight hours before an official search is begun, and it was awfully soon to file a missing person's report, the investigators heard the anxiety in Terry's and Jennifer's voices, and with their permission, activated a missing person's report at once.

Still, at this point, there could be some reasonable explanation for all four of the Powells being gone.

Jennifer Graves finally reached Josh Powell's cell phone at 5:27 that afternoon. At first she felt relief, but when she asked him where he was, and he told her he was at work, she knew that didn't compute.

"You're lying, Josh," his sister said. "We know you're not at work. Where are you?"

Josh then changed his story and told Jennifer that he and the boys had been camping.

"Well, you'd better get home. The police are there, and Susan is missing."

"How much do you know?" Josh asked Jennifer.

"What do you mean," she responded. "Why did you ask me that?"

Josh hung up.

Twenty minutes later, in an attempt to avoid unnerving Josh Powell more, West Valley City police detective Ellis Maxwell borrowed Jennifer Graves's cell phone and used that to dial Josh's number. Josh picked up, seeing his sister's number on the Caller ID.

Maxwell identified himself and told Josh to return to his house as soon as possible.

"I have to get my sons something to eat first," Josh said. "Then I'll be home."

It was close to an hour before Josh drove up. Detective Maxwell walked up to the passenger side of the minivan before Josh could exit the driver's seat.

"People have been looking for you," Maxwell said. "Why didn't you answer your cell phone or call someone all day today?"

"I had to keep my phone turned off to save the battery," Josh replied. "I don't have a phone charger."

That was a ridiculous excuse. Maxwell could clearly see Josh's mobile phone resting on a front seat console.

The phone was plugged into a cigarette lighter phone charger.

Josh appeared to be shocked to learn that people— including his own mother and sister—had been concerned enough about his family's safety to call the police. He said he and the boys were fine. And as Maxwell peered into the backseats, he was reassured to see Charlie and Braden Powell, who did, indeed, appear to be in good shape.

But where was Susan? No one saw her get out of the minivan.

Detective sergeant Ellis Maxwell, who would soon be appointed the lead detective on the "missing person" case by West Valley City police chief Thayle "Buzz" Nielsen, asked Josh to get the boys settled and then come to police headquarters so they could talk more about where he'd been. And, of course, he also wanted to talk about where Susan Powell might be.

Josh agreed to come down, and that evening he and Maxwell talked.

Josh said he had taken Charlie and Braden out camping about midnight in the Simpson Springs area of the west desert, farther west than the Cedar Fort area in Tooele County.

Josh explained that he wanted to test his new generator to be sure it was working well. That seemed dangerous to Maxwell. What if the generator *didn't* work well, or if dangerous fumes filled the minivan where boys only two and four were sleeping? Maxwell noted that, but he didn't argue with Josh, who continued talking.

"I actually thought it was a little after twelve thirty A.M. on *Saturday* night—not Sunday," he explained. "I was confused and I missed a whole day of work. That's why I didn't call my company—I believed that I'd be fired if I called in."

That didn't make a lot of sense, either, but Ellis Maxwell moved on to his next question, "Where do you think Susan is?"

Josh shrugged. "I have no idea. All I know is that she should have gone to work today."

Maxwell observed that Powell showed very little concern or anxiety about the police questions concerning Susan. The detective found that strange.

After that first interview ended, Josh gave his consent to the West Valley City police to search both his house and his vehicle. The minivan did appear to be packed for camping. The investigators found the new generator, blankets, a gas can, tarps—and a shovel. They also found Susan Powell's cell phone in the center front console. It was turned off. On further inspection, they discovered that the digital sim card was missing.

Asked why Susan's mobile phone happened to be in the van if he had seen her last at home, Josh had no explanation. All he knew was that she was there, sleeping in their house when he, Charlie, and Braden went camping after midnight. Susan hadn't felt well enough to join them so they had left without her.

"Why didn't you guys check with Susan today?" Josh

asked. "You could have asked her where the boys and I were."

Josh appeared to be surprised when they told him that no one had been able to locate Susan, that she hadn't shown up at the Wells Fargo offices.

As for his winter camping trip with Charlie and Braden, Josh made it sound as if it was the most natural thing in the world to have a late-night adventure with his boys on a snowy night in December. If they had been ten and twelve, that might be—but they were two and four.

Josh had no idea where Susan had gone. Her bicycle was still in the garage, but then she wouldn't have been able to ride it with snow on the streets and sidewalks.

Although he was mystified about where Susan might be, he didn't see why the investigators were asking so many questions about his camping trip.

That, in itself, struck detectives as peculiar.

Why *anyone* would take toddlers out to camp in a blizzard at midnight was the question on everyone's mind. And it would keep coming back to niggle at investigators in the months to come.

After his van was thoroughly searched, the West Valley City investigators moved on to the Powells' house. Susan Powell wasn't there—sick, alive, or dead. Outside of Josh, Charlie, and Braden, there was no one there. But it wasn't exactly normal inside, either. The couch was wet, as if it had just been shampooed. Two fans were pointed at the couch, whirling away, perhaps in an effort to dry it off. There were some unidentified stains on the tile floor next to the carpet portion near that couch. If something terrible had happened, criminalists would have to test all of the wet and stained items.

Although the probe into the whereabouts of Susan Powell was growing more ominous, there were still plausible reasons for the wet couch and fans. Little boys are well known for spilling things.

All of the items that Susan would surely have taken with her if she decided to leave Josh and her boys were still in the master bedroom: her clothes, makeup, purse, credit cards, cash, identification, driver's license, and her keys.

And her cell phone had been found in Josh's Chrysler van.

One of the more modern tools of forensic science is the ability of detectives to follow cell phone "pings" from the towers that are sprinkled all across America. Ellis Maxwell and his crew now subpoenaed Josh and Susan's phone records to see who—if anyone—either of them might have called on Sunday or through the daytime hours of Monday. The last call made or received on Susan's phone was at 2:29 P.M. on Sunday. That proved to be a call Susan had made to JoVonna Owings, who came over to visit shortly thereafter.

Josh's mobile phone records showed that he had used his phone Sunday at 12:14 P.M., when he called his father's cell phone.

There was no more activity on Josh's phone until 3:02 P.M. on Monday, when JoVonna's son, Alex, called.

Alex didn't know what to say to a man he knew his mother had been trying to find all day and he hung up. But Jo-Vonna called Josh only a minute later.

She asked him where he was, and was he aware that Susan hadn't come to work at all that day? Josh said he and the boys were just driving around the West Valley City area, and that he didn't know that Susan had missed work.

And then Josh drove about twenty miles before he called Susan's mobile phone to leave a voice message for her—asking if she needed a ride home from work. At that point, he *knew* Susan hadn't gone to work, so there was no point in leaving that message for her.

JoVonna Owings had just told him that Susan never made it to work. And he must have seen Susan's phone on the console in the minivan. It looked very much as though he was frantically trying to set up alibis for himself.

Chapter Six

Simpson Springs in Tooele County is about eighty miles south and west of West Valley City. It was once a main stop on the Pony Express route as stagecoaches and riders crossed through Utah in the mid-1800s. Simpson Springs was highly desirable then for the quality and plentitude of water available there.

In modern times, the U.S. Bureau of Land Management has a campground at Simpson Springs and the Future Farmers of America have constructed a replica of the original Pony Express station, but few tourists visit the historical site in the darkest days of winter. And hardly anyone camped overnight there in December.

It was much too cold for tent camping, and even in the Powell minivan, the 10 degree temperature and fierce winds would have been hard on Charlie and Braden.

Josh said the weather hadn't deterred him from his quick trip with the boys; he and Susan often took them to the west desert to camp. He still couldn't understand why the police had to be involved.

The Utah detectives spread out, talking to everyone

they could locate who had known Susan Powell: Amber Hardman, Kiirsi Hellewell, JoVonna Owings, Susan's family, Josh's mother and sister. Everywhere they went, they were told that Susan would *never* have abandoned her boys. They also learned that Susan and Josh had been having marital problems, financial troubles, and disagreements so wrenching that Susan was considering filing for divorce.

West Valley City police chief Buzz Nielsen's detective team also learned that Josh was the beneficiary of a number of insurance policies written on Susan's life.

"How much? How many?" Ellis Maxwell asked.

The answer and then the validation by the companies who had written the policies was staggering.

"One and a half million dollars . . ."

Detective Larry Marx discovered that Susan Powell had opened a safe deposit box at the Wells Fargo bank on West Amelia Earhart Drive in Salt Lake City. It was in her name only and no one else could open it, and yet she had accessed the box only twice. Ellis Maxwell reviewed and evaluated what was in the safe deposit box.

There was a folded letter inside, addressed to her "family and friends." It was stapled securely all around the edges. Inside, Susan wrote a warning that the contents should never be shown or given to Josh, adding: "I don't trust him."

The letter was titled "Last Will and Testament for Susan Powell," and it was dated June 28, 2008, almost eighteen months earlier.

Susan wrote that Josh Powell, her husband, had threatened to "destroy me" if they should ever get divorced. If that happened, she knew that her children would have neither a mother or a father.

She wrote that they had been having marital problems for the prior four years—which meant the trouble had begun in 2004, shortly after they had moved to Utah. She asked that if something should happen to her, whoever read this letter should contact her sister-in-law, Jennifer Graves.

Susan also stated that if she should die and it looked like an accident, someone should investigate. "It may not be an accident—even if it looks like one."

As Susan's disappearance moved to the top of the headlines and nightly news in the Salt Lake area, one man who had attended a Wells Fargo Christmas gathering of Susan's fellow employees and their spouses in December 2008 recalled talking to Josh at that event. His wife, Amber, worked with Susan, and Scott Hardman strived to be polite, but, like many of Susan's friends, Hardman avoided being stuck with Josh. Josh loved to argue and debate about almost anything. Their 2008 conversation hadn't seemed that ominous at the time, but now Scott Hardman watched the barrage of media bulletins about Susan's disappearance and felt uneasy. He called the West Valley City police and was put through to detective Larry Marx.

Marx interviewed Hardman, taking notes. Scott recalled talking with Josh Powell a year before Susan disappeared. Somehow they had gotten on the topic of fictional television crime shows. Josh, who watched a lot of television, held forth on how he visualized the perfect murder and that he knew how to get away with it. The subject turned to how a killer could hide a victim's body where it would never be discovered.

Not exactly a Christmas cheer discussion, but that was Josh. Hardman couldn't remember just what method of murder Josh would employ, but he did recall where Josh would hide a body.

Hardman told Detective Marx that Josh had pontificated that an abandoned mine shaft would be the ideal place to dispose of a corpse. All one would have to do would be to throw a body in, knock some of the surface shaft timbers and rocks loose, and the deep hole would collapse in upon itself, burying everything on the bottom.

"No detectives are going to risk their necks going down inside a mine like that," Josh said. "It would be too dangerous. There are a lot of abandoned mines in the west desert, but the police wouldn't take a chance on looking there."

Detectives Marx and Maxwell knew how perilous such a search would be. A conservative estimate of the number of old mines in Utah is between fifteen thousand to twenty thousand! Most of them have been scoured clean of coal, copper, garnets, or other minerals, and some of them are still burning at the bottom. The Utah Abandoned Mine Reclamation Program is striving to fill mines in, or at least place grates or fences around the openings on the surface.

By 2012, they hoped to have blocked entrance to at least six thousand deserted mine shafts.

If anyone stumbles into these mines, they will probably be killed. Dog owners are warned to keep track of their pets when they are in the west desert area.

Now that Susan Powell had seemingly vanished into thin air, the thought that her body might lie at the bottom of a mile-deep mine shaft seemed possible. And horrifying.

But which one—and *where*? The West Valley City police detectives kept this option to themselves. They didn't want to risk the lives of volunteers who might take it upon themselves to search for Susan in mine shafts. It was early in the probe, and they still hoped she might be alive or that they could find her in a less precarious spot. If that didn't happen, they were prepared to go into the old mines themselves.

More than eight hundred miles away in Puyallup, Washington, Chuck and Judy Cox had no idea that their daughter was missing. On the morning of December 7, 2009, Chuck received a phone call at work from Jennifer Graves.

"She asked if I had spoken to Susan lately," Chuck recalls. "I told her I'd talked to Susan the week before. Then she told me that Susan, Josh, and the boys were missing! She asked me to talk to my other daughters to see if they had heard from Susan, and of course I said I would."

But Susan's sisters hadn't heard from her. Chuck called Jennifer back that afternoon to see if she knew anything and she said that Susan was still missing, although Josh had called her.

"We were discussing what could have happened—and I had my phone turned to speaker. Judy was listening in.

"Then Josh called Jennifer and she put him on her speakerphone—so we all heard him. She asked him where he was and told him everyone was looking for him. Then he told Jennifer what she knew was a lie. He told her the boys were safe and Susan was at work. She told him Susan wasn't at work and straight-out asked him, 'What have you done?'"

At that point, the line went dead. All Chuck and Judy could do was wait. They knew the West Valley City police were at Josh and Susan's house and hoped to find out what was going on after the police questioned Josh.

"We didn't hear anything until the next day," Chuck said. "Josh called me just before noon. He said he didn't have any idea where Susan was. The last time he saw her was eleven thirty Sunday night, and she was getting ready for bed. I didn't challenge his story—because I might have inadvertently helped him come up with a more believable one. I also didn't want him to know that we overheard his conversation with Jennifer."

Josh's lack of concern alarmed Susan's parents. He told them that the police had interviewed him a few times.

Chuck and Judy were dumbfounded and frightened. They worried about what could have happened to Susan. They even half expected her to show up at their door. They knew that it was possible she and Josh had had a big fight and that she'd finally left him. Susan and Josh had been arguing recently about the endless phone calls between Josh and his father, Steven Powell. After hearing Josh talking for hours to his father, Susan was usually annoyed. Josh wouldn't allow her to talk to her sister Denise for fifteen minutes, but he burned up the phone lines with Steven. Even though they had managed to move far away from her father-in-law, Susan still felt creepy if she even heard his name.

Although the Coxes could understand why Susan would leave Josh, and separate herself from his family—except for Jennifer and her husband, Kirk Graves—they seriously doubted she would ever have left Charlie and Braden behind. Her boys were her life.

Josh was summoned to the West Valley City police headquarters again on that same day—December 8. He agreed to come in, but he arrived nearly four hours late. Ellis Maxwell repeated the same general questions he had asked Josh the day before. And Josh gave him the same peculiar answers. He had gone camping with his sons, returning the next day. They liked to camp—winter or summer.

Josh's response to the detectives was much less responsive than it had been. He asked to leave the interview prematurely, which he was subsequently allowed to do. He requested an attorney and said he wasn't going to answer any more questions. This would, indeed, be the last good chance for Detective Maxwell and his fellow investigators to talk with Josh Powell about the night of December 6.

Josh voluntarily surrendered *his* cell phone, but their technical experts discovered he had surreptitiously removed the sim card before he handed it over. With both his and Susan's sim cards missing from their phones, any record of pings from cell phone towers was gone. This would have been a prime avenue to track Josh and the boys as they drove into the west desert to go camping as a snowstorm beat down on the blue minivan.

Josh Powell might have been a difficult employee, frequently fired, socially inept—but he was very intelligent. His technical knowledge just might make up for his dimwitted alibis. He was an electronically savvy suspect.

There was, however, one disturbing aspect to this second interview, something that made him look guiltier than before. Never once did Josh Powell ask about Susan. Nor did he ask what the investigators were doing to find her. It was almost as if he had dismissed her from his life. Where most innocent husbands would have been frantic, Josh Powell had moved on only two days after Susan disappeared.

On that same day, detective Kim Waelty of the West Valley City police gently interviewed Charlie Powell. Charlie remembered that his mommy had gone camping with them.

"But she didn't come back home with us," he said. "And I don't know why."

He was only four, and Waelty didn't question him further.

Although he learned that the West Valley City detectives were talking with Josh, Chuck Cox said he couldn't imagine that Josh would have hurt Susan. He knew his son-in-law was something of an oddball, but he couldn't picture him being violent.

On December 9, 2009, the West Valley City Police Department contacted the Pierce County Sheriff's Department in

Washington State. Susan and Josh Powell had moved from Puyallup—in Sheriff Paul Pastor's jurisdiction—and it appeared that most of their family members on both sides still lived there.

Pierce County Sheriff's Department captain Brent Bomkamp assigned detective Gary Sanders to work with the Utah detectives in the search for Susan Powell. From that date on, the two law enforcement agencies would cooperate and share information, even though the missing-person case had occurred in Utah and was the West Valley City department's case.

Armed with a search warrant for the house on West 3945 South, in West Valley City, the Utah investigators removed boxes and bags and what looked like computers. The detectives shook their heads when someone tried to ask them a question. From the beginning the Utah investigators were playing their cards very close to their vests, only grudgingly releasing information to the media, who clamored for something—anything—they could use by their deadlines. If the West Valley City officers had found anything significant in Susan's disappearance, they weren't saying.

Nor was Josh talking much. He refused any more police interviews. Initially he'd talked to a few reporters, and the police investigators subpoenaed television stations for raw footage of those interviews—to study and learn exactly what he had said.

With every day that passed, things looked more ominous for Susan. Police and volunteers searched the Simpson Springs area on the possibility that she *might* have gone along on the camping trip but hadn't come back. But it was a vast area and there were so many places in the west desert where she—or her body—might be hidden.

As always, the spouse or lover of a missing person is the first suspect. But Josh Powell had yet to be declared even a "person of interest," to use the more obscure term police use currently to identify those under suspicion for a crime.

Josh Powell seemed nervous, but some members of the general public felt that any husband would be if his wife had disappeared. They were unaware at this point of his disinterest in her fate as he talked to detectives. Josh speculated to reporters that Susan might have gone off with another man, leaving him and the boys behind. No one who knew Susan Powell believed that.

Moreover, Susan had left her purse and cell phone behind. Josh pointed out the message he'd left on her cell phone, trying to sound convincing that he had believed she had gone to work on Monday. It was there on *his* outgoing voice mail, saying "I'll pick you up after work."

He would only have had to call from one cell phone in his Chrysler to another. Where he and the boys were at that point cannot be proven, although he claimed to be in West Valley City.

It was undoubtedly the women of the Salt Lake City area who doubted Josh in the beginning. They knew that very few women run off with other men, leaving their purses, keys, credit cards, makeup, and cell phones—not to mention their beloved children—behind.

Mothers don't do that. Men leave—but mothers stay, except for the minuscule number of women who seem to have been born with no maternal instinct. And Susan Powell was not one of those.

The Utah investigators felt the same way, although they didn't reveal what lab tests had shown. They were fully aware that they were probably searching for a badly injured victim . . . or a body. The stains on the couch and floor of the Powells' house had been analyzed and tested for DNA. Although the couch had been washed, criminalists discovered that the discoloration was human blood, and the DNA inherent in it was Susan Powell's.

Susan had bled on that couch, although it was difficult to pinpoint just when that had occurred. The fact that the sofa had been shampooed on the date she vanished suggested that she might very well have been injured in the house before she was forced—or carried—out.

From the neighbor's description of someone arguing in the night, Susan was probably alive when she left her home.

Chapter Seven

Susan had been missing for only seven days when Josh called his day-care provider to let her know that Charlie and Braden wouldn't be coming back. "You'll probably never see them again," he added.

He also contacted Susan's chiropractor and asked that all her future appointments be canceled.

Three days later, on December 17, Josh used his power of attorney to withdraw Susan's IRA accounts from the Wells Fargo bank.

On December 19, Josh, with Charlie and Braden in tow, drove to Puyallup, Washington, through winter storms. He didn't contact his in-laws, but Chuck and Judy Cox, along with their friends and relatives, were startled to see Josh during a vigil for Susan on December 20. Josh had Charlie with him, and they stood in the pouring rain as people lit votive candles in plastic cups.

Josh let Charlie play with the cups, apparently unconcerned that he could be burned. Josh set himself apart from the Cox family, and they found it eerie to see him standing in the rain with an enigmatic expression on his face. The vigil honored Susan and the hope that she might be alive somewhere, but it also added to the agony to know that she wasn't there.

It was an odd, sad Christmas. The Coxes had short visits from Charlie and Braden, but only after one of Josh's old friends talked him into it. He brought the boys to their grandparents for a few hours on Christmas Eve and delivered them again for Christmas Day dinner.

Chuck and Judy wondered how Josh could have left the home he'd shared with Susan at Christmas. Wouldn't it be more natural that he would stay there, waiting for her to come home or to at least have some word of her?

And then it was a New Year: 2010. Josh let their grandparents see Charlie and Braden for a short while in January, and then he balked. He refused to return Chuck and Judy Cox's phone calls or emails. Worried, they drove to the subdivision where Josh was living and found their grandsons playing on a community swing set. They were allowed to spend half an hour visiting with them.

After that, Josh told Chuck that they must never come to his neighborhood again, and that if he had anything to say, it had to be by email. That was self-defeating as Josh didn't reply to their emails.

On January 3, Charlie was attending a primary class at church in Puyallup. His world had changed so rapidly in less than a month. He was acting up some, and his teacher told him that she would have to go get his mom or dad.

Charlie looked at her with no emotion on his face and said, "My mom is dead."

Crystal Lewis, his teacher, hadn't known that Charlie was one of the children of Josh and Susan Powell, but suddenly it all became clear. The small boy with the blank face was dealing with a lot of pain.

On April 10, Chuck and Judy were surprised to get an answer to an email. Josh said he would allow them to come to see the boys at Bradley Park—but they were not to bring anyone else. No cousins, no friends. They had no choice but to agree. As soon as the Coxes arrived at the park, the boys started running around. And then Steve and Michael Powell showed up, saying they just happened to be in the area.

"For the next hour," Chuck said, "we watched Charlie and Braden play on the swings and jungle gyms with fifty other children, while Josh and Steve took pictures of them.

"After that, no more visits were allowed."

It was so painful for the sad grandparents. Sometimes, they caught fleeting glimpses of the boys. Once, they went to the Home Depot store and spotted them but Josh wouldn't let them talk to their grandsons. On another Saturday, they decided to try again. Josh refused to let Judy hug Charlie and Braden, and he demanded that they leave the store.

Josh subsequently filed a restraining order against them, claiming that Chuck was guilty of "domestic violence" because he didn't leave the Home Depot on Josh's orders. The judge, of course, tossed that out but did place anti-harassment orders on each of the Coxes "just to be safe."

It was bizarre. Susan had been missing for months, Josh was the main person of interest, and yet he still had custody of Charlie and Braden and made outrageous demands.

The weeks became months, and there were no sightings of Susan Cox Powell. Residents in the Salt Lake City area called the West Valley City detectives with various tips and theories, none of which were of much help. For chief Buzz Nielsen's force, the growing media attention was almost threatening. They had followed other cases where alleged murder victims had vanished and seen those cases become media circuses. There was the Laci and Scott Peterson case near San Francisco at Christmastime in 2002. And then Drew Peterson, the Illinois policeman suspected in 2007 for the murders of two of his wives: Kathleen Savio, whose death in her bathtub had initially been deemed accidental, and Stacy Peterson, who had simply disappeared one night, leaving her children behind with Drew Peterson. Only eighteen months before, two-year-old Caylee Anthony had vanished in Florida weeks before her body was located, and her mother, Casey, became the "person of interest."

Laci's and Caylee's bodies were not found for some time after they were murdered; Stacy hadn't been found at all.

Now it looked as though the disappearance of Susan Powell was turning into the latest high-profile "possible homicide" case, and the police in the city of 129,000 didn't want to make a mistake. They had never dealt with a possible homicide case where a victim's body had never been found. They weren't even convinced she was dead, and Chief Nielsen was worried that they couldn't get a conviction without a body.

There *have* been such convictions, and I have written about them, but out of the two thousand or more cases I have covered, bodyless murder cases are definitely in the minority.

The West Valley City Police Department wanted to be sure that they didn't rush into an arrest and trial without enough evidence for prosecutors to work with. If a defendant was found not guilty, double jeopardy would attach and he or she could never be tried again—even if Susan's body was found.

Both law enforcement veterans and laypeople grew impatient with chief Buzz Nielsen and his investigators, as they seemed to drag their feet. Josh Powell's explanations of where he and the boys had been the night Susan disappeared seemed bizarre, even unbelievable. His affect was all wrong.

After spending Christmas in his father's house, Josh had continued to behave suspiciously. On January 8, he returned to West Valley City with a moving van and his brother John. Rather than stay in the last place he'd seen his wife, Josh and some of his relatives began to pack up the house on West 3945 South, preparatory to his move to Washington to live with Steven Powell. He put the house up for rent or sale and soon found a renter.

To many, it felt as though Josh was erasing his life with Susan—indeed, that he was *erasing* Susan herself.

Or, perhaps, he already had—and only Josh knew where her physical body was.

The Powell case became the current darling of the national media—from the tabloids to *People* magazine to Nancy Grace. In an era where certain criminal cases have so many unresolved questions and news bulletins, news of the missing mother became for a while the next "big thing."

Josh now lived in Washington State, back in his father's house, along with his brothers John and Michael, and his sister Alina. He wasn't under arrest; he hadn't even been called a suspect.

Charlie went to a nearby school and Josh allegedly found employment, although he wouldn't tell reporters where he worked.

Where Chuck Cox had once been quoted as saying that he didn't think Josh would have hurt Susan, he no longer felt that way. He couldn't understand why his son-in-law wouldn't cooperate more with the police in Utah; *he* was the last to see Susan. Surely Josh knew things—no matter how seemingly unimportant to the case—that might help find her.

Steven Powell joined Josh in saying that they believed Susan was promiscuous, and that she almost certainly had gone away with a lover. When they learned that Steven Koecher, a Utah man in his thirties, had vanished within the same time frame that Susan had, both men suggested strongly that this was her secret lover.

That was ridiculous. Police found no links whatsoever between the two. They had lived some distance apart, and

Susan never knew the missing man. Only Steven and Josh Powell insisted there was a connection.

Susan's family organized media "blitzes" to keep people looking for her. There was always the danger that people would forget about Susan and they didn't want her to be forgotten. If she *was* alive somewhere, if she was suffering from amnesia after a physical domestic violence incident, they wanted to keep her face in front of the public so that someone, somewhere, might recognize her.

The Coxes retained two attorneys to represent them. One was a Seattle attorney whom they had seen frequently on television, Anne Bremner, and she would prove to be expert in keeping Susan's case alive.

Anne is very attractive, tall and willowy with long blond hair, a natural for television. Most readers will have seen her on one national show or another; she has appeared on dozens of shows to comment on criminal cases and give her analysis of case law.

She spends many hours each month flying all over America. She has no hobbies; she has no time for them— but she loves her cats.

I have known Anne for more than twenty years, and I'm well aware that she has a soft and giving heart, and she is an attorney who fights for the underdog. She probably works too many cases pro bono (without charging the client) than she should, but she is the epitome of what a lawyer should be—smart, clever, and interested most of all in justice. Such a stance hasn't made her rich, but it has given her the satisfaction of knowing she has done the greatest good for the most people.

Bremner has worked for decades on the state's side of criminal trials. She is far from anti-police; in fact, she has been the legal counsel for the Seattle Police Department for many years. Anne graduated from Stanford and received her law degree from the University of Puget Sound. From 1983 to 1988, she was a King County deputy prosecuting attorney, and she specialized in trying defendants in sex crimes. She won two hundred of those cases, taking dangerous offenders off the streets.

She is a trial attorney who has spent twenty-seven years working on highly visible cases. She represented Washington State attorney general (later governor) Christine Gregoire, and was the attorney for the Des Moines, Washington, police department in the case of elementary teacher Mary Kay Letourneau, who was arrested and convicted of second-degree rape of one of her students, Vili Fualaau, then thirteen. Anne Bremner was also on Amanda Knox's defense team of lawyers, when the University of Washington student was jailed in Italy on charges that she was an accessory in the murder of her roommate. After being in prison for years, Amanda Knox was finally acquitted.

In another landmark case, Bremner spoke for the city of Seattle in a national test case by the American Civil Liberties Union involving the riots that accompanied the World Trade Organization convention in 1999.

Now Anne Bremner stepped in to help Susan Powell's family in their almost hopeless search for their daughter. Either Anne or her paralegal, Misty Scott, vowed to be there for the Coxes in court, or, if necessary, at their home to help them bear up under the stunning revelations that occurred frequently.

Steve Downing, the Coxes' other attorney, would do his best to help Chuck and Judy Cox and Jennifer and Kirk Graves have reasonable visitation with Charlie and Braden. Anne Bremner volunteered to speak for them pro bono, and file civil suits if that was what was needed.

The West Valley City detectives had discovered a good deal of evidence—both physical and circumstantial—that would have spurred on most law enforcement agencies to seek arrest warrants. But chief Buzz Nielsen didn't want to move ahead with charges too rapidly.

Nielsen's detectives had found no unidentified fingerprints in the house on West 3945 South, a common occurrence when both a victim and a suspect share the same house. They expected that they would find Josh's, Susan's, and the little boys' prints. The only way Josh's prints would have been of important evidentiary value would be if they'd been left in blood.

Only the Utah and Pierce County, Washington, detectives knew what was embedded in Josh's computers, seized with a search warrant by the West Valley City police shortly after Susan disappeared. There were disturbing files. A computer technician discovered them on the hard drive; they were pornographic with incest themes, peopled with children's cartoon images of familiar characters like SpongeBob SquarePants, the Simpsons, and Superman. Only they weren't funny; their content was clearly adult-to-child incestuous acts. The investigators and child psychologists who were contacted later feared that children could watch these cartoons and believe that such activities were normal—even funny.

What was going on in Josh Powell's mind?

On May 11, 2010, Steven Powell gave the West Valley City investigators consent to search his house in Puyallup, Washington—the house where he, Josh, John, Alina, Charlie, and Braden were currently residing. There were several Utah detectives participating as well as FBI Special Agent Gary France. Steven gave France permission to look in a locked cabinet in his bedroom.

Inside, France discovered image after image of Susan Powell. Perhaps it shouldn't have been a surprise to the officers who searched for something that might lead to Susan; Steven had been interviewed by investigators a number of times and he never held back on his "love" and infatuation with his daughter-in-law.

And yet the photographs of Susan had clearly been taken by someone without her knowing it. They were egregious invasions of her privacy. Even though she probably hadn't known about Steven's stalking with a camera, she must have sensed something dark and chilling while she lived in his house. It was no wonder that she had been uncomfortable—even afraid—of Steven Powell, and that she had done her best to avoid him, even going so far as to want to leave her own family and move far away to another state.

In some of the images Susan was clothed, but in others she was in various stages of undress. It appeared that the photographer had been able to peer through a slightly open door and watch her when she thought she was alone. One photo showed her in her underwear in the bathroom, doing her hair, while another view was of her in a dress with her legs slightly apart—enough to reveal her panties. There were some odd totally nude photos where Susan's head had been pasted over the original models' heads.

There were other pictures, this time many shots of a man's erect penis while he was masturbating. And as the camera drew back, the man masturbating to Susan's image on a television screen was Steven Powell. He simulated oral sex with an unknowing reflection, but it was still shockingly invasive.

Special Agent France found a number of videotapes labeled "Susan" in the locked cabinet, along with women's undergarments.

"Where did you get these pictures and tapes of your daughter-in-law?" Gary France asked Steven Powell.

"Some I took," he answered easily, "and some I copied off of Josh's computer without him knowing."

Steven Powell didn't seem embarrassed about his sexual obsession with Susan. Rather, he appeared almost proud of the "secret love" he believed they shared.

Police detectives see any number of shocking things that laymen never encounter, but Steven's fantasy sex life shocked those who searched his house.

They didn't know at that point that they had only seen the tip of the iceberg.

Chapter Eight

West Valley City detective Ellis Maxwell and Pierce County detective Gary Sanders had shared what information they knew as the months passed. Maxwell said that his department had recovered one of Susan's journals early on from her office at Wells Fargo in December 2009. This diary had begun in January 2002. Susan noted inside that she had kept personal journals since she was eight years old and that those were "packed away." The one she kept at the Wells Fargo office described the arguments and unhappiness in her marriage to Josh Powell, troubles that had apparently begun in 2005 and continued until the last time she made an entry, on October 26, 2009—less than six weeks before she vanished.

Susan had also written about her father-in-law in a time period that began in December 2002 and continued to 2007. Obviously, even the move to Utah in 2004 hadn't succeeded as far as her escaping Steven Powell was concerned.

Susan wrote that Steven was a negative influence on Josh, that he was a pedophile, and she commented on how hard it was for her to forgive Steven for what he had said to and about her.

"I don't want him in *my* life, in Charlie and Braden's lives," she wrote. "I really, really wish that Josh would cut his father completely out of *his* life!"

Josh and Steven Powell had told friends and even the media that they had about seven to nine of Susan's journals in *their* possession. When the Utah detectives had asked for the originals and/or copies of those journals to help them in their search for her, Steven Powell said he would give them only copies. And there was a proviso before he would do even that. He wanted the most recent of Susan's diaries that the West Valley City police had.

But then Steven changed his mind. He called Deputy U.S. Marshal Spencer and said that neither he nor Josh was interested in releasing Susan's writings to the police, and that they didn't intend to cooperate with the investigators any longer.

Josh had begun a website called susanpowell.org within a week or so of Susan's vanishing. Now he and his father began to post excerpts from her journals going back to 1999, when she was in her mid-teens. They chose sections when Susan and her best friend, Brittainy Cornett, complained about their parents—not uncommon for teenagers—or wrote about crushes they had.

Josh and Steven were clearly setting out to destroy not only Susan's image—but her family's, too.

Rather than worry about Susan's fate or trying to find her, both Josh and Steven Powell became more nasty in degrading her. They posted a link to a journal entry they believed Susan had written about Judy Cox, detailing what she considered "abuse." As it turned out, Susan hadn't written that at all: Brittainy had jotted it into Susan's journal when she was upset with *her* mother.

In November 2010, *Salt Lake Tribune* reporter Nate Carlisle managed to obtain an interview with Josh, who had been avoiding the media *and* the police for almost a year. Now, he told the *Tribune* that Susan was an "extremely unstable" woman and that her mental illness had caused her to abandon him and their sons. The only way to get her to come back would be for the story of her disappearance to be dropped. As it was, he opined that she would probably be too embarrassed to face public opinion.

Josh blamed Susan's family for her running away. They had always wanted her to be perfect, he said, "A saint with no fallibility."

He told Carlisle that his wife's family had to stop lying about him and learn to accept Susan's flaws.

"She doesn't have as much strength as they think she does," he said, with tears in his eyes. But Josh insisted she was "a good person, and a good wife, and a good mother."

Josh kept to the same story he'd given all along, reminding readers that it hadn't been cold in his van that night, since he had purchased a generator and a heater only two weeks before. Josh was sure that Susan had gone with him to buy the generator. He couldn't remember the name of the store, however.

Steven Powell backed his son up. He dismissed the

damp carpet and couch in his son's home. Susan had been cleaning them. As for the red splotch, he said it was "probably juice or something."

Josh Powell said he wouldn't talk to the West Valley City police again; there was no point. Steven described his missing daughter-in-law as a woman who was "very sexually and financially motivated." He said she told her friends about many sexual adventures before she married Josh.

How Steven Powell could possibly know what Susan had told her friends was a mystery. But as time passed, Josh's father would hint more and more broadly that he and Susan were sexually involved. It became clear that Steven was unnaturally obsessed with his daughter-in-law, just as Susan had told Kiirsa Hellewell.

Susan Powell's disappearance might have been dismissed by her husband and father-in-law, but no one else forgot it.

Another new year arrived: 2011. No one had seen or heard from Susan Powell, and any paper trail she might possibly have left was nonexistent.

A long time after the fact, Robin Snyder, who worked in a Comfort Inn motel in Sandy, Utah, which is about sixteen miles south of West Valley City, had tried to contact detectives about a troubling incident on December 7, 2009, but no one had returned her call to a tip line. More than two years later, she tried once more to report what she had seen and heard.

"This man and his two little boys came into our complimentary breakfast buffet at the inn," Robin said. "I work there—help filling up the coffeepots, put out fruit and rolls, juice and that sort of thing. When I got to work about 6:30 that morning, they were sitting at a table."

One of the little boys had looked up at Robin and asked: "Do you know what happened to my mom?"

"No," she'd replied. "What happened to your mom?"

The man, who she assumed was their father, kept his face averted as she talked to the older boy. But before he could answer, another guest asked for more coffee. When Robin Snyder turned back, she saw the man hustling the boys out the door to the parking lot. Later, she recognized images of the Powell family as the story broke on television, and said there was no doubt that they were the father and sons she had seen in the Comfort Inn.

The Cox family's vow to keep Susan's memory alive was working. Everyone in America seemed to recognize Josh, Charlie, and Braden Powell.

"The boys didn't even get to eat their sweet rolls," Robin Snyder recalled. "They all left, all of a sudden." It had seemed at first as though the child had been telling her a joke, or about some incident involving his mother. She hadn't taken his question in a literal sense. But now she wondered if he was indeed asking her where his mother was. Maybe he didn't *know* what had happened to his mother.

Worse, maybe he did. She decided that she would have to go to the West Valley City police in person and tell them about the incident.

*   *   *

During that brief encounter in the Comfort Inn, it couldn't have been more than seven or eight hours since Josh supposedly left the house to take Charlie and Braden camping, and only about five or six hours since the sick neighbor woman on West 3945 South had overheard a couple arguing outside her window, and a vehicle racing away.

Had Josh really gone on a freezing camping trip—or had he gone into the desert on a macabre errand, accomplished it, and then checked into the motel with his boys? Maybe he hadn't even registered at the motel, but had pretended they were guests there to establish an alibi for the hours in between.

The latter seemed likely. Charlie and Braden were older in 2011 and in the two years since their mother left their home, they were becoming much more verbal. For months Braden had said, "Mommy's in the mine," although he gave few details. At one point he suggested, "Maybe my mommy was looking for crystals."

Hunting for crystals *was* something Susan liked to do when they went camping in the west desert in good weather. Charlie and Braden could be confused about *when* they went camping. But as he grew older, Braden gave more details. Later he tried to explain what happened that frigid night to Steve Downing, one of the attorneys who represented Susan's family.

"We went camping," he said. "Mommy was in the

trunk. Mommy and Dad got out and then Mommy disappeared."

Braden was also a talented young artist and he drew lots of pictures at YMCA summer camp. One was chilling. It was of the Powells' minivan. Josh was driving, and Charlie and Braden were in the backseat.

But Susan was in the trunk.

"Why was your mommy in the trunk?" Braden was asked.

He shrugged his shoulders and said, "I don't know. My mom and dad got out, but my mom got lost."

Whether his sons said anything to Josh about what they remembered, no one knows. If they had, that might account for what appeared to be the exacerbation of his nervousness. The bags under his eyes were puffier, and his whole face drooped.

Despite their earlier support of Josh, the Cox family had long since come to believe that Josh had, indeed, hurt Susan and almost certainly killed her. It was a stab in their hearts every time Charlie talked about his mommy being "lost."

Chuck, particularly, vowed to keep the search for her before the public, and appeared on nationwide network shows as well as local shows. Susan's photos became familiar to millions of people. And yet no one reported any sightings of her that seemed to fit.

Susan had left absolutely no paper trail, and she hadn't called anyone. If she was alive someplace in the world, it had been impossible to trace her whereabouts.

In the summer of 2011, Josh and Steven Powell continued their campaign to convince the public that Susan had a sordid past.

On July 14, Josh and Steven appeared on the *Today* show on NBC. They bragged that they were in possession of two thousand pages of Susan's journal entries. During their interview, the cameras panned over a laptop computer in the background so the viewing audience could glimpse Susan's handwriting in red and blue ink. Josh and Steven even allowed the show technicians to reveal some of the sections that Susan had written.

Steven told the media that Susan's journals were very important because she had detailed her relationships with many men and wrote about her "sexual fantasies." He all but crowed as he said he and his son would be releasing more and more of Susan's diary pages, and also upload them to the website they had set up in an effort to locate her.

It was ridiculous; most of Susan's "relationships with men" entries were about girlish crushes, and not even vaguely titillating.

Detectives Gary Sanders and Ellis Maxwell were very concerned by the obstructive behavior Josh and Steven were demonstrating. They wouldn't share Susan's journals with the law enforcement departments who were desperately trying to locate her, but they were prepared to pick and choose from her personal thoughts and post them for the world to see.

Steven Powell and his children believed that they were within their rights as they castigated Susan. They had not shown one scintilla of concern about her fate, but that may well have been part of Steven and Josh's insistence that she had run off with the man who went missing in Utah/ Nevada about the same time she did.

The missing man—Steven Koecher, thirty, of St. George, Utah—hadn't been seen since December 13, 2009. His car was found parked in a cul-de-sac in a posh neighborhood in Henderson, Nevada, near Las Vegas. Wrapped Christmas presents were in the car. A security camera in a nearby home snapped frames of a man resembling Koecher walking away from that vehicle. Koecher's mother told reporters that he hadn't known Susan Powell. The *only* connection they had was the proximity of the dates they vanished, and Steven and Josh Powell had seized upon that coincidence to add weight to their espoused theory that Susan had run off with another man.

Koecher is still missing as this is written. In the last year, his mother has been widowed and has lost her father to death, but she still keeps her Christmas tree lit year-round, hoping that her son will return. Koecher is blond, blue-eyed, and five feet, eleven inches tall.

Aware that public opinion wasn't on their side, Steven Powell claimed *he* had no idea why his family was unpopular. "Why don't people try to get to know us?" Steven asked rhetorically. "If they did, I think they'd like us."

Perhaps. Perhaps they would not have.

Steven's comments about how sexually involved he had been with his daughter-in-law became more snide and sickening. He actually told reporters that Susan was an "exhibitionist" who sometimes appeared partially undressed in front of him, that she flirted with him. In an interview with KOMO-TV in Seattle, he described his relationship with her as clearly romantic—and physical, stopping just short of saying they had been intimate.

If only in his own mind.

This, of course, warred with what Susan had told her closest girlfriends and her sister Denise. Steven Powell had made her skin crawl.

Chuck Cox had reportedly heard that the West Valley City police expected to arrest Josh Powell in the summer of 2011, but it was the middle of August and Josh, Charlie, and Braden were still living with Steven.

No arrests had taken place.

Since 2009, Chuck Cox had appeared on more than forty television and radio shows, including *Good Morning America, Today, Dr. Phil,* and *Larry King Live,* to fulfill his promise to his daughter that he would "shout her name from the rooftops" until she was found, and he wasn't about to stop.

On August 20, 2011, Chuck and Judy, along with members of their family and friends, stood in the Fred Meyer mega-store parking lot in Puyallup and handed out fliers with Susan's photo and announced to shoppers that their daughter and sister was still missing.

Suddenly Chuck Cox and Steven Powell met head-on. It was definitely not a friendly encounter. Steven confronted Chuck and began shouting that he was deliberately embarrassing the Powell family at the store where they shopped. That was true about the Fred Meyer store, but it was also the store where Chuck and Judy shopped regularly, too.

Fred Meyer employees knew Josh Powell well; he was a problem customer, and clerks dreaded seeing him entering the store.

"He's always complaining," a department manager said later. "Nothing suits him, he returns stuff—and I think everybody who works here knows him."

But the conflict in their parking lot had nothing whatsoever to do with Fred Meyer—"Freddie's," as northwesterners call it. It was strictly between Chuck Cox and Steven Powell, and television reporters rapidly got word of it and clustered around them.

Steven Powell accused Chuck Cox of humiliating his family, warning people against them—especially against Josh—and he was dismissive of any suggestion that Susan had come to harm.

As he and Josh had been doing of late, Steven Powell smeared her reputation and continued in his monologue about how she had run off with another man, leaving his poor son to grieve.

A few minutes later, Josh came driving up and joined them. Tears ran down his face as he maintained his stance as a cuckolded husband, left to raise two small boys alone, reviled by the public because of what his father-in-law was saying.

Chuck Cox was angry; he had held his temper for twenty-one months, waiting and hoping for word of his precious daughter. Now he reminded Steven Powell that he was the one breaking a restraining order by showing up and interrupting them as they handed out fliers. He was clearly more in control of the situation than either Steven or Josh was, but he was upset, too.

There seemed to be a disconnect of empathy on the Powells' part as their voices rose. Beyond Josh's showing up at the December 2009 vigil shortly after Susan vanished, neither he nor his father had demonstrated any concern for her family's pain.

More than ever, the Powells simply wanted it all to go away. In less than four months, Susan would be gone for two years. All that time without a word. Steven Powell was furious that Chuck wouldn't just let it drop. Why did he have to keep talking about it, and handing out his damned fliers? Didn't he know how upsetting this was to their mutual grandsons?

Probably less upsetting than losing their mother.

Neither grandfather was deterred by the media teams who stood by with mikes and cameras watching what one reporter called "a surreal scene."

Did either man know what was about to come to a head in this tangled case? When Josh drove up and broke into tears, it would seem so. The world was closing in on him.

Chapter Nine

The Utah police were searching in the west desert of Utah and also near Ely, Nevada. Breaking news bulletins shouted that "remains" had been found, and that they could be what was left of Susan. But the decomposed body was soon identified as a Mexican citizen—a male.

Then there was another find of what looked like a human body. But that rumor kept diminishing. First, there was supposed to be a body. And then charred bones. And, finally, the news that only ashes were found. Unidentifiable ashes. Impossible to tell if they were human or animal. Or wood, for that matter.

In the mines that were shallow enough to explore, searchers found nothing but rubble. They risked their own lives for several days, all to no avail.

Susan might very well be at the bottom of a mine, but if she was, the person or persons who had hidden her there had made sure she would never be found.

*   *   *

In Puyallup, only five days after the parking lot argument, the case was about to explode wide open. Detective Gary Sanders had written an affidavit to obtain a search warrant to search Steven Powell's house again. The Pierce County Sheriff's Department was seeking permission to search for Susan Powell's journals, photographs, digital media to "include but not limited to" laptop computers, desktop computers, or any type of device that could store digital media copies of Susan's journals.

Searchers would also seek images or papers that contained password information to access encrypted digital media. And "any other fruits or instrumentalities determined to be evidence of the crimes of aggravated kidnapping, homicide, and obstruction of justice."

Photographs and videotape of the interior and exterior of the Powell home, garage, or other structures on the property would be searched for, along with three Dodge Caravans and a light blue Chrysler Town and Country minivan.

The search warrant was granted on August 24, 2011, by a Pierce County Superior Court judge.

On August 25, at least fifteen law enforcement officers, some from the West Valley City, Utah, police department and some from Pierce County, met for a briefing at Pierce County's South Precinct. They were told what to look for at Steven Powell's house and what was to be seized (if located). A tentative time to execute the search warrant was being discussed at 2:15 that afternoon when Ed Troyer, the public information officer for the sheriff's department, got a phone call from a television news team saying they had heard "something was going to be going on at the Powell residence."

Troyer notified Ellis Maxwell, who conferred with Gary Sanders. They agreed that they should move ahead with the search warrant as soon as possible. Neighbors around Steven's tan and white house witnessed a group of squad cars parked in front, and then a phalanx of officers gathered near the front door.

One of Steven's male relatives answered the door naked. Steven Powell was not at home, but Josh, Charlie, and Braden were, along with Alina and John Powell, Josh's siblings. It was a very hot afternoon, and once the residence was secured, the Powell family members were asked to wait outside, where it was a bit cooler. Embarrassed by the stares of neighbors, Josh asked if they could move to the backyard. That was fine with the search team; they particularly wanted to avoid upsetting the little boys.

Charlie and Braden knew Pierce County detective Teresa Berg and leapt into her arms when she arrived, and they also seemed secure with Adam Anderson, the head of the Forensic Unit.

Luckily, they were young enough that they didn't understand what was happening.

Alina Powell was angry at the intrusion and kept going back into the house, staring down the officers who asked her to stay in the backyard. It was all very uncomfortable—but there was no other way to do it. The investigators couldn't take any more risks that Steven or Josh might destroy possibly vital evidence.

Gary Sanders and Ellis Maxwell logged in the names of

all the law enforcement personnel who entered the house, noting their times of arrival and departure.

What would they find inside? In the prior search warrant, now more than a year in the past, Steven Powell had been agreeable and seemed to hold nothing back. In fact, he had actually seemed pleased that the FBI agent came along on that search. But since then, Steven had grown annoyed and resistant to requests from both Utah and Pierce County detectives.

After Adam Anderson had finished taking photos of everything stipulated in the search warrant, the men and women searchers swarmed over the house. Once again, seasoned detectives would be taken aback by what they uncovered as they combed the contents of every room.

At 3 P.M., Josh Powell asked if he could have his mobile phone and Bluetooth, and Ellis Maxwell went to Josh's bedroom and returned with them. Then Josh said he wanted to take his sons and leave. Gary Sanders and Maxwell searched the blue minivan, found nothing of evidentiary value, and released it to Josh.

Josh told Charlie and Braden that they were going to McDonald's, and he was allowed to leave with his boys.

Josh didn't come back until after the investigators left. Ellis Maxwell noted that Josh had not asked one single question about how the investigation into his wife's disappearance was going, or if this search warrant meant that the detectives had new information.

The main intent of this massive exploration was to find anything inside that might have evidence bearing on Susan Powell's vanishing. The "surreal" sense of this case was exacerbated. The law enforcement officers didn't find as much as they thought they might about the night of December 6, 2009, when Susan vanished, but they found items that shocked even veteran investigators.

For almost two years, everyone had focused on Josh Powell, the oldest of the Powell sons. But West Valley City chief Buzz Nielsen had often said that he didn't feel confident enough in the evidence they had to arrest Josh.

Not without Susan's body.

As it turned out, Josh, the apple, hadn't fallen far from the tree as he'd downloaded sexually suspect sites into his computers. Steven Powell's bedroom, closet, and bathroom yielded more items that showed his almost-psychotic fixation with Susan.

Ellis Maxwell and Gary Sanders had been designated as the *only* detectives at the Powell house who would sift through possible evidence to determine what would be seized. They began their onerous task.

The earlier search warrant had yielded the surreptitious photographs that Steven had taken of Susan. On August 25, 2011, there was more—much more. Searchers found several VHS and 8mm videocassettes, many with Susan's name on them, women's underwear, used tampons, a length of long brown hair that appeared to have been pulled from a sink drain, and more still photographs of Susan, both dressed and in her undergarments.

There were also several spiral notebooks where Steven had written about Susan. Although he began his notations sounding like a shy, insecure, lovesick schoolboy, he progressed rapidly to detailing his unbelievably salacious sexual fantasies about Susan. He used the most degrading four-letter words to describe parts of her body and his own frequent masturbation while he thought about her.

Steven Powell appeared to be convinced by his own delusions, believing that his daughter-in-law harbored lust for him! He hypothesized that when Susan sat quietly, looking away from him, she was actually masturbating in her mind and reaching silent climaxes because she was so sexually turned on.

A hundred. Two hundred. More than three hundred pages filled with typed entries or Steven's sprawling handwriting. He read quiet seduction and temptation into everything Susan did.

Steven recalled in an early notebook that he had professed his love to Susan openly on July 13, 2003. He was dismayed and puzzled when she seemed to avoid him after that. If he saw her at all, she was with Josh.

In December 2003, Steven was helping Susan and Josh pack for their move to Salt Lake City.

"She was at least somewhat friendly, though not visibly happy," he wrote in his spiral notebook. "Toward the end of the day, she was posing again, doing her sexual thing with me. She sat on the floor with her body facing me for about five minutes with her legs spread wide, and her right knee bent with her heel nearly touching her crotch. We had just unassembled her bird's cage, and she was idly playing with the screws with one hand, picking them up and dropping them on the carpet . . . When Josh left the apartment for about five minutes, she turned her head to the right and held it there, so that I was facing her left profile and had opportunity to look her over and drink her image in. I just stood and stared at her, neither of us speaking, moving my eyes from her beautiful face to her crotch, her face to her crotch. Back and forth. She knew what I was doing, and I knew she was letting me do it . . ."

Steven concluded that Susan was deliberately responsible for his getting an erection and that she herself was agitated and aroused.

"When she gets aroused, she becomes quiet like that, and plays a little cat and mouse game. She plays the demure act, as if trying to avoid the attention she knows I am paying to her."

This excerpt from Steven Powell's journals is mild when compared to his other writings about Susan, his erections, and his masturbation sessions several times a day. He seemed to be in a perpetual state of priapism.

Steven had written a number of songs, all inspired by his "love" for Susan. The one that seemed to describe his obsession best was "I Will Love You in a Secret Way."

For years he had peeked at her, stalked her, taken furtive photos of her in her most private moments, and frightened her as she sensed that his interest in her was nothing like what a father-in-law should feel for his son's wife. Now, in this journal, it was Christmas Day 2003, and Steven panicked at the thought of Susan moving far away from him.

He wanted to see her one more time, and she had refused to come to his house again. Steven Powell had heard Josh mention shopping at Costco, so he drove to the mammoth store, hoping to get one more glimpse of Susan before she left the state.

"Pulling out of a parking space, I scraped someone's bumper and had to deal with that," Steven began. "Luckily, he accepted a twenty-dollar bill to buy a bottle of touch-up paint. I was agitated because I was afraid I would miss an opportunity to see Susan if she was at Costco. When I got to Costco, they were *there!* Their van was parked next to the tire-install bays and Josh was outside talking to someone.

"Susan was still sitting in the van, reading. Neither noticed me even though I drove by facing Susan and looked at her. I flipped around and parked where I could videotape her. It was too dark to get a good image of her in the van, but she got out to go into the store and I caught her from behind mainly. She turned around, apparently to yell something at Josh and I got a dark grainy shot of her face . . ."

Steven pasted many still shots from his videotaping in the spiral notebook to illustrate his memories. Susan was trapped, unknowing, within his cameras.

He didn't leave. Neither Susan nor Josh was aware that Steven waited outside Costco for almost an hour, hoping to get more videotape shots of Susan. He did capture more grainy shots, some of which were of Susan looking over her shoulder. Steven wondered if she was looking at him, letting him know that she knew he was there.

Steven Powell went on for eleven more pages detailing his stalking of Susan at Costco. And then he added nineteen pornographic pages about how he lusted for Susan.

It would be an invasion of her privacy, of her very soul, to quote those pages, so I won't. The two detectives—one from Utah and one from Washington—were appalled by Powell's journals. He went on so long in his obscene fantasies that they almost became boring in their repetition. Oddly, he had made no effort to hide them, possibly thinking that the investigators would never come to search his house again.

Susan could never have guessed how dark her father-in-law's mind really was. His scrutiny and imagination went far beyond anything she could have visualized. Did Josh know? Probably not. Once more, Steven Powell appeared to have no guilt about the way he coveted his son's wife.

After Josh and Susan had moved to Utah, Steven began a new journal. Although he still proclaimed that Susan had opened up a new view of the world for him, a view that showed him that younger women *did* find him "sexy and attractive," he noted that no woman could ever replace Susan, because they were meant to be together. "I am the voyeur," he said. "She is the exhibitionist."

But it didn't take long before Steven Powell became fixated on another woman in her twenties. She worked for a company that often had booths at trade shows that Steven attended.

Joan* was a beauty contest winner, engaged to be married soon, and had been friendly to Steven—friendly as a woman might be to someone her father's age. When he emailed her, she usually responded politely and kindly.

Now Steven believed that this new woman was coming on to him. As always, he began his journal entries sounding like an infatuated high school boy, but he soon descended into vulgarity and intensely disturbing scenarios.

In the hot August afternoon, Ellis Maxwell and Gary Sanders seized Steven Powell's journals as possible evidence in Susan Powell's disappearance, astonished by the sexual snake pit the search warrant was uncovering.

Chapter Ten

Susan's journals were also in Steven Powell's house. Her private thoughts since she was seven or eight through her marriage to Josh *were*, indeed, in her husband and father-in-law's possession.

Moreover, Steven confessed in one of *his* journals that he had snuck into Josh and Susan's apartment and read Susan's journals. He had told neither of them about that intrusion, although he was unhappy when he didn't find anything positive about himself.

Shortly after he arrived, Lieutenant Phil Quinlan of the West Valley City Police Department, who was at the Powell house for the search warrant, asked Alina Powell if she would speak with him. She agreed, and they talked in the backyard. Quinlan asked if Alina had any information that might help them investigate the fate of her missing sister-in-law. Alina shook her head slightly. She told Quinlan that initially she had wondered if Josh might have had something to do with Susan's absence. But Alina said she'd spoken about that with her brother in several candid conversations, and she had come to believe he wasn't involved.

"I'm supporting Josh," Alina said. "Unless there is any evidence that could prove he had anything to do with it."

"If you found out anything like that, would you report it to us?" Quinlan asked.

She nodded and said she would. Then she asked Quinlan why police had been searching mines out in the area near Ely, Nevada.

"We had to," the detective lieutenant answered. "We had some evidence that Susan might be there."

"I think it was all a ruse to put pressure on Josh," Alina argued.

All the while Quinlan talked with Alina, Josh kept wandering back to where the interview was taking place. He seemed to be concerned that his sister was openly speaking to law enforcement, and he kept urging Alina to leave the property with him. She hadn't really said anything to implicate Josh, but apparently he was worried that she had.

When Josh left shortly with his boys to go to McDonald's, Alina remained at her home.

Lieutenant Quinlan was one of the investigators who searched Steven's bedroom. He tried to open a two-drawer filing cabinet with several keys on a nearby ring, with no success. When he drilled the lock with a power drill, the drawers opened easily. Quinlan stared at a curious object in the top drawer. It was flesh-colored and made of latex.

As he looked closer, Quinlan saw it was a reproduction of female buttocks and genitalia. It had a labia, vagina, and anus.

Also in this filing cabinet were more pictures of Susan, including her wedding photos. But someone had cut Josh's face out of the frames, so that only Susan's face remained.

The search wasn't over.

Beyond Steven Powell's perverted obsession with Susan, the investigators were taken aback to find that he had other sexual perversions. The elder Powell was apparently a voyeur, watching and filming young females in his neighborhood. There were scores more photographs, forbidden shots of little girls and teenagers.

Susan's was a missing-person case under the West Valley City Police Department's jurisdiction and the evidence seized so far had to do with her. But now the search team had discovered a possible crime in Pierce County.

They found many, many computer file folders and subfolders containing pictures of prepubescent and slightly older girls. The shots had obviously been taken by someone in Steven's bedroom, someone who had focused on neighboring houses in this subdivision, which had large houses on small lots. Building codes allowed for six-foot fences, but there was no protection from someone aiming cameras from an upstairs room.

Through Steven Powell's window, and then a window in the next lot, across a room and down a hall, a camera had been aimed stealthily at two little girls in an upstairs bathroom.

There was no question of *their* innocence as they had taken baths, used the toilet, dressed, and undressed. They had no idea that a man old enough to be their grandfather was aiming a camera with a telephoto lens at them in their most private moments.

But that wasn't all. Steven Powell's files held what proved to be *two thousand* pictures he—or someone in his bedroom—had taken of young girls and those who appeared to be in junior high and high school. The camera lens had zoomed in to focus on their breasts, buttocks, and genital area.

Some of the teenagers were playing basketball in a driveway, and, in a few of the shots, a car's license plate was visible.

The images were in subfolders labeled "Neighbors," "Taking bath-1," "Taking bath-2," "Open window in back house," and "Brandi* on 191st."

Some had been taken in daylight, some at night, and the dates on them spanned several years.

The evidence of voyeurism and child pornography was now in the hands of Pierce County sheriff's detectives. Identifying the victims, however, wouldn't be easy. Some of the nearby houses were rentals, and several had been sold to new owners over the years.

Pierce County prosecuting attorney Mark Lindquist, Sheriff Paul Pastor, and their respective staffs had grown increasingly frustrated as the probe into Susan Powell's disappearance moved at what seemed to them a snail's pace for almost two years. Susan was, basically, a resident of Pierce County, as were most of her relatives and friends, and Lindquist and Pastor wanted to do everything their offices could to bring about arrest warrant(s) for whoever was responsible for her fate.

The problem was that the missing-person case was within the domain of the West Valley City police. Gary Sanders of the Pierce County Sheriff's Department had been involved with the case since three days after Susan vanished, and a few dozen lawmen and criminalists from the sheriff's office had also taken part in this case, which had grown more convoluted and weird as time passed.

Prosecutor Mark Lindquist had said privately that if this had been his case, he would have charged Josh Powell with murder early on. "There is direct evidence. There is circumstantial evidence. There is motive," Lindquist pointed out. "There is everything but the body."

Mark Lindquist finally had probable crimes that had occurred in *his* jurisdiction that involved either Steven or Josh Powell. If exploring the story behind the thousands of clandestine photographs found in the August 25 search warrant should lead back to Susan, there might finally be a break in her case.

Lindquist and two of his deputy prosecutors—Mary Robinett and Grant Blinn—met with detectives from Washington and Utah. They devised a plan to locate the nameless victims, girls who probably hadn't even known they *were* victims of a sexually obsessed man with a camera.

Gary Sanders and detective Bob Bobrowski from the West Valley City force suggested that they start with the subfolders with titles. Investigators would go to the neighborhood where Steven and Josh Powell lived and attempt to locate the girls caught in the voyeuristic photographs. It meant door-to-door canvassing, one of the oldest police techniques in law enforcement history. Yet it is also one that still can be counted on to elicit information.

Sanders, Maxwell, Bobrowski, detective Kevin Johnson, and sergeant Teresa Berg began by tracing the license plate that showed in some of the bedroom pictures through the computers at the Washington State Department of Motor Vehicles. The plate came back to homeowners who had once lived just across the street from Steven Powell. This would be where "Brandi on 191st" had resided.

On September 19, 2011, the canvassing team contacted Brandi's parents, who had long since moved to Alabama. They stated unequivocally that their teenage daughters had *never* posed for any of the mystery photographs and that they certainly hadn't given the mystery cameraman permission.

The detectives moved on to the house directly behind Powell's residence. This was a likely target because Steven's bedroom window faced the side of this residence where a window was on the same level.

No one was home.

Three hours later, Gary Sanders and Ellis Maxwell returned and spoke with Loretta Schaller.* She said she had lived there for less than a year and had no young daughters. She was renting the home from a man named Burt Mallett* and provided Mallett's address. Mrs. Schaller agreed to let the detectives in to look at the layout of the house.

Upstairs, Sanders recognized the bathroom and its fix-tures as the room where the younger girls, who appeared to be about seven and eleven, had been photographed. This bathroom, however, was on the far end of the residence from Steven Powell's house and his bedroom window.

"The only line of sight to be able to photograph this bathroom would be from Steven's bedroom window," Sanders wrote in his report. "And the bathroom door of the other house would have had to be open at the time."

Ellis Maxwell took pictures of the "target house's" interior before they left. Then Sanders contacted Burt Mallett.

"We own it, but we only lived there for a little while," Mallett said. "Then we rented it out."

"To anyone with young girls?" Sanders asked.

"Yeah . . . to a couple that had two little girls—sometime around 2006 to 2008. Not sure which. I'm not very good with dates."

By checking databases, Gary Sanders determined that a John and Sally Mahoney* had lived in the house from June 2006 to August 2007. They currently lived in a house they had purchased a short distance away. When he drove to their home, Sanders encountered Sally Mahoney and her daughters, Lily* and Robyn,* as they pulled into their driveway.

Sanders instantly recognized Lily as the older girl in the surreptitious photos. He approached Sally and asked if he could speak to her without her daughters being present. She sent the girls into the house and Sanders explained why he was there. He first showed her pictures where her daughters had clothes on. She identified them easily, but then she asked him if there were other photos she didn't know about. When he told her there were—images of her girls bathing, changing their clothing, and using the toilet—she began to cry.

The thought that someone had taken pictures of her vulnerable little girls was devastating to Sally Mahoney. She said she had never given her permission for her daughters to be photographed in the nude, in their own bathroom. She was appalled that someone had done so.

"My youngest daughter, Robyn, was afraid about being in the bathroom upstairs, with the door shut—I don't know why," she explained. "So I told her she could leave the door open and shout down to me to be sure I was there and they were safe.

"Now, I guess they weren't safe at all," Sally added, with tears streaking her face.

The investigators continued to call on nearby homes, and they found other residents who recognized the teenagers in the photos they held out.

Still, most of the hundreds of pictures were of the younger girls—Lily and Robyn Mahoney. They weren't sexually mature; they were innocents, preyed upon by eyes they didn't see. Robyn must have sensed that someone evil was watching her. Perhaps that was why she insisted on leaving the bathroom door open. Ironically, that open door was where the telephoto lens snaked through.

*   *   *

The time had finally come. Patrol cars parked along the street near the Powells' tan and white house shortly after 11 P.M. on September 22. It was dark out and there were no whirling blue lights or wailing of sirens to announce the presence of law enforcement officers outside.

Gary Sanders asked one unmarked patrol unit to drive by the Powells' house to see if there were vehicles in the driveway. They made three passes and noted only two cars, but they weren't the ones driven by Steven Powell. On the fourth pass, the patrol officers saw Steven Powell pull into the driveway and emerge from his Department of Corrections state-owned van.

At 11:14 P.M. on September 22, 2011, Steven Powell was arrested on a Pierce County Superior Court warrant. He was booked into the Pierce County Jail in Tacoma twenty minutes later. He was arraigned the next morning and charged with fourteen counts of voyeurism for the photographs he'd furtively taken of young girls, and one count of possession of child pornography. Bail was set at two hundred thousand dollars.

He did not comment or protest his arrest.

Back at the house he owned, John, Michael, Alina, Josh, Charlie, and Braden now lived for the first time in years without the man who had wielded absolute authority over them.

Chapter Eleven

Chuck and Judy Cox were worried sick about their grandsons. They had had virtually no contact with Charlie and Braden for months, and they wondered what was going to happen next. They wanted very much to have Susan's little boys with *them,* where they could be sure they were safe.

Within days of Steven Powell's arrest, workers from the Department of Social and Health Services removed Charlie and Braden from the house they had been living in since a few weeks after their mother disappeared. Everyone—except for the Powell family, including, of course, Josh—was concerned about what the secrecy, probable brainwashing by their father, the police presence, and the loss of their mother were doing to the boys. Charlie was now six, and Braden, four.

Judy and Chuck Cox received many emails, letters, and calls from people who wanted to help them keep the boys safe.

"I got a call from a marine officer," Judy recalled. "He said he had six children himself, and he offered to 'take

Josh out' if we said the word. Of course I told him that we didn't want that—that we would never be part of anything violent. But I thanked him for his consideration."

Shortly after Steven Powell's arrest, Braden and Charlie were temporarily placed in a foster home while their situation was assessed.

Josh wanted them back, but Chuck and Judy Cox intervened, asking to have the boys stay with them. Luckily, their grandsons spent very little time in the foster home before Pierce County Superior Court judge Kathryn J. Nelson ordered that they be placed with the Coxes until the best place for them to be was determined.

For the time being, Josh Powell would have three-hour supervised visits with them every Sunday morning. That meant an observer, approved by Child Protective Services, would have to be present during the entire time Charlie and Braden were at his house. Josh was not pleased, and could not understand how anyone had the right to take his children away from him, or to criticize him as a parent.

Judy Cox remembers that reuniting with Charlie and Braden was not a completely joyous occasion. The boys had been through so much, and they were very cautious. Clearly, they had been programmed by their father, and probably their grandfather. They had been told how terrible the "Mormon Police" were, and that "the bad Mormons" were trying to take them away from their dad.

"They were robotic," Judy says. "I don't know what all they had been told about us, but we knew that Josh and Steven Powell never hid what they thought from Charlie and Braden, even if it upset them. They discussed *every-thing* in front of the boys."

In the past two years, Susan's little boys had been through constant change and upheaval. Their mother was gone, and they had left the only home they knew back in Utah and come to live with their dad's father, brothers, and sister. And now they had been moved once again, to their mom's family.

It wasn't surprising that they didn't know whom to trust, or if they could trust anyone. Josh hadn't made the change of custody easy; as far as he was concerned his sons *belonged* to him. He owned them, and he had done everything he could to turn them away from the Coxes. He seemed unable to comprehend what his sons were going through, and he hadn't made their lives any more secure.

Chuck, Judy, Chuck's sister, Pam, Denise, and their friend Laurie Nielsen took Charlie and Braden to Chuck E. Cheese, the beach, a nearby park, and an amusement park on several different jaunts. They hoped the boys would have fun, and they seemed to.

And yet, when a social worker assigned to the boys' case asked them what they had been doing at their grand-parents' house, the little boys said, "Nothing . . ."

Judy reminded them of the places they had all gone, and the boys nodded carefully. They were tiptoeing on eggshells, afraid that they wouldn't get to go back to their father if they said they were happy with their maternal grandparents.

"They finally told their caseworker that they *did* have fun with us," Judy recalls. "We all understood how confused they were. And we tried to put them at ease whenever we could."

The Coxes live in a big house in the country on acreage. They grow vegetables and flowers and their place is sheltered by a ring of cottonwood and evergreen trees. There was plenty of room for two little boys to run, and Charlie and Braden were showered with love, not only by their grandparents, but also by their aunts, uncles, and cousins.

Gradually they began to relax. But there were setbacks. One that broke Judy Cox's heart occurred when Charlie was playing with his aunt Denise's son.

"They were tossing an 'eight-ball' back and forth, and Charlie threw it at his cousin too hard. Before we stopped to think, one of us shouted at him not to do that."

Charlie had almost stopped being worried, but he was shocked when he was reprimanded.

"He walked over to the glass door in the lower level," Laurie Nielsen remembers. "And he started to cry. He kind of looked up at the sky and said, 'Mommy, Mommy, where *are* you? I *need* you!'

"We felt like crying, too. He hadn't forgotten Susan at all, and he couldn't understand why she had left him. His emotions were so fragile."

Still, as the weeks—and then months—went by, the boys were feeling safer all the time. Josh's sister Jennifer and her husband, Kirk, sided with Susan's family and felt the boys were much safer with them than with Josh. Because Chuck and Judy were in their mid-fifties, the two families decided that it should be Jennifer and Kirk who eventually raised Charlie and Braden, along with their own children.

But it was much too soon for that. Steven Powell was in jail throughout the fall of 2011, awaiting trial. His children, all but Jennifer, visited him faithfully, and none of them would talk to the media as Steven's trial dates were delayed again and again.

In an effort to have his sons returned to him, Josh Powell grudgingly agreed to undergo a psychological evaluation. He met with Dr. James Manley on October 27.

Dr. Manley's report was couched in "tactful" psychology terms that were maddening to those who loved Susan. He wrote of Josh's "parenting skills," and of his devotion to his sons, blaming Josh's tirades about the Mormons and Susan's family on his stress because he was a murder suspect.

That was, of course, a given—even if you weren't a licensed psychologist. Josh Powell *was* stressed; police agencies and the general public considered Josh a prime suspect. The circumstantial evidence that continued to be uncovered made him look more and more guilty.

Manley, a psychologist—not a psychiatrist—*was* concerned that Josh drifted off the subject of his sons too often as he spoke about what *he* was going through. Even so, Manley's remarks were reminiscent of homicide detectives who sometimes refer to violent criminals as "this gentleman" in their reports when they really should say "the defendant" or "the convicted man/woman."

Most killers aren't "gentlemen."

"Across his supervised visits," Manley wrote, "Mr.

Powell has demonstrated a strong foundation of parenting skills and an unwavering desire to parent his sons. His demonstrated inability to curb his inappropriate commentary about the 'Mormon Police' and the Cox family during a recent family therapy session is concerning."

Dr. Manley waffled, however, in his evaluation of Josh. He suggested that Josh have counseling to help him deal with the disappearance of his wife, giving the impression that Manley felt his subject had nothing to do with whatever had happened to Susan.

Manley's opinion of Josh Powell was that his "stability is not secure . . . Once these matters have been resolved, when he is no longer a subject of investigation, when he can amend his communication style and address other identified parenting concerns, father's reunification with his sons may be warranted."

Christmas 2011 came and went. No one had stepped forward to bail Steven Powell out of jail, so he spent the holiday locked up, awaiting trial. Charlie and Braden had their scheduled visits with their father, and their observers noted that they were obviously very attached to Josh. Child protective authorities, however, were still troubled by the strange incestuous cartoons found on Josh's computers in the week after Susan vanished.

For some reason, Dr. Manley had not seen the four hundred images on Josh's computers with Dennis the Menace, Rugrats, SpongeBob SquarePants, et al. in roles where the story line featured children having sex with their parents.

When he finally had access to them in January 2012, he took a firmer stand and suggested that Josh Powell should undergo a psychosexual examination before any decision was made about custody of Charlie and Braden.

Chuck and Judy Cox were also worried about what sexual fantasies Josh might be hiding, particularly after his father's arrest for voyeurism and child pornography. They didn't know why their grandsons preferred to run around naked, even when it seemed inappropriate.

"We were playing with the boys one afternoon, taking pictures of them—with their clothes on, of course—and being silly," Judy recalled. "Charlie was jumping up and down on his bed, and I lifted my camera. All of a sudden, he said, 'No—no—we need to have the lights out.' I began to wonder *who* had taken after-dark photos of him and Braden."

They took a lot of photographs and videos of the boys. Laurie Nielsen still has a video on her cell phone where Braden stands in a pile of leaves and Charlie runs around tossing golden maple leaves in the air. Braden clearly believes that Laurie is using a still camera, while Charlie knows he is in a "movie." After a few minutes without moving, Braden says to Laurie, "Take the picture!"

At first Susan's sons lived in a small bedroom in their grandparents' house, but Chuck worked on plans he had drawn up to expand his house so that they would have their own large room. He began to add a wing on to their house, with a basement apartment for his mother, Anne

Cox, who had recently been widowed when Chuck's father died. They ordered bunk beds for the boys.

It wasn't always easy, looking after two energetic little boys, but Chuck and Judy knew Susan would want Charlie and Braden to be with them. There had been no leads that might help the West Valley City police detectives find her, but her children were safe.

Chuck Cox did much of the carpentry work himself and had a lot next to the house partially excavated to make a pond.

"Charlie said I had to put a little island in the middle," Chuck remembers. "He said that the ducks that swam in the pond would need a safe place to be—where nothing could get them. So I piled up some dirt to make the island."

The first thing in the morning, the boys ran to the window of the big room that would soon be theirs to check on their ducks.

Charlie was quite an accomplished artist, and he drew pictures and gave them to his grandparents, aunts, and friends. But he always asked to have them back. That was part of his cautiousness. After a little over four months with Chuck and Judy, the two boys were much more relaxed than when they first moved in, but they still looked forward to Sundays with their father.

Caseworkers who accompanied those visits observed Josh's interactions with his sons. He cooked breakfast or lunch with them—usually tacos or enchiladas—and was careful to let them participate, even though the result was sometimes a little messy. They played games and built simple projects. Charlie and Braden seemed to enjoy themselves, although the Child Protective Services caseworkers noted that Josh seemed to be putting on a show for their benefit.

He also became flustered when the boys didn't obey his instructions instantly.

Charlie still asked for his drawings back, and his mother's family members quickly handed them over. It seemed to make him feel safe to keep his little collection.

On Thursday, February 3, 2012, Josh Powell appeared before Pierce County Superior Court judge Kathryn J. Nelson for a hearing involving his sons' custody.

"I have proven myself as a fit and loving father," Josh told the Court, "who provides a stable home even in the face of great adversity . . . It is time for my sons to come home!"

With Steven Powell in jail on charges of voyeurism and child pornography and with the disturbing findings in Josh's computer of cartoon characters engaged in sordid incestuous activities, authorities were very concerned about Josh having full custody of his sons, or even of allowing him nonsupervised visits with them.

Josh continued to fight hard against Chuck and Judy Cox. He wanted his sons back, and he was outraged that his in-laws had even temporary custody of them. He had been without them for four months; they *belonged* to him and he wanted them back. *Now.*

Judge Nelson ruled that Josh Powell would have to undergo a psychosexual examination before she could make a judgment on whether he would have Charlie and Braden returned to his custody. She would not consider his arguments if he didn't agree to the examination.

In any case, she said the two little boys would remain with the Coxes until at least late July 2012. Josh would retain his rights to supervised visits with his sons.

A psychosexual evaluation is one of the more intrusive examinations anyone can undergo. It is a tool used by psychologists and psychiatrists to evaluate the possible risks inherent in the test subjects. Most often it is used to winnow out imprisoned sex offenders to decide which of them might be safe to move back into society, or if they are even ready to be paroled to halfway houses or less strict programs. But there are many reasons to ask for psychosexual evaluations. When children are involved in a case, every effort is made to protect them.

The professionals who had studied the Powell situation for two years were very concerned with the salacious cartoons on Josh's computers, and with Josh's inability to modify—or just plain lack of interest in modifying—his behavior and remarks when Charlie and Braden were present. He resented most of the world, felt people were ganging up on him, and refused to accept criticism for *anything* he did.

Psychosexual evaluations include delving into police reports, children's protective agencies' records, criminal and correction histories, interviews with the subject and his or her family, his or her sexual patterns and history, alcohol and drug use, stress level, use of pornography, employment, education, medical history, and myriad other very personal areas.

Sometimes a device—the penile plethysmograph—is attached to a male subject's penis to chart if he becomes erect while viewing certain videos or photographs.

A kind of genital lie detector.

The plethysmograph is used in this country in 58 percent of psychosexual evaluations; in Washington State it is a standard part of the examination—although not *always* required.

For Josh Powell, who appeared to have lived with sexual secrets for most of his life, such an evaluation would be devastating—and humiliating. And yet when two small boys' safety was concerned, it had to be done.

Josh left Judge Nelson's courtroom angry, perhaps angrier than he had ever appeared in public before.

The evaluation was scheduled for the week of February 7 to 11, 2012. He would still have his regular Sunday morning time with Charlie and Braden, including a visit on February 6.

Chapter Twelve

On Saturday evening, February 5, 2012, Charlie Powell was working on an art project. He asked Laurie Nielsen, who was like a member of the family to him, to help him find some pictures of vegetables.

"He needed three different kinds," Laurie remembers. "I think it was a tomato, an ear of corn, and peas or string beans. I suggested that he draw and color them himself because he was such a good artist. And he did a really good job. When he was finished, he brought his drawings over to me, and, of course, I admired them.

"When I started to hand them back—because he always wanted his projects back—he said, 'No.' I asked him why, and he told me they were for me. He grinned and said I could keep them! I know it doesn't sound like a huge move forward—but, for Charlie, it was. He finally felt safe enough to share."

The boys' great-aunt Pam, Chuck's sister, read to them before they were tucked in. Everything seemed more normal than it had been for a long time.

Sunday turned out to be an uncommonly sunny day for western Washington in February, especially since there had been blizzards and power outages earlier in the week in the mountains. Usually, Charlie and Braden were eager to go to Josh's house, but, for some reason, this time they weren't.

It was a relatively new place for them; Josh Powell had told authorities that he'd moved out of his father's house in Puyallup and into a rental in Graham, Washington. It would be just for him and his boys.

No one knew that he didn't really live in the house in the middle of a cul-de-sac; it was barely furnished, although he had enough furniture in the living room and kitchen to make it *look* as if he lived there. Caseworkers assumed that he just hadn't gotten around to unpacking yet.

There had been any number of things that Josh Powell did between his court date on Thursday and Sunday morning. He didn't broadcast his activities, but in retrospect, they demonstrate how carefully he prepared for what he was about to do. But no one could see that from the other end.

He wasn't crazy—not in the legal or medical sense.

In many states, supervised visits with children or estranged spouses don't take place in private homes. That isn't always the case in Washington. The ideal situation is to have a central place where involved parties won't meet. Visits are often staggered, particularly when one parent delivers a child or children to the other in a very intense custody battle. One can come in a door, leave the children with a social worker, and the other parent enters fifteen or thirty minutes later through a different door. That helps to defuse potential arguments. Indeed, in Montana, if one parent is even late for a visit, supervising caseworkers are instructed to call police at once so that feuding parents won't run into each other.

And there should be security officers present to protect all parties. Marriages that began with promises of love forever can become dangerous, particularly when the parents are fighting over where their children will live, who will support them, and numerous other problems.

Of course, in the Powell case, there was no mother fighting to keep her children with her. Susan was gone. Even so, experts on supervised visits would never allow a woman supervisor to go to the private home of a man known to be upset and angry by a recent judge's ruling.

There are all different degrees of people referred to as *social workers.* Some may be kind people who have had a weekend of "training" to prepare them for their assignments—which can include supervised visits. I was a social worker for more than a year after I graduated with a BA degree from the University of Washington. I worked for the Washington State Department of Public Assistance and handled mostly welfare applications, client visitations, and monthly welfare checks for those who qualified. My daughter, Laura, who works in another state, went to college for seven years to attain a master's degree in social work. She has counseled children, their parents, and geriatric clients. She has also overseen supervised visitations, but only in a neutral building with safety procedures in place and adequate security, and never in a private home.

In Washington State, Governor Christine Gregoire signed into law SB 5020 on April 15, 2011, which protects professional social workers in the state. The legislation prevents someone without a degree in social work from working in a job titled "social work." Only those with a degree from an accredited school of social work will be allowed to fill those positions. The National Association of Social Workers (NASW) is hoping all states will follow suit.

Elizabeth Griffin-Hall is a sweet-faced, plumpish woman in her sixties. In February 2012, she worked for a company that was under contract to Washington State's Child Protective Services which provides human services workers to accompany children in supervised visitations. She has neither a four-year degree nor a master's degree, although she has undergone training provided by her employer. Although the media continually referred to Griffin-Hall as a "social worker," that term was not accurate.

For Charlie and Braden Powell, she was like another grandmother, someone who cared for them, cuddled them, and went along when they visited their father. There is no question that Griffin-Hall loved the boys and was quite involved with them emotionally.

On the morning of Sunday, February 6, Charlie and Braden balked at going to their father's house. Usually they were anxious to go—but this Sunday morning, they wanted to stay with Chuck and Judy Cox. They didn't know about the strange test the judge said their father had to have, and if they had known, they wouldn't have understood it. But they felt safer all the time with their grandparents and their mom's relatives, and they didn't want to leave.

Chuck and Judy had to coax the little boys to get dressed for the visit, reminding them how much fun they had with their dad. They didn't want to make them go to visit Josh, but it was the law, and they had to follow Washington's guidelines.

Josh said negative things about them to Charlie and Braden and they didn't want to confuse their grandsons, so they tried to speak as well of Josh as they could.

Finally, Charlie and Braden changed out of their pajamas and said they would go with Elizabeth Griffin-Hall to Josh's house. Griffin-Hall carefully put them into car seats and fastened the straps. They began to get a little more enthusiastic about their weekly visit as they got closer to the town of Graham.

They didn't have anyone else with them; there was no deputy to stand by for backup. It would have been a prudent idea to have law enforcement protection, considering how angry Josh Powell had been after court three days before.

It wasn't very far to Josh's new rental. Griffin-Hall pulled in front of Josh's house and unbuckled Charlie and Braden, following closely behind them as they ran toward the front door.

Josh opened the door, and the boys ran in. Griffin-Hall

recalls that Josh looked "kind of sheepish," in the glimpse she saw of him. He had opened the door just enough for his sons to get inside, and then he slammed it in her face. Hard.

She could hear Josh telling Charlie, "I have a really *big* surprise for you!"

And then she heard Braden cry out in pain. She thought at first that he must have tripped or banged his foot on something; he'd injured it a few days before.

Elizabeth banged on the door and the windows, asking Josh to let her in. But he didn't. She ran around the house to look into the windows but couldn't see what was going on.

And then she smelled gasoline. What could that mean? There is something frightening about any strong smell that emanates from where it shouldn't be. Gasoline smells inside a house? They had to come from inside; there were no cars around that were running, nobody outside lighting a trash fire. Her car was turned off.

When she got no response at all from her knocking and pounding, Elizabeth Griffin-Hall ran back to her car where her purse and cell phone were. She didn't have the physical power to try to break into Josh's house, and she couldn't see anyone else around.

She called 911.

What happened next was a tragedy of errors. For some unfathomable reason, the operator who monitored Griffin-Hall's call didn't take her seriously. True, she was frightened and spoke very rapidly. But many 911 callers do. She told him that she was in front of Josh Powell's house, that her two charges were inside on what was supposed to be a supervised visit. But she couldn't get in, and she smelled gasoline. She tried to find the address, although she could feel herself panicking and had trouble locating it in her purse or her car. She dropped the slip of paper with the address on it, and had to pick it up. The 911 operator sounded impatient.

Griffin-Hall did not immediately respond to the questions he asked her—probably because they made little sense to her. What did it matter when Josh's birthday was or how much he weighed? As she failed to answer, the operator paid less attention to her comments about Josh's court hearing, that he was a suspect in his wife's disappearance, and how she feared for the boys. Desperate, she asked how long it would be before deputies could get there.

And the operator said, "We have to respond to life-threatening emergencies first, ma'am."

She told him that this could very well be a life-threatening emergency, but he didn't seem to comprehend what she was saying. That was not all his fault. She spoke breathlessly and it was somewhat hard to make out her words. Still, the 911 operator's repeated questions about who was supervising *her* were patronizing and puzzling, and she couldn't make him understand that *she* was the supervisor in this situation.

"I tried to get in," she told the 911 operator. "I begged him to let me in . . ."

She gave the address once more, and finally she believed that help was on the way.

But it was too late. She had been on the phone six minutes. Maybe it wouldn't have mattered how quickly deputies and the fire department vehicles were dispatched. From where Elizabeth Griffin-Hall stood in front of the house next door to Josh's, she watched in horror as a tremendous roar shook Josh's house, and flames and smoke boiled out, shooting twenty feet or more toward the sky.

Clearly in shock, Elizabeth tried calling her supervisor, and then the fire department dispatcher because she hadn't seen a fire truck yet. She gave the address again and answered more needless questions. She knew in her heart the boys were gone; they couldn't survive in that burning hellhole. But she didn't want to accept that yet.

In the end, she just hung up. Neighbors huddled along the street, watching in horror. They didn't know who lived there. Most of them thought the house was empty, which was understandable since Josh had never actually moved in.

Graham Fire Department deputy chief Gary Franz told reporters that the roof was gone when they got there. It didn't take them long to "tap" the fire as they knocked down walls that had turned to cinder. Franz commented that Elizabeth Griffin-Hall was lucky to be alive. If she hadn't gone out to her car to grab her cell phone, she undoubtedly would have died, too.

The firefighters found three bodies: an adult and two small boys.

Josh Powell looked to have been sitting on a five-gallon gas can when he lit a match. It had virtually melted into him, and he was burned beyond recognition. He would ultimately need to be identified by a forensic dentist to be sure it was really him.

Charlie and Braden had suffered "chopping" wounds to their heads and necks from an axe, although forensic pathologists would determine they were not fatal wounds.

Miraculously, the little boys lay beside each other, with no visible burns at all. They were holding hands.

Postmortem examination would prove that all three of them had died of carbon monoxide poisoning.

Probably everyone in Washington and Utah can remember where they were and what they were doing when they heard that Charlie and Braden Powell had perished in an explosion and conflagration, set by their own father. It was like when Mount St. Helens erupted, when John F. Kennedy was assassinated, when Pearl Harbor was attacked.

I was standing at my kitchen counter when a friend called to tell me. I refused to believe it, but then I had to. I was angry at first, asking over and over in my head, *Why didn't they have deputies backing them up?*

Like everyone else, I wanted to blame someone. Anne Bremner called to tell me that Chuck had already arrived at the burned-out shell of the house, and that her paralegal, Misty Scott, was at the Coxes' house. Chuck and Judy were in shock but they were holding together. They had been through so much loss. I didn't see how they could survive this.

Anne and I had planned to have dinner together on that awful Sunday night, and we did—but we just stared at each other in wordless denial as Anne's cell phone rang constantly with calls from television and radio shows, and news services.

The only comfort was that we both believed that Charlie and Braden were now with their mom.

Chapter Thirteen

Fourteen hundred mourners attended memorial services for Charlie and Braden. Their teachers brushed back tears as they remembered them, what an exceptional artist Charlie was, how they both loved bugs and frogs and ducks. They were such new little souls, and their lives had been blighted by the man who had destroyed them— almost from the beginning.

The boys were buried in a single casket in Puyallup's Woodbine Cemetery. One day, if they should ever find Susan's remains, Chuck and Judy Cox would lay her to rest with her little boys. Her relatives had a graveside service, and were even gracious enough to allow Terrica Powell and her children to have their own small ceremony of remembrance there. But they were horrified when Josh's mother wanted to bury Josh close to Charlie and Braden in the same cemetery!

With some of her family, Terrica Powell visited Woodbine and chose a plot that overlooked the boys' grave. A grave was quickly dug and plywood put over it, but the Powell family hadn't yet paid for it when Chuck found out about their plans. The Cox family threatened to sue the city-owned public cemetery if they allowed the man who killed their grandsons to be buried there.

Once again, they sensed Terrica Powell's almost complete lack of sensitivity in some areas. Why on earth would she think they could ever have any kind of peace visiting their grandsons when Josh's remains were so close?

When Chuck spoke to her and asked her to reconsider, Josh's mother was surprised that they were upset about her plans. It hadn't even occurred to her that burying the killer so close to his victims might be inappropriate.

It was a new problem for the city. Anne Bremner said she would seek a temporary restraining order to block any efforts to bury Josh near Charlie and Braden. "For him to be buried near those kids is unthinkable," she said. "For God's sake, for them to lose Susan first, and then the boys, and now this? Just give these people a break."

Steve Downing, the Coxes' other attorney, could scarcely believe the Powells' plans, either, saying with black humor, "Same cemetery . . . different destinations."

But when he spoke with the Coxes, he realized that they would never feel comfortable passing by Josh's grave. The Powells' plans had to be stopped.

Terrica and Alina seemed determined, and someone had to make a move quickly. Since Terrica hadn't paid for the plot, Sheriff Paul Pastor and Pierce County Sheriff's Department public information officer Ed Troyer came up with the money from their own pockets to purchase it immediately. Crime Stoppers, a longtime support group for police and victims of crime, helped. When the *Ron and Don* radio show on KIRO-CBS in Seattle told their listeners about it, they were overwhelmed with donations—fifty thousand dollars' worth—from all over America.

The Woodbine Cemetery has voluntarily reserved the hillside for only children's graves. Chuck and Judy Cox will use a portion of the money raised to buy a headstone for Charlie and Braden, and a Christmas Box Angel statue will be placed where it overlooks their graves. Richard Paul Evans's book *The Christmas Box* was the inspiration for the statues. Today there are more than twenty-five in place in America, and nearly one hundred more are in the planning stages.

The Coxes and Pierce County Crime Stoppers, along with detectives on the case, have used part of the fifty thousand dollars as seed money to help carry out the Christmas Box Angel memorials, which will eventually cross this country.

On December 6 each year, vigils are held at all the Christmas Box Angel sites. That is the date of the death of the fictional child in Evans's book, and is also celebrated as Children's Day in many parts of the world.

Coincidentally, that is also the anniversary of Susan Cox Powell's disappearance from her Utah home. Chuck and Judy Cox plan to have Braden and Charlie's angel statue be in place by December 6, 2012.

Pierce County detective Gary Sanders and his fellow investigators on the Powell case asked Troyer's group, as well as prosecuting attorney Mark Lindquist's staff, to join them in another mission to commemorate the two small boys they could not save in time. It is called "Charlie's Dinosaur."

Sanders saw one of Charlie's last drawings—a dinosaur—when the Pierce County detectives served a search warrant. The young detective envisioned a living memorial to Charlie and Braden.

Charlie's dinosaur drawing has been transformed into the logo for "Charlie's Dinosaur," a project aimed at donating backpacks filled with school supplies, clothes, blankets, and food to children in need.

"*Whatever* they need," Troyer says of his department's detectives' goal. "It has to be new; a lot of these kids have never had *anything* new in their lives."

Josh Powell is not buried in the Woodbine Cemetery. He has been cremated and his family will put his ashes in an unknown location. With all the strong feelings and the anger at what he did, it would be an open invitation to vandalism for the public to know where his remains are.

Public information officer Ed Troyer announced that his department's investigators had found that Josh Powell planned the destruction of his sons and himself very carefully. Since he was gone, the question of premeditation didn't matter much in a legal sense. It is interesting, however, for those who study the psychology of abusers and killers.

Before the dread Sunday of February 6, 2012, Josh withdrew seven thousand dollars from his bank account, gave away Charlie's and Braden's toys, and took loads

FIRE AND ICE

Susan Cox Powell was a happy, loving young woman. She disappeared one night in December, leaving behind her beloved little boys, Charlie and Braden. Her husband, Josh, said that she had run off with another man. (*Cox family*)

Susan and Josh as an engaged couple in January 2001. They would be married in three months. He was seven years older than she was, and yet he looked as young—or younger. (*Cox family*)

In 2001, Susan worked as the co-manager of the Orchard Park Retirement Residence, a job she shared with her bridegroom, Josh Powell, shortly after they were married. She thought it was a great opportunity for advancement, but Josh criticized his bosses and was let go. (*Cox family*)

Susan and Josh on his birthday in 2001. He looks about fifteen, and he had always lived at home with his father until a few weeks before he met Susan. She thought of him as an "older man" with an independent life. Far from it. He depended on his father, Steven Craig Powell, to help him make decisions. (*Cox family*)

The bride and groom: Susan and Josh Powell, holding one another under a Japanese cherry tree outside their reception. Judy, her other daughters, her sister-in-law Pam, and many friends catered the reception. Steve Powell paid for the rehearsal dinner but complained about the price. (*Cox family*)

Susan in her wedding gown. The photograph is damaged because it went through a terrible fire in February 2012. Miraculously, this and most of the other pictures in this section survived the fire, although they remain singed on the edges. (*Cox family*)

Josh Powell puts a lacy garter on his bride Susan's leg just before their wedding at an LDS temple near Portland, Oregon. The future lay ahead of the young couple. (*Cox family*)

Susan and Josh and their attendants at their wedding reception. It was a wonderful affair. Josh's mother asked if she could take the leftover food, flowers, and decorations home to Spokane, where she planned another reception. Surprised, Judy Cox demurred and shared those things with her family. (*Cox family*)

Susan laughing as she dances with her dad at her wedding reception. He had warned her, "You don't marry a 'project,'" but stood by her when she could not be dissuaded from marrying Josh. Through the years ahead, Chuck and Judy often bailed Josh out financially. (*Cox family*)

Susan and Josh Powell celebrate their first Christmas as a married couple. They both seemed to be very much in love. (*Cox family*)

Susan Cox attacks a giant slice of pizza in March 2001, a month before her wedding. (*Cox family*)

Susan Cox Powell on a visit to the west desert country in Utah. These photos are eerie because many investigators and her family and friends believe that she may lie at the bottom of one of the thousands of abandoned mine shafts in the west desert. (*Cox family*)

Susan and Josh Powell had two precious sons. Braden is on the left, and Charlie is on the right. They loved animals of all kinds. And they worried about them. Charlie was an excellent artist, talented beyond his years. (*Cox family*)

January 2002. Susan in the Temple Square in Salt Lake City. She was a faithful member of the Latter-day Saints (Mormon) Church. This was only eight months after she and Josh Powell were married. (*Cox family*)

Susan in October 2002. She believed that her marriage to Josh would be forever, and she was happy to be with him, even though she was a little concerned that he changed jobs so often. (*Cox family*)

Susan in an impish mood. One of her husband's male relatives believed that she was secretly in love with him. He was totally besotted with her, and she was afraid of being alone with him. (*Cox family*)

Susan right after Christmas 2001. It was her first Christmas married to Josh Powell. Even though many people didn't care for him, she believed he was only shy and that she could make him happy. (*Cox family*)

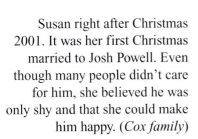

Steven Powell, left, and Josh at a trade show. Steve was never without a camera or two. After Josh and Susan were married, Josh talked to his father on the phone almost every day—for hours. That was one bone of contention between the newlyweds. Susan felt Steve interfered too much.

Susan plays cards and visits with members of Josh's family. At first she enjoyed being with all of them, but later on she wanted to leave Washington State and move to Utah so she and Josh could concentrate on their own family.

Susan and her dad, Chuck Cox, are tired at the end of a western hoedown party. Chuck and his wife, Judy, did their best to look out for their four daughters, but the girls made their own choices. (*Cox family*)

A holiday dinner at Chuck Cox's parents' home. Chuck sits at one end of the table, and his father at the other. Anne Cox, Chuck's mother, is in the kitchen cooking. The elder Coxes lived in a log cabin house. (*Cox family*)

Author Ann Rule in Salt Lake City doing research on the Powell case. Standing in the same spot where the Coxes and Powells stood in happier days.

The Powell and Cox families pose in Temple Square in Salt Lake City. Susan's parents are to her left—Judy Cox, with Chuck behind her. Josh's family are to his right. As bonded as they look here, the two extended families rarely saw each other. (*Cox family*)

Chuck's sister, Pam, adored her great-nephews, and they felt the same about her. When they visited their maternal grandparents, the boys began to feel safe again, although they missed their mother tremendously. Left to right: Charlie, five, Braden, three, and their aunt Pam in March 2010. Susan had been missing four months when this picture was taken. (*Cox family*)

Charlie and Braden with their mother in a photo taken by Chuck Cox, their maternal grandfather.

Braden and Charlie all dressed up for Halloween 2011. They were growing more secure with Judy and Chuck Cox all the time. Behind them is Susan's large photo, which the Coxes keep in front of their fireplace. (*Cox family*)

The Powell house, on fire.

02/05/2012 12:25

119

The aftermath of the terrible fire that destroyed three lives.

Josh Powell at a court hearing. He was ordered to get a psychosexual evaluation. This was something he refused to face. (*KOMO-TV, ABC Seattle*)

Behind Josh are his missing wife's parents and friends. Far left is Judy Cox, then Chuck Cox. (*KOMO-TV ABC Seattle*)

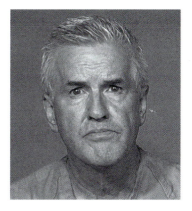

Steven Craig Powell, sixty-two, just arrested for fourteen charges of voyeurism and one charge of child pornography, September 2011. No one knew the strange secrets he hid inside. Was he part of a grotesque, cruel plot—or only obsessed with his son's wife?

Detective Gary Sanders of the Pierce County Sheriff's Department was the lead investigator into the Washington State portion of some very puzzling and macabre cases. He and his team located the spot where a stalker viewed his victims through a camera lens. Sanders worked closely with detective Ellis Maxwell of the West Valley City, Utah, police department.

Pierce County Sheriff's Department public information officer Ed Troyer had to keep explaining to the public why his department could not move forward on an arrest. He was as frustrated as all law enforcement personnel in his county. The problem? Susan Powell disappeared in Utah—not Washington State.

Pierce County sheriff Paul Pastor's investigators, along with prosecuting attorney Mark Lindquist, kept waiting for a "go-ahead" to serve an arrest warrant on Josh Powell. Tragically, it never happened.

Prosecuting attorney Mark Lindquist, along with the Pierce County Sheriff's Department, wanted to arrest members of the Steven Powell family—but they were not the primary investigators in the beginning. It was supremely frustrating for the Washington detectives, sheriff, and prosecutors. (*Mark Lindquist*)

Anne Bremner, nationally acclaimed attorney, volunteered her expertise pro bono to Chuck and Judy Cox as they sought first to find their daughter Susan, and later to gain custody of their grandsons. (*Anne Bremner*)

of books, papers, and other belongings to a landfill and a Goodwill store. He bought several five-gallon cans of gasoline and a small axe.

Josh had always lived through his computers, seemingly connecting with them more easily than he could communicate with people. He sent an email message to his attorney, apologizing for what he was about to do: "I'm sorry," he typed. "Goodbye."

He also wrote to his pastor and his family, saying, "I'm sorry. I just can't live without my boys."

Josh's emails were coherent as he left instructions on how to handle his affairs after his death.

"He sent the emails only minutes before he set the fire," Ed Troyer explained. "There was no way anyone could have stopped him."

Josh Powell didn't mention Susan in any of his final correspondence. Whatever he knew about where she was, he would take it to his grave.

If he hadn't viewed the boys as his possessions, he could have chosen to kill only himself—but the boys belonged to him, and if he couldn't have them, then no one could. He also could have planned a more humane way to kill them. Why he used an axe and fire, instead of sleeping pills or other methods by which Charlie and Braden could have gone to sleep peacefully and never have endured Josh's "big surprise," is puzzling. But he had, indeed, purchased the hatchet and gasoline for a specific purpose. A deadly purpose.

And appalling. He was angry at the world that was closing in on him, humiliating him, and taking away his power and control. Maybe he was even angry at his sons for wanting to be with anyone but him.

Chuck Cox was in church when he got word of the tragedy. His bishop drove him to the fire-gutted house.

"That house burned completely," he remembers. "He wanted the whole place to go. They're gone [Charlie and Braden], and I said, 'Okay, what do I do now?' "

Chuck and Judy had always been aware that Josh was capable of doing something "drastic."

"I knew that it was possible," Chuck continued. "I knew that he was capable of doing something if he was pressured and pushed. If he felt there was no hope, he was capable of ending their lives and his life. But to do it in such a manner—by burning your own children—I just couldn't believe that would've happened."

In his jail cell, Steven Powell was notified of the deaths. He was stoic, but jail officials put him under suicide watch, just to be sure *he* wouldn't do something drastic, too.

Alina Powell, Josh's younger sister, blamed law enforcement and their "malfeasance" for causing the fiery deaths of Josh, Charlie, and Braden. She was convinced that both the Utah and Washington investigators had hounded Josh until he could take no more.

After Braden and Charlie were laid to rest, the recriminations continued to abound. Chief Thayle "Buzz" Nielsen flew up from West Valley City to offer any help he could, and tears filled his eyes as he spoke of the boys. It was not clear if it had been Nielsen's decision to delay in arresting Josh Powell for so long—or that of Salt Lake County district attorney Sim Gill.

Too late. There was obviously nothing that could be done now that an entire family was either dead or missing. The consensus is that Susan is also dead. Her parents will probably never have the slight comfort of finding her body and giving her a proper burial.

More information on the physical evidence found in Susan's disappearance was finally released after Josh murdered his sons. The West Valley City investigators revealed that they had located a comforter with Susan's blood on it in a storage locker. This shocked her parents.

Chuck Cox decried the more-than-two-year wait for Utah authorities to arrest Josh. "If Josh had been in jail, the children would be safe."

No one disagreed with that.

Pierce County sheriff Paul Pastor's detectives *had* known about the macabre finds and details Chief Nielsen's investigators discovered since December 2009, but there was nothing the Washington team could do. Susan's disappearance wasn't their case.

"Obviously," Ed Troyer said, "it was frustrating. We were always waiting for the phone call to go arrest him."

And that phone call never came. Buzz Nielsen's detectives worked hard, sometimes around the clock, and they were frustrated, too. In a sense, from the beginning it was a game that no one could win. If any arrests were made too soon and there was no conviction, Josh Powell could have gone free, never again to be tried for Susan's murder.

If they waited too long . . .

Well, of course, they did. And two innocent children died in a monstrous conflagration.

In this case, the risk of an acquittal was far outweighed by the terrible danger that stalked Charlie and Braden Powell.

What began with ice ended with fire. It didn't have to be this way.

Epilogue

Steven Powell's trial on voyeurism and pornography charges lay ahead. It had been postponed from November 2011 to March 2012, and actually began in Pierce County Superior Court judge Ronald E. Culpepper's courtroom in May.

On Monday, May 7, 2012, Steven Powell went on trial on fourteen counts of voyeurism. The single charge of possession of child pornography had been thrown out. Powell appeared calm, almost disconnected, from the legal process taking place.

Alina Powell was there to support her father, and Susan Powell's parents and family also attended the proceedings.

It wouldn't be easy to pick twelve jurors and two alternates from the seventy-person jury pool; the Powell saga had had a great deal of publicity, both locally and nationally. Six potential jurors said they didn't think they could be fair, and several others had reasons not to serve. Even so, Pierce County deputy prosecutors Grant Blinn and Bryce Nelson and defense attorneys Mark Quigley and Travis Currie managed to winnow out seven men and seven women who felt they could judge the testimony and evidence from each side without undue influence from pretrial media coverage.

Would Steven Powell's explosive journals be allowed into evidence by Judge Culpepper? Having read some of his sexually obsessed entries about his daughter-in-law Susan, and other young women, I could understand why Blinn and Nelson wanted them in, but also doubted that Judge Culpepper would find them admissible. They had shocked and sickened me even after so many years working within the justice system wearing one hat or another, and surely their very vulgarity and depravity would strike many of the jurors as disgusting.

In the end, Steven Powell's journals were not permitted in this trial. Seeing the small man in his suit, shirt and tie, his hair now snow white, no one would suspect what went on in his head.

Judge Culpepper went out of his way to keep Susan Powell's "ghost" out of the courtroom. These legal proceedings did not involve her disappearance. He would allow very little—if any—testimony about Susan. And still, those in the gallery who knew her story felt her presence.

Whether the jurors did, no one knows.

In his opening statement, Deputy Prosecutor Nelson told jurors, "This case is about a secret. That secret is that Steven Powell is a voyeur."

Prosecuting attorney Mark Lindquist's team made every effort to spare the unknowing targets of Powell's intrusive cameras from being upset. Pierce County Detective Gary Sanders narrated the series of photos that had been taken from a window in the defendant's house, explaining that the angles, distances, and point of view could only have come from Steven Powell's bedroom window. Sanders and other police personnel executing the search warrant had found a box in Steven's bedroom with a CD containing the surreptitiously taken intimate pictures.

The gallery could not see the pictures of two young girls in their bathroom, and that was as it should be. They had been photographed taking a bath, undressing, using the toilet, and the powerful telescopic camera lens had often been focused tightly on their private parts.

Gary Sanders told jurors about tracking down the families who had lived in the Powell's neighborhood in 2006 and 2007 until they located the little girls' mother, and of how she reacted when she found out that someone had watched them stealthily.

Cross-examined by defense attorney Mark Quigley— who clearly wanted to suggest that there were three or four males living in the Powell house at the time who might have taken the photos—Sanders said whoever held the camera had to have been standing at the window of Steven's bedroom on the second floor. And, of course, the pictures were found hidden in Steven Powell's bedroom.

The woman whom I have called "Sally Mahoney" for her privacy's sake and her two daughters, now in their teens, testified. "Sally," "Lily," and "Robyn" were identified by their initials, per Lindquist's office's attempt to preserve their identity.

Sally told jurors that she had never given any permission for her daughters to be photographed, and the girls testified that they didn't know someone was watching and filming them.

Grant Blinn asked "Robyn Mahoney" if she ever felt afraid when she lived in the rental house near the Powell residence.

She shook her head. "I felt safe."

"Why?" he asked.

"I was in my house," she explained.

If ever children should feel safe, it *is* in their houses with loving parents close by.

Mark Quigley wisely declined to cross-examine either girl.

Jennifer Powell Graves, Josh's sister who had long since sided with the Cox family, testified for the state about the males who had lived in Steven's house in the middle years of the first decade of the twenty-first century. Her recollection was that two of her grown brothers were not living there at the time.

She also testified that she had seen a journal entry, written in what she recognized as her father's hand, that noted that the author enjoyed taking pictures of girls and women wearing skirts and shorts.

Steven Powell did not take the witness stand. That probably was a relief for his attorneys; he had blurted out so many odd statements over the past few years when he was interviewed by radio and television reporters, particularly about his belief that he and Susan Powell had had a special and secret sexual relationship.

Nor did Mark Quigley and Travis Currie mount a defense. They called no witnesses.

Suddenly, the trial was over.

The jury quickly found Steven Craig Powell guilty on all fourteen counts of voyeurism. His sentencing was set for June 15.

The public believed that Powell could get as little as four years in prison or as much as ninety years if the sentences ran consecutively.

Prosecutor Lindquist said that his office would seek a ten-year sentence. That seemed very short to most people, but there were statutes in place at the time of the crimes against the Mahoney girls that might impact the sentencing. Powell's defense attorneys announced that they were asking that their client serve only a year in prison.

Many people who had followed Susan's case since 2009 hoped that there might be some kind of plea bargain. If Steven Powell would tell where Susan was, maybe he would get a shorter sentence.

"They didn't offer," deputy prosecutor Grant Blinn commented about such a possibility. "And we didn't ask."

It probably would have been fruitless anyway. Steven Powell had been a sphinx when it came to any questions about Susan's fate. Investigators doubted he would suddenly open up now, particularly if he had any guilty knowledge of her disappearance.

June 15 arrived, and Judge Culpepper had to cope with

a difficult legal decision. Were the fourteen instances of voyeurism involving the Mahoney girls a *series* of separate offenses? Or should they be viewed by the Court as a continuing single act?

Quigley and Currie cited several voyeurism cases in Pierce County. One convicted man had had *sixteen* convictions of voyeurism, and his sentence was only nine months!

Quigley argued that his client should be dealt with the same way. *To be fair.*

Blinn pointed out that Steven Powell had shown no remorse at all for his crimes, and that he had never even admitted his behavior was wrong.

For those who wanted to see Steven Powell go to prison for the rest of his life—and many did—Judge Culpepper's ruling was astounding. And yet his choices were limited under the law.

Culpepper termed Powell "the ultimate creep of a neighbor," as he pronounced sentence. "I think it's appropriate for him to be punished for what he did. Not for what somebody suspects. Mr. Powell obviously has a long-standing sexual deviance. There's something seriously wrong with Mr. Powell's view of women in the world."

And then, to everyone's shock, he sentenced Steven Powell to only two and a half years in prison! With credit for time already served, and time off for good behavior, Powell will probably be in prison for less than a year. He will remain in isolation while he is evaluated at an interim facility, and likely will remain isolated in his final prison.

If he is out in the general prisoner population, his chances of survival could be slim.

On the day her father's case went to the jury, Alina Powell began a website castigating law enforcement. Alina believes her father and her brother are innocent of any criminal acts, and are merely victims of public opinion and devious investigators.

Although Judge Culpepper did his best to see that Steven Powell was not convicted because of suspicion that he might have had something to do with Susan's death, questions remain. Steven asked for time off from his job within days of Susan's disappearance in Utah. Many believe he went to Utah. During that time, Josh rented a vehicle and put eight hundred miles on the odometer. Is it possible that Steven was part of a plot to kill Susan? Perhaps he was like Josh was with his sons. Rather than give them up to Susan's parents, Josh killed them. If Steven could not have Susan, then perhaps he didn't want Josh to have her, either. Maybe he manipulated his weak son into destroying her. Possibly he went to Utah to help Josh hide Susan's body where no one could ever find it?

An investigation into that possibility is ongoing.

It's sad to visit at Chuck and Judy's home, to sit in the room that was once meant for Charlie and Braden, and to look at the island in the duck pond, an island where the little boys said the ducks would be safe. Their photos are there in their grandparents' house, along with a giant picture of Susan. It seems as if the front door will suddenly open and all three of them will come running up the stairs.

But, of course, they won't.

Judy longs to have Susan's scrapbook—the one she kept from the time she was a little girl. But Steven has refused to give it to her.

Chuck thinks he burned it.

Steven Craig Powell is far from out of the woods legally. On the day he was sentenced to prison, Anne Bremner served him with papers as she filed a civil suit against him on Chuck and Judy's behalf alleging "general outrage" for his criminal acts.

In the third week of August 2012, Anne Bremner flew to Utah to present a request to the city council of West Valley City. On behalf of Chuck and Judy Cox, she asked that the West Valley City Police Department release their investigative files on the disappearance of their daughter, Susan Cox Powell.

Susan's case had stalled and been virtually dead in the water for many months. Her parents had been allowed only glimpses of any discoveries the Utah police investigators had found over the almost two years since Susan vanished. And what they *had* learned was excruciatingly painful— details on Susan's note, obviously written as she feared she might be murdered, and descriptions of the amount of her blood found in the home she shared with Josh.

It was like pulling adhesive tape slowly from a wound,

and it hurt far more than if the Coxes could know it all in a complete reveal.

"It's been horrible for Chuck and Judy," Bremner told the city council. "They just want to see it all at once, especially if there is something more upsetting coming out." The Seattle attorney pointed out that Susan's case wasn't moving forward. "*Who* are they investigating?" she asked. "And for *what*?"

She asked the council members to look at what chief Buzz Nielsen's department was doing on the probe and to find out for themselves if the investigation was dormant or not, reminding them that it seemed to be going nowhere. Under Utah's victims' rights laws, she felt the Coxes had every right to read the files on their missing daughter and her now-dead husband, the prime suspect.

West Valley City police advisor Clint Gilmore insisted that the council didn't have the authority to release the Powell records. "The case is still active," he said. "This is an ongoing investigation. We want to solve this case, and to disclose anything would jeopardize it."

Whether he was being actively investigated in Utah for any part he might have played in Susan's disappearance—and, perhaps, murder—Steven Powell *was* the target of great interest for the Pierce County sheriff's detectives and prosecutor Mark Lindquist's office.

"We have to wonder," Bremner said, "if there is information on his [Steve Powell] being there at the time of Susan's disappearance, about phone calls he made to Josh, his calling in sick after she disappeared, and about his criminal obsession with her. What did the West Valley City Police know about that?"

Steven Powell *had* called in sick on December 8 and 9, 2009. Although he kept in touch with coworkers via the Internet, no one had actually seen him during that time. One coworker recalled that he had told her around Thanksgiving that he planned a camping trip in Utah with his son Josh in the near future.

There were other issues. The Cox family was in a legal tussle with the Powells over millions of dollars in insurance money. The money didn't matter to them, but it would be a bitter pill to see members of Josh's family profit from the loss of their daughter and their grandsons. They needed to know what had taken place in a missing person's probe that had lasted for almost three years.

But Anne Bremner's plea to the West Valley City council members didn't convince them. They debated over what she had said, but came back with their refusal to release the city's police records on Susan Powell.

And so the saga continues, still full of secrets and lies. There will never be full closure for the Cox family that has lost so much, but it is desperately important that what is hidden from them will one day be revealed.

They deserve that.

TWO STRANGE
DEATHS IN
CORONADO

Chapter One

In the wee hours of July 13, 2011, the only sounds at the Spreckels Mansion on Ocean Boulevard were the engines of the few cars that passed by, and the soft lapping of the Pacific Ocean as waves washed over the massive beach rocks that spell out CORONADO.

The dark-haired woman was beautiful even in death, and the moonlight dappled her naked body, but it is impossible—even now—to determine just where she was when it was first discovered. She could have been moving slightly in a mild breeze beneath one of the bedrooms' balconies, a shiny thick orange-red rope around her ankles, securing her wrists behind her back, with her lower legs several feet off the ground.

There is also the possibility that she rested on the grass and never came off the balcony above her at all. The red rope might have crushed her neck in another kind of strangling. Or someone's strong hands could have choked the life out of her. There is even a chance that she was killed someplace else and carried to the place where she was found.

Only one person said that he saw her as the sun rose; only he came forward to speak about discovering the horror of her death. He told Coronado, California, police detectives how she was when he first observed her, and recalled the sequence of events rather dispassionately. Shock, of course, makes different people react in different ways. One couldn't even attempt to know how he felt on this Wednesday morning of July 13.

Her name was Rebecca, and she was the girlfriend of billionaire pharmaceutical tycoon Jonah Shacknai. She was thirty-two. He is Adam Shacknai, Jonah Shacknai's brother. He is forty-eight.

When Adam talked with investigators about "Becky's" death, they were puzzled by what dark force loomed over Jonah's home. The discovery of the exquisite woman's corpse was a second shock. Becky Zahau had been vibrantly alive only hours before. Her death was an unfathomable blow to two already grieving families. It made no sense.

It made just as little sense as when Jonah's small son fell from an upper-story landing of the mansion, apparently clinging to a huge cut-glass chandelier for seconds before he crashed down to the foyer, unconscious and terribly hurt, only two days before Becky's death. Jonah's son's full name was Maxfield Shacknai but his family usually called him Max or Maxie, and he was only six.

At the time of Becky's death, Maxie, the youngest of Jonah's three children, was still alive—but in extremely critical condition in a drug-induced coma. Doctors warned

Jonah and his ex-wife Dina—who was Maxie's mom—
that it was unlikely their son would survive.

And now Becky was dead.

The very wealthy are not immune to scandal, tragedy, and
police investigations. Consider the Kennedy family and
their trials for alleged crimes behind the walls of luxurious
estates in Florida and Connecticut. Or the 1966 murder
of Illinois senator Charles Percy's daughter Valerie in the
Percy family's estate in a suburb of Chicago as her twin
slept nearby, unaware.

Being rich doesn't assure safety—not at all; sometimes
it attracts aberrant minds. And sometimes it seems that
those who have too many wordly goods pay for it with terrible losses that they could not foresee.

Jonah Shacknai owned what was known as the Spreckels Mansion. Jonah, fifty, was rumored to be a billionaire,
an entrepreneur much like the Spreckels sugar barons
generations earlier. He and Becky and Jonah's extended
family used the mansion as a summer place, arriving
from Scottsdale, Arizona, on Memorial Day and returning to Shacknai's even more lavish desert home around
Labor Day.

For the very wealthy, the Coronado mansion was the
equivalent of a summer cottage. It was a little worn around
the edges, and some rooms hadn't been redecorated since
the mid-twentieth century. But it was as cozy as such
a huge property could be, and the breeze off the ocean

across the street was a welcome change from baking Arizona in the summertime.

The Duke and Duchess of Windsor stayed at the Spreckels Mansion once—probably in the 1930s or '40s—and their bedroom suite was completely redone for the occasion. That bedroom was still in pristine condition, with especially made twin beds joined by a lavish double headboard of imported wood. The rest of the mansion is genteelly shabby, and in need of repair—or at least it was in 2011. The guesthouse was in better shape.

Jonah Shacknai's mansion had five stories. The lowest level was the basement; the first floor/main level consisted of a foyer, living room, sunroom, dining room, sitting area, butler's pantry, kitchen, laundry room, and a half bath. The second floor had two bedrooms (an office and guest room/office) and a bathroom. The master bedroom and en suite bath were on the third floor, along with three smaller bedrooms—one each for Jonah's children: Max, Cameron,* and Josh.*

And the top floor was the attic.

The guesthouse was bigger than many families' homes. It had a living room, three bedrooms, a kitchen, and three bathrooms.

The history of the Spreckels estate is well-known, with so many memories and tales of generation after generation of an impossibly rich, famous and infamous family written about in books, newspapers, and gossip columns.

With two disasters in as many days, one might wonder if the place was haunted, cursed by something that emanated eerily from events that had happened a century earlier.

It seems unlikely; what occurred in 2011 couldn't have any connection to the original owners. Indeed, it was John Spreckels who built Jonah Shacknai's summer place; the other Spreckels mansion, in San Francisco, was constructed to suit the taste of his brother Adolph Spreckels, who, along with his descendants, was far more involved in scandals and violence. John was the brother and uncle whose life was more circumspect.

The Spreckels family had no connection, of course, to those who lived there a century later. Nonetheless, the magnificent grounds and huge, once-luxurious rooms seemed steeped in the Spreckels' stories, too. For more than a hundred years, the mansion has stood through storms, earthquakes, baking sun, stock market upswings, depressions, and wars. Surely the stoic walls had absorbed a sense of history.

But, of course, the walls said nothing. The old trees had grown above the roofline and the lush foliage sheltered the mansion more every decade. It seemed to be an estate that anyone might envy.

Chapter Two

When I first heard about double tragedies in the wealthiest enclave of posh Coronado, California, I found them both appalling and intriguing. I still do.

I've been to Coronado a few times, although I never got to stay at the fabulous Hotel del Coronado, which is located close by the Spreckels Mansion. I've only driven through the circular driveway to view it close up. It is a luxurious and expensive place to stay—and on the book tours that took me to Coronado I was housed farther down the road, at more mundane hotels.

A few miles south of those and closer to Mexico, the odor of sewage drifts up from Tijuana. I had little choice but to keep my windows closed and air conditioners on.

But the Hotel del Coronado has remained majestic and sacrosanct. It has been featured in any number of movies—many of them horror based. An historic edifice, the hotel is said to have its share of ghosts.

Coronado itself is rife with millionaires' estates. And along Ocean Boulevard, the real estate is prime. Huge homes rise in stately profusion with wide and deep velvet green lawns, fragrant night-blooming jasmine, bougainvillea, camellias, hibiscus, bottlebrush, and other exotic trees bursting with blooms. Most of the mansions are built of stucco with tile roofs; there are many outbuildings that sprawl across the large lots: separate guesthouses, servants' quarters, pool houses, and, of course, aquamarine pools. Many of the properties are protected by delicately filigreed iron gates with sturdy locks, closed off from the traffic along Ocean Boulevard and keggers on the beach.

Just beyond the busy street, the Pacific Ocean pushes against the shore, later to ebb as the moon's cycle changes.

John D. Spreckels, born in 1853, created the Coronado mansion where Maxfield Shacknai and Becky Zahau were to die mysteriously. He was at first a newspaperman and millionaire sugar baron, and he branched out into many other fields.

The Spreckels clan have lived in luxury to this day, and yet some of their ancestors exhibited bizarre, almost psychotic tendencies. Some wonder if a black cloud might have remained in their grand houses long after they died off.

The more shocking scandals appear to have trickled down through Adolph's line. In 1884, Adolph shot Michael de Young, the cofounder of the *San Francisco Chronicle,* because he was furious about an article suggesting that Western Sugar Refiners, the family corporation, had defrauded their shareholders. Charged with attempted murder, Adolph pleaded temporary insanity and was quickly acquitted due to his "mental incapacity."

Adolph and Alma had three children—two daughters

and a son. Adolph Jr. was a disappointment, said to have a mean streak, often acting out with violence. That may have been because most of his family called him "Little Adolph." A daredevil, Adolph Jr. was piloting a hydroplane on Green Lake in Seattle in 1936 when his throttle stuck and the boat went airborne over the crowd, fatally injuring a bystander in a wheelchair. Little Adolph himself was badly injured and had to have a series of surgeries on his arm and face to *almost* restore them.

Adolph Jr.'s seduction of women wasn't hampered by his scars. He had half a dozen or more short-lived marriages, and many affairs with beautiful actresses. His sixth wife was movie star Kay Williams, who left him after an unfortunate vacation on Balboa Island, where she complained that he'd beaten her. The story made headlines all over America.

Kay Williams Spreckels had two children with Adolph Jr.—Joan and Adolph III, known as "Bunker." Bunker was born in 1949 and he was five years old when his mother divorced Adolph Jr. He admired his mother's new husband, movie star Clark Gable, who was kind to him and taught him about guns, hunting, and women.

Bunker lived a life most teenagers wanted to emulate. The handsome youth was a champion surfer. He went steady with Miss Teen California. He expected no inheritance because his father, Adolph Jr., was spending millions at an alarming rate. Bunker was sure it would all be gone before his father died. But Adolph Jr. passed away unexpectedly before he could spend all his money; at twenty-one, Bunker Spreckels rented an armored car and went to the bank where he had $51 million waiting for him. He demanded it in cash and took it to a secret location he called his "Bat Cave," where he kept treasures he didn't want anyone to see.

Bunker Spreckels was a brilliant, blond youth who believed in living fast, dying young, and making a handsome corpse. Sadly, his prediction came true. Despite his multiple skills and Adonis-like looks, he died at the age of twenty-seven.

His grandfather Adolph built the Spreckels mansion in San Francisco, a spectacular structure now the home of author Danielle Steel. And his uncle John designed the Spreckels estate in Coronado, on Ocean Boulevard. John spent many happy years there. He also had another home in Coronado, his "bay-side" property, which is now the Glorietta Bay Inn, and he called that his "beach house."

As of this writing, the house on Ocean Boulevard where Jonah Shacknai and Rebecca Zahau lived has been sold to a corporation. The asking price was $16.9 million!

Becky Zahau came from modest beginnings, and she was a little dazzled by the beach estate with its main house *and* guesthouse, twenty-seven rooms in all, and a northeast wing with two apartments and a six-car garage. A mixture of Italian Renaissance and Beaux-Arts architecture, 1043 Ocean Boulevard boasted an exercise room and a ballet studio, and the basement had not one—but *two*—wine cellars.

The path up the wide sidewalk to the mansion, with its

carefully trimmed low hedges and a hundred feet of purple flowers on either side, was like an entry to paradise. Inside there were marble fireplaces, winding stairs, thick carpets, chandeliers, and balconies. Windows gave a commanding view of the Pacific Ocean.

By the summer of 2011, even though the last of the Spreckels family had long since moved on, the grand estate, in a gentle state of disrepair, was still called the Spreckels Mansion. It probably always will be.

And this was where half the family who occupied it suffered disastrous fates.

Chapter Three

Jonah Shacknai shared custody of his son Maxie with his second ex-wife, Dina, who lived close by. Becky Zahau loved the little boy as if he were her own. Jonah also spent a lot of time with his two older children by his first wife, Kim. His daughter, Cameron, was fourteen, and his older son, Josh, was eleven. They, too, lived most of the year in Scottsdale. Jonah's older children were not as accepting of Becky as Maxie was. That was to be expected—especially with a teenage daughter who wanted her father to herself.

According to Jonah's close friends, he was very happy to be living with Becky, and had achieved a serene and loving relationship after two rather chaotic marriages—the most combative one with Dina, who was a child psychologist.

When Jonah and Becky were traveling or at their home in Arizona, a couple who lived in one of the apartments oversaw the estate. They also cleaned, and supervised garden workers.

On Sunday, July 10, 2011, Becky's younger sister,

Zaré,* arrived for a three-week visit. Zaré adored her twenty-years-older sister and was delighted to fly from St. Joseph, Missouri, to Southern California for a long visit. Becky was just as happy to see her little sister, and Jonah was always gracious to members of her family.

Becky's background was as different from Jonah's as it could possibly be. She was born in Burma, the second daughter of a man who worked with Christian ministries. He was imprisoned by the military regime there for fighting for religious freedom in Burma. He later sought political asylum in Germany so his family would have the chance of a better future. Becky was quite young at the time, and she and her older siblings grew up there. They were raised in a Protestant church.

Most of Becky's immediate family migrated to America—to the St. Louis, Missouri, area.

Jonah was born on the East Coast to Gideon and Selma Shacknai and raised in Suffern, New York. He and his brother, Adam, were from a tight-knit, high-achieving family. Selma was an educator and therapist during most of her adult life. Gideon came to America as a young man of twenty-one, and soon got his citizenship.

Jonah and Adam grew up in the Jewish faith. Jonah is a handsome man, with dark hair, tall and charismatic. His acumen for business is remarkable, and he became wealthy at a comparatively young age because of that.

Jonah and Becky had been together for a little less than two years when Maxie fell on Monday, July 11.

In the tense days while Maxie fought for life, Becky did everything she could to make things a little easier for Jonah.

Jonah himself was staying at the Ronald McDonald House across from the Rady Children's Hospital in San Diego, so that he could be close to Maxie, who hadn't regained consciousness since his terrible fall.

No one knew exactly how Max's accident had happened, because there were no witnesses—or none that came forward. He was a very active little boy who played soccer almost as soon as he could walk, and whose physical coordination was perfect. Why had he fallen?

One theory was that he had been going too fast on his Razor scooter on an upper landing and hadn't been able to stop before he hit the railing. It looked as though he had grabbed on to the crystal chandelier in an attempt to save himself, but the light fixture, the scooter, and Max had all ended up in a heap on the carpet far below, just inside the front door.

Some thought he might have been sliding on the banister, lost his grip, and tried to hang on to the chandelier. The scooter might have been downstairs already, beside one of Maxie's soccer balls.

The chandelier chain had been found to be cut cleanly, rather than torn apart. That could have been done by paramedics who lifted it off the child as rapidly as they could.

The doctors at Rady were doing their best to save Maxie's life. They were initially puzzled, however, that he was so near death when his physical injuries didn't seem that bad. He had no broken bones, and he was currently undergoing tests to see if he might have an undetected genetic heart malfunction, possibly a "long Q syndrome." This is a stealthy defect, one that kills some children and young athletes without warning by throwing off the heart's rhythm until it stops beating.

(After his fall, Maxie's heart *had* stopped beating, however, for perhaps as long as twenty to thirty minutes, according to an anonymous medical professional with a screen name of "KZ" who posted her opinion on "The Hinky Meter," an Internet opinion posting site in Southern California. *Hinky* is, of course, a well-known police term for something suspicious.)

Maxie was resuscitated, but it probably was far too late to prevent massive brain swelling.

Perhaps Maxie hadn't fallen over the second story railing because he was chasing a soccer ball or going too fast on his scooter. There was a possibility that he had fainted when his heart faltered, and he tumbled over the rail. At this stage of the probe, there was even a dread possibility that someone had pushed the little boy over the railing— either deliberately or accidentally.

So, as far as anyone knew, Rebecca and Zaré had been alone in the mansion with Maxie while his father, Jonah, was working out at a private gym in the Hotel del Coronado, only a few blocks away.

Becky and her little sister had apparently been in separate bathrooms, bathing and washing their hair when it happened. The mansion was so large that it was *possible* that someone else *could* have been inside without either

Becky or Zaré realizing it. But who would want to hurt Maxie?

Becky's near-hysterical call to Jonah's cell phone right after she found Maxie injured was nearly unintelligible. Jonah hadn't even tried to figure out what she was saying. He immediately started running for home, arriving only a few minutes later to find paramedics working over Maxie.

Now it was the morning of Wednesday, July 13, and it was touch and go whether Max would live. Jonah was devastated. It had taken him a long time to locate his second wife, Dina—Max's mother. She evidently had been home—but ill—when efforts were made to reach her.

Although Jonah and Dina had gone through a contentious divorce, this was their beloved child, the one good thing to come out of their marriage. They sat beside Max's bed watching him and praying, hoping against hope that he would open his eyes and be the healthy, active little boy he was only two days before.

At the moment, no one but Adam Shacknai knew yet that Becky was dead. Adam Shacknai didn't live in Coronado; he lived in Memphis, Tennessee, where he worked as a tugboat captain. The Shacknai brothers were close in age, but worlds apart in lifestyles. Although Jonah and Adam didn't see one another often, Adam was almost always invited to family events.

When Gideon Shacknai called Adam to tell his son about Max's accident, Adam dropped everything and flew to San Diego, arriving on Tuesday evening, July 12. He had apparently come to offer what comfort he could to Jonah.

Becky picked up Adam Shacknai at the airport shortly after she put her thirteen-year-old sister, Zaré, on a plane for Missouri. Zaré had stayed only a day or so; with everyone worried sick about Max, it seemed wiser to postpone her visit to another time.

On this Wednesday at 6:48 A.M., Adam Shacknai called 911. Indeed, he called three times and he both frustrated and worried the dispatcher, saying first, "I got a woman hung herself . . . I cut her down."

Adam either could not—or would not—give the address where the dead woman was. It took the third call for the emergency operator to elicit the information that something terrible had happened at 1043 Ocean Boulevard. She immediately sent EMTs and Coronado police officers.

A mystery within a mystery within a mystery had just begun to bubble from a secret place—an inscrutable series of conundrums almost impossible to explain.

Chapter Four

The first patrol officers to arrive at the scene were led to the rear courtyard, where the slender body of a woman lay on the dew-damp grass just below one of the balconies in the main house. She was completely naked except for some kind of blue clothing—a shirt, perhaps—that was wound several times around her neck. A length of reddish nautical rope cinched her neck. Her wrists were bound behind her back with the same rope; another length of the rope secured her ankles. It appeared to be a waterskiing towrope; the handle was still caught up in it.

Adam Shacknai told the Coronado police that he had wakened early and was on his way to the main part of the mansion to get a cup of coffee in the kitchen when he saw his brother's girlfriend suspended from the balcony with a rope around her neck. He said he raced into the kitchen to find a knife so he could cut her down.

"She had that cloth wedged in her throat," Adam said. "I took it out."

The rope around Becky's neck had been cut, and the investigators saw that the other end of the rope dangled from the balcony above her. There was a round patio table, its wood weathered, that appeared to have been placed under the balcony rope. One leg was broken.

"I moved that table over," Adam said, "so I could reach her to cut her down."

The patrol officers tried to find a pulse, but she had none. They began resuscitation but were very relieved when the EMTs from the Coronado Fire Department arrived.

Only six minutes had passed, but it seemed like hours.

Paramedic John Feliciano quickly checked the woman, and then shook his head. "She's cold to the touch—and rigor mortis is already beginning in her jaw."

For rigor to be noticeable, Becky Zahau would have to have died hours before. Feliciano pronounced her dead. She had been for some time.

At 8 A.M., chief Lou J. Scanlon entered the Coronado Mobile Command vehicle that was parked in front of 1043 Ocean Boulevard. He saw a tall man with dark hair and black-rimmed glasses standing inside, and suggested he take a seat. Officer Robert Kline was the only other person present, and he said to Scanlon, "This is Adam—the brother."

Chief Scanlon had already heard that Adam was the brother of the property owner, that he had been staying in the guesthouse at the rear of the estate and had discovered the woman's naked body.

"This must be traumatic for you," Scanlon said. "Officer Kline will stay here with you."

At first Adam Shacknai seemed not to hear what he'd

said. And then he blurted, "This is fucking crazy. I don't think my bedside manner is that bad—"

What did he mean by that? Possibly he was in shock, Scanlon guessed. It seemed off the wall.

Adam Shacknai said nothing more to Lou Scanlon and stayed in the motor home with Officer Kline.

Shortly after eight, the Coronado Police Department asked San Diego County sheriff's detectives and criminalists from their crime lab to respond to the mansion on Ocean Boulevard.

No one in the sheriff's department knew exactly what had happened—no more than that a woman's body had been discovered less than two hours earlier.

At 8:39 A.M., San Diego County homicide sergeant Dave Nemeth conducted a hastily arranged briefing. The word was that there had been a "suspicious death" in Coronado. The deceased was said to be Becky Zahau, who resided at the Spreckels Mansion with her boyfriend, Jonah Shacknai.

It promised to be a high-profile case, and the sheriff's office quickly agreed to aid the much smaller Coronado Police Department. The investigation into Becky's death would be handled by the San Diego Sheriff's Homicide Team #2, with detective Angela Tsuida as the lead investigator. Coronado police sergeant Mitch McKay was at the death scene and he briefed the crew of San Diego County sheriff's detectives who gathered there.

Each two-detective partnership would have a specific

assignment. Some of them would interview possible suspects and witnesses, and some would gather physical evidence; fingerprint experts would lift what prints they could. There would be literally hundreds of photographs taken—both on the scene and from helicopters circling like hungry hawks above the posh neighborhood.

Already the pilots could see nearby residents sitting on their roofs and high balconies, trying to get a glimpse of what was going on in the courtyard where detectives swarmed. It was sad that the dead woman had no protection from prying eyes, some behind binoculars.

Who lived in this estate? What had the neighbors heard—if anything? It was a new age, and forensic computer experts and those trained in retrieving phone calls in and out would strive to find whatever might lie hidden inside electronic devices.

Detective Brian Patterson began writing an affidavit for a search warrant of the home, outbuildings, and vehicles. Detectives D. Hillen and Hank Lebitski were assigned to interview the man who had called 911: Adam Shacknai. Detectives Todd Norton and M. Palmer would interview Jonah Shacknai.

The dead woman still rested on the grassy courtyard. There was no urgency now; she was gone and could not be brought back. But once a homicide victim has gone to the medical examiner's office to await autopsy, and the crime scene is released, nothing can be reconstructed exactly as it was, so it is essential that detectives spend hours—sometimes even days—at the initial crime scene.

The teams of San Diego detectives wanted to keep it untouched by outsiders as long as they could.

They did not erect a temporary tent over Becky Zahau's body to give her some privacy from onlookers, as homicide investigators often do. Becky was dead, but it upset her family when they heard how long she had lain exposed to the world.

San Diego County medical examiner Dr. Jonathan Lucas was notified, but it would be late afternoon before he arrived at the scene.

For now, CRIME SCENE: DO NOT ENTER tape marked areas where no one but the investigators were allowed to go. Too many "looky-loos" can cause vital evidence to be lost forever. Even department brass were asked, albeit politely, to stay outside the tape.

As their fellow detectives went over the perfectly manicured grounds for anything that might be of evidentiary value, Hillen and Lebitski interviewed Adam Shacknai at the Coronado Police Department headquarters. With Shacknai's permission, their conversation was taped.

It was, however, a rather brief interview, lasting less than an hour. Adam repeated his recall of the prior evening, adding some details. After having a quick dinner with his brother, Jonah, and Becky, who had picked him up at the airport, they dropped Jonah off at the Ronald McDonald House and then returned to the Spreckels Mansion. Adam said he slept in the guesthouse and, as far as he knew, Becky had retired to her room in the main house. He believed that they were the only two people present at the estate during the night.

The Memphis tugboat captain said he was crossing the square of grass below the balcony of Becky's bedroom/office when he saw her hanging there. Luckily, he had been able to find the right drawer in the large kitchen where knives were kept, and he grabbed one and raced back to cut her down.

When Adam hadn't been able to revive her, he said, he called the 911 operator.

As many people close to Becky would do, Adam Shacknai agreed to be processed for evidentiary purposes. Asked if that was okay with him, he said, "All right—okay."

Detective Angela Tsuida called and asked if Shacknai would be willing to give them his shoes and fingerprints. Adam agreed to that, too. Denys Williams, an evidence technician with the San Diego County Sheriff's Department, took a number of photographs of Adam, some with his shirt removed. She then took swabs from his mouth, and retrieved head hair samples and fingernail scrapings.

When Williams was finished, Hillen and Lebitski came back into the interview room and spoke with Adam on tape for about six minutes. When he was asked if he would be willing to take a polygraph test regarding the statement he had given them about finding Becky, Adam said he had no objection to that.

The detectives tentatively set up a lie detector test for

5 P.M. Then they dropped Adam Shacknai off at a car rental kiosk at Lindbergh Field, at his request.

Shortly before five, Detective Hillen phoned Adam and asked if he was still willing to take the test. Adam said he wanted to speak to his brother, Jonah, about it, and Hillen said that was fine—he would call him back in a few minutes.

Hillen did so.

"I have nothing to hide," Adam said. "I'm willing to take the test."

It was 5:30 when Adam Shacknai arrived at the San Diego County homicide offices to meet with polygrapher Paul Redden. Once again, Hillen reminded him that he was not compelled to take the test, and that he was present of his own free will. Adam nodded.

And then his cell phone rang. He said he didn't recognize the number and let it go to his text mailbox. But it rang again a few minutes later. Adam checked the caller ID and saw that it was a message from an attorney's office.

"My brother must have called a lawyer for me," Adam said. "What do you think he wants to say to me?"

"I think," Hillen said truthfully, "that he would tell you not to take the polygraph test."

Adam Shacknai mulled that over, but he didn't change his mind and said he had no reason to talk to an attorney. Four times Detective Hillen explained to Adam that he was in the sheriff's office voluntarily and he didn't *have* to take a lie detector test.

And four times Adam said he had nothing to hide.

He grew nervous only when Redden began to hook him up to the leads for the polygraph: blood pressure, breathing patterns, galvanic skin response, and heart rate. He asked about what the lie detector test could say—even when the leads were attached to an innocent person.

Redden assured him that it didn't matter how nervous a subject might be: if he was telling the truth, the polygraph would show that.

Redden began the test at 6:40 and continued for two hours. At first he asked only innocuous general questions. He noted his subject's response to deliberate "lie questions."

Finally, he began to question Adam Shacknai about the past few days' events.

Paul Redden gave Adam Shacknai *four* polygraph tests. He asked the following relevant questions:

1. Regarding the death of Rebecca, do you know for sure if anyone did anything to her that resulted in her death?
   (SUBJECT answered "No.")
2. Regarding the death of Rebecca, did you, yourself, do anything to her that resulted in her death?
   (SUBJECT answered "No.")
3. Regarding the death of Rebecca, were you in the guest room that she was found hanging from at anytime during the night?
   (SUBJECT answered "No.")

Redden charted two more tests with similar questions.

4. Did you, yourself, do anything to Rebecca that resulted in her death?
   (SUBJECT answered "No.")
5. Did you physically do anything to Rebecca that resulted in her death?
   (SUBJECT answered "No.")

RESULTS

At the conclusion of the polygraph examination, a careful evaluation of all the subject's polygraph charts revealed insufficient physiological responses necessary to make a determination. It is my opinion, as the Examiner, based on careful analysis of all the subject's polygraph charts that the subject was inconclusive when he answered "No" to the above relevant questions.

Respectfully,
Paul Redden
Polygraph Examiner

Adam Shacknai elaborated next to Redden, Hillen, and Lebitski on the statement he had given earlier in this endless day. He said he had received a phone call from his father in New York on Tuesday, telling him that his nephew Max had fallen and hit his head. His father said Max was in a coma, in serious condition.

"I called Rebecca, my brother's girlfriend," he said. "I told her I would fly out here from Memphis to give whatever help and support I could. I told her I would rent a car at the airport, but she said she would pick me up—since she was dropping her sister off at the airport anyway."

Becky *had* picked him up, and they drove to Rady Children's Hospital, where they picked up Jonah and his best friend, Dr. Howard Luber. Then they drove back to the airport, Adam recalled. Adam said he believed that Dr. Luber was in San Diego to support Jonah after Max fell.

"We dropped him off so he could fly home to Arizona," Adam said. "Then we drove to the Fish Market restaurant where the three of us—Jonah, Becky, and myself—had dinner."

After they ate, Becky drove back once again to the hospital. "Jonah showed me his room at the Ronald McDonald House."

Finally, Adam said, he and Rebecca had driven to Jonah's mansion on Ocean Boulevard. He estimated they arrived there between 7:30 and 8 P.M. That would have been 9:30 to 10 on Adam's Central time.

"Rebecca told me to stay in the guesthouse, and she went into the main house," Adam recalled. "I've stayed there four or five times before when I visited Jonah."

Asked how well he knew Rebecca, Adam replied that he didn't know her well and didn't even know her last name—but he had met her occasionally over the last year.

"Did you see Rebecca again last night?" Redden asked. "After you went to your room in the guesthouse?"

"No. I didn't see her or talk to her. I went to the guesthouse, drank a Diet 7Up, and called my girlfriend."

Adam said he'd taken an Ambien sleeping pill and gone to bed. He recalled getting up during the night to go to the bathroom, and falling back to sleep until a quarter after six in the morning.

Evincing no embarrassment, he said he'd begun his day by pulling up a porn site on his iPhone.

"I wanted some breakfast," he told Redden, "and I showered and got dressed. I was going to go to the main residence and ask Rebecca if she wanted to go out to breakfast with me."

But he had opened his door and seen a red rope hanging off the balcony of the big house with a body suspended from it. At first he thought it was a prank and that some kids were "messing around"—but then he'd recognized that it was Rebecca, so he'd run inside the main residence and grabbed a knife so he could get her down.

"I had to pull the patio table over to her body so I could reach her," Adam said. "I stood on the table, cut the rope, and put her on the ground. I called 911, and started CPR on Rebecca—after I pulled a blue scarf out of her mouth. The dispatcher asked me for the address, and I ran around to the front of the house so I could tell the location. Then I went back to Rebecca, and the police were there within a couple of minutes."

Adam Shacknai said he hadn't heard anything during the night. In fact, he had noted how very quiet it was.

The detectives asked more probing questions, but Adam denied any knowledge or involvement in Rebecca's hanging, and he said he had never been in the room next to the balcony where Rebecca had hung herself.

*   *   *

Adam Shacknai had neither "passed" nor "failed" on the four lie detector charts.

And so the San Diego County sheriff's investigators were back to square one. Adam's frank admission about his early-morning porn session was a little startling, but not an admission of any guilt.

Adam *had* taken Ambien the night before. Recent studies have shown that many people have proven to react strangely to this sleeping pill. Without being aware of it, they walked or drove in their sleep. Sometimes they ate, drank, swam, made phone calls, did all manner of activities when they were actually sound asleep and had no memory at all of any of it. Indeed, one man who was charged with the drowning murder of his wife had used the "Ambien defense" at his trial, insisting he had no memory at all of attacking her in the middle of the night.

But Adam wasn't claiming he had had a somnambulant misadventure during the previous night. Not at all. He was sure he had gotten out of bed only once, and that was to use the bathroom.

Chapter Five

The probe into Rebecca Zahau's mysterious death
had barely begun. Dozens of investigators were working
on one aspect or another of the case. It was near dusk at
7:18 P.M. on July 13 when medical examiner Dr. Jonathan
Lucas and Investigator Dana Gary arrived to remove her
body. Lucas was scheduled to perform the autopsy the
next morning—Thursday, July 14.

There was nothing new for curious neighbors and by-
standers to see and it would soon be too dark to work the
crime scene effectively. Uniformed officers would guard
the Spreckels Mansion until morning.

The detectives who were looking for witnesses weren't
ready to pack it in yet. They were prepared to canvass as
many homes and businesses as they could even if it took
far into the night.

Adam Shacknai was only the first person of possible
interest that detectives had talked to. He was not without
experienced legal representation. Even in his despair,
Jonah Shacknai was trying to help his brother, and he had

a coterie of attorneys to call upon, as any wealthy businessman has.

It was probably Jonah who had retained Paul Pfingst, the lawyer who had texted Adam just before he took the polygraph tests. Unable to reach Adam, Pfingst knew the private number to call at the sheriff's office where he could get a message to Adam as soon as possible. His intent had indeed been to advise Adam, as Detective Hillen had predicted, that he should avoid the polygraph machine—at least at this point in the investigation.

Since the results were inconclusive, it didn't really matter.

Earlier in the day, Paul Pfingst had gone to the Spreckels Mansion before Rebecca Zahau's body was removed. He was one of the few people besides the EMTs and law enforcement personnel to be allowed onto the property. Pfingst was photographed talking with the detectives on the *other* side of the CRIME SCENE tape. In one shot, a detective has an arm around Pfingst's shoulder.

Although he was currently in private practice as a criminal defense attorney, Paul Pfingst was familiar to many of the investigators. He had served two terms as district attorney of San Diego County, and he had forged friendships with law enforcement and forensic pathologists then.

Even so, it was almost unheard-of for a defense attorney to be allowed inside a possible crime scene so early in an investigation.

And it was troubling to some.

*   *   *

July 13 was the longest day any of the participants and investigators remembered. Detectives Norton and Palmer had been assigned to speak with Jonah Shacknai. They were not insensitive men, and they winced inwardly as they looked into the misery-filled eyes of this man who probably *was* a billionaire and could have anything money could buy. But there are things money can never buy. Now Jonah Shacknai was in the midst of losing two people he reportedly loved a great deal. Becky was gone, and his son Max was clinging to life by a thread.

Nevertheless, Jonah was willing to answer any questions the detectives might have for him. He said that his brother, Adam, had called him at 6:58 that Wednesday morning and told him that Becky had taken her life. "I was shocked," Jonah said slowly. "I couldn't talk. And then I called him back and he said that she had hung herself."

Jonah Shacknai's world was crumbling rapidly. Not even forty-eight hours had passed since Max had fallen. "I was at the gym Monday—at the Hollywood Athletic Club at the del Coronado—when I got a call from Rebecca. She was crying and saying something about Max. I wasn't sure what she was telling me, but it sounded bad. I just ran home the few blocks . . ."

Jonah recalled that he got there in time to see his son being loaded into an ambulance, and he'd noted the still-wet splotch of blood on the foyer's carpet. A patrol officer from the Coronado Police Department had driven him to Sharp Coronado Hospital right behind the ambulance. Once there, an ER team found Max in such critical condition that he was moved quickly to Rady Children's Hospital in San Diego.

Jonah said he'd never left Max's side all that day, not until the doctors told him Monday evening that Max would be having tests for an hour, and sent him home. His best friend, Dr. Howard Luber, drove him there, where he took a quick shower, made some sandwiches, and packed a few personal items. "I drove myself back."

Jonah said he had hoped to stay at the Ronald McDonald House across the street from the hospital, but there were no vacancies Monday night, so he checked into a nearby hotel. He didn't want to be more than a few minutes away from Max's hospital room. He got a few hours' sleep but spent most of his time beside his son's bed.

Jonah said he had attempted to locate his ex-wife Dina, but he'd gotten no answers when he called her phones. He was able to reach her twin sister, Nina Romano, in San Francisco. Dina had finally responded to police knocking on her door early Tuesday and spelled Jonah in the hospital.

Jonah verified that Becky had put a shaken Zaré on the plane for St. Joseph, Missouri. Not long after, she picked Adam up on his flight from Memphis. He appreciated that she was doing everything she could to help him, taking care of details that he was too distraught to attend to. He knew that she longed to talk with him, to be updated about how Max was doing—but she had tried not to bother him.

"I called her when I could," Jonah said.

Jonah's memory of late Tuesday evening differed slightly from Adam's. He recalled that he, Adam, Dr. Luber, and Becky ate a quick dinner together. And *then* Becky drove Luber to the airport in time for his flight before she and Adam headed for the mansion.

"I called Becky at midnight—last night," Jonah said. "She didn't answer."

He hadn't really been concerned. He figured she could have been asleep, or taking a bath. She had planned to stay alone in the big house, and Adam had a room in the guesthouse. As far as Jonah knew, there was no one else on the estate on Tuesday night. Even Ocean, their dog, had been left with friends.

Becky Zahau may already have been dead at midnight. She was certainly dead by the time seven more hours had passed.

Jonah told the two investigators that he was trying to piece together what could have happened—both with his little boy's devastating fall and his girlfriend's shocking death.

"Max was an extremely good athlete—he was great at soccer, even at his age," Jonah said. "We played 'hall soccer' inside the front door."

"Did he slide down the banisters?" Norton asked. "Or try to climb that chandelier? Was he a daredevil?"

"No—he climbed *trees,* but—"

"Was Rebecca depressed?"

"No, no." Jonah was adamant that Rebecca would not have chosen suicide.

"Was she on meds?"

"No. She took care of herself," he said, explaining that she was very health-conscious, being careful to eat proper foods and to exercise regularly. "And she wasn't unhappy. Of course she felt terrible about Max."

Jonah Shacknai occasionally broke into tears, which seemed genuine. And certainly understandable.

He was positive that Becky hadn't been depressed, nor had she evinced any suicidal ideation. Naturally, she was sad and worried—they all were—about Max. But Becky was not a woman easily disheartened or given to moods.

"Things are suspicious—" Detective Palmer began, and Jonah Shacknai looked up suddenly.

"*Are* they?" he asked, startled.

"Do you think that she would kill herself?"

"She might have felt responsible—for Max," Jonah said slowly. "But no—*no*! She would not have added to my troubles—unless she was so overwhelmed with guilt. No."

Once again, Jonah asked what seemed suspicious. Palmer hadn't answered him before.

"We can't really answer that right now as we're in the midst of an investigation," Todd Norton said. "That's why the Coronado police called us in—to find out what happened."

Jonah Shacknai himself was never a suspect in Becky's death. The Ronald McDonald House had security cameras at all its entrances and exits, and even in the hallways that led to rooms. The investigators were able to obtain images of Jonah at the entrance doors to the McDonald House, and in the corridors, arriving and leaving his room. They could absolutely place the times Jonah had gone to his room and then left to sit with Max, and his return to the McDonald House to catch a few hours' sleep. They had videotape of where he was on Tuesday night.

Jonah told Norton and Palmer that Becky's relatives

were on their way from Missouri and wanted to stay at his estate.

"Probably they can't. We haven't released the scene yet," Norton said. "But we do need you to sign a permission form that allows us to search your property."

Jonah had no objection to that. At this point he still had very little information about how and where Becky perished. He asked where she had been found, and Todd Norton told him she was lying on the grass courtyard below the balcony outside the bedroom where her computer was when the first police arrived.

Asked if he could think of anyone who might have wanted to hurt Becky, or might be obsessed with her, Jonah pondered that.

"She was an extremely beautiful woman," Palmer said. "Was there anyone who stalked her?"

"Her ex-husband contacted her almost every day," Jonah said. "His name is Evan Solanev.* He lives in Arizona. He texts her and they're not creepy but kind of strange. Like, 'Can we have lunch?' and 'I'll do anything.' He's very religious, but he seems to be well on the other side of wanting her back. She showed me his messages. They were married for three and a half years. He was studying to be a nurse, and Rebecca is—was—a nurse."

Asked about Becky's friends, Jonah said her older sister, Mary Loehner, was her best friend, and that Becky didn't have close friends in Coronado.

"She took our Weimaraner, Ocean, to the park often. He's protective—but not aggressive. We had a guard dog but it died last year, and we're looking for another."

"Any particular reason?"

"No. No threats or anything like that. We tried one out two weeks ago, but it didn't work out."

Once again, Jonah Shacknai looked up sharply. "Do I *need* protection?"

"No—not at this point. We'll let you know if you ever do."

The San Diego detectives learned that Becky had arranged for Ocean to be at the Camp Diggity Dogs kennel for a few days after Max's fall because she felt that was better with "people coming and going."

The investigation was embryonic at this state. Palmer and Norton hadn't even been inside the house yet—and they said quite honestly that they didn't know what had happened.

"I need a change of clothes," Jonah said. "Can I go in and get some?"

"In a few hours."

Shacknai asked the detectives to be very sensitive when they spoke with Becky's family. "They're very religious."

"How is your son doing?" Palmer asked.

"He's very critical," Jonah sighed. "Very, very critical condition."

Jonah Shacknai hadn't said anything that would indicate he was at all estranged from the dead woman. Indeed, he spoke very tenderly about her. But he also seemed anxious that there might be someone in the shadows, someone who could be hazardous to him and his children. Given the hellacious losses he had had to deal with for two days, that was understandable.

*   *   *

San Diego County deputy sheriff Dan Pearce was assigned to the San Diego County District Attorney's High Tech Crimes Task Force (known as CATCH). He is a Certified Forensic Computer Examiner (CFCE) and has achieved the Master Level of Computer Forensic Science Certification. In layman's terms, Pearce has the knowledge to trace what has happened inside computers, on the Internet, and cellular phones. Highly trained technicians such as Pearce can use Cellebrite's Universal Forensic Extraction Device (UFED) to extract data from approximately 95 percent of the smartphones, PDA devices, and cell phones in use today. Information can be extracted without changing the original data on the source phones.

Becky's cell phone showed that a call had come in at 11:48 P.M., and that was probably Jonah's last call to her. If there had been a text or voice mail message from him, it was no longer there. It could have been accidentally—or deliberately—erased.

Joe Friday of *Dragnet* never heard of computers, cell phones, smartphones and all the other devices available in the twenty-first century, and most criminals don't realize what trails they now can leave behind.

On July 13, Deputy Pearce examined a Hewlett-Packard laptop computer, whose only active user account was Rebecca Zahau, and an iMac computer whose single user account was Jonah Shacknai. Both of the computers were from the guest room/computer room with the balcony where Becky Zahau had allegedly hung herself. He also had her Samsung cell phone.

Pearce reached three conclusions:

1. A review of the Internet history showed no searches were conducted for the terms: suicide, rope, knots, or hanging.
2. A review of the Internet history from Becky's computer during the last twenty-four hours showed numerous searches and viewing of pornography, including lesbian and anime pornography. [The latter is a Japanese style of animated cartoon, often with violent or sexually explicit content.]
3. There were *no* documents found related to suicide.

What were the investigators to make of the Internet links that someone had connected to in the hours during which Becky Zahau died? Would *she* have searched for pornography? In her grief over Maxie, concern for Jonah, and the chaos they were all living in, why would she seek out such X-rated links on the computer? The only other person on the estate that night was Adam Shacknai.

Adam had already told detectives that he'd watched porn on his cell phone early on the morning of July 13—before he left the guesthouse and discovered Becky hanging from the balcony. He said he'd never been in the mansion itself the night before; he'd gone directly to the guesthouse where his room was. The computers were in the main house.

It was confusing. Was it perhaps possible that someone had killed Becky and deliberately roamed on the computers to make it look as though *she* had been watching erotic sites?

It seemed unlikely.

Among the items seized on the Shacknai estate was a Japanese video titled *The Housemaid*. Its scenario was chillingly similar to aspects of the life Becky lived—a beautiful maid who was in love with her wealthy employer, who adored his child. It was an erotic love story.

Quite possibly, Jonah wasn't as close to his brother, Adam, as he was to his longtime best friend, Dr. Howard Luber. Luber was like another brother to him, a man with whom he shared his deepest feelings. The two men had known each other for sixteen years. After they met at a dermatology seminar in Hawaii, they had become best friends. They usually spoke every day.

When the investigators asked Dr. Luber about Jonah's relationship with Becky, the dermatologist said they had been together for just under two years.

"They have—*had*—a special relationship," he told detectives. "Jonah found a great deal of happiness with Rebecca—much more than he did in either of his marriages. They were very compatible and she brought tranquility into his life. Before that, his marriage to Dina could be chaotic. But Jonah and Becky were both involved in nutrition and exercise.

"Some people frowned on the difference in their ages—he was more than fifteen years older than Rebecca—but he ignored that. He loved her."

Jonah Shacknai was a PhD and Howard Luber was a medical doctor, and they had both lived in New York when they first became friends. Eventually, they and their wives moved to the Phoenix-Scottsdale area and they often double-dated or shared family activities. At that time, Jonah was married to his first wife, Kim. The men's wives were also good friends.

Jonah had started his business in 1988, and he was wildly successful in the pharmaceutical and beauty products field. Eventually his corporation, Medicis, was responsible for putting "Restylane" on the market. The substance was quickly in demand for plumping up and erasing wrinkles and restoring a youthful look. Actresses, models, and everyday women swear by it. And so do a lot of men, but they're not as vocal about the treatment that takes years off their appearance.

Other companies rushed to imitate Restylane. And there were other pharmaceutical products that Jonah Shacknai spearheaded, all of them successful.

Luber had known Jonah through both of his marriages and now understood his contentment with Becky Zahau. With her gone forever, he knew his friend would be hit hard. Especially now that he faced losing Max, too.

Dr. Luber acknowledged that Jonah's brother, Adam, hadn't known Becky very well. He lived and worked thousands of miles away from Arizona *and* California. The life of a tugboat captain was a world away from Jonah's lavish lifestyle.

And on his current trip west, Adam surely had had virtually no chance to get to know Becky better. He had been in Coronado only a dozen hours before he said he'd discovered her naked body, hanging.

Chapter Six

The Coronado Police Department and San Diego County investigators had, of course, *two* incidents to investigate further. Maxie's tragic fall and Becky's death were inextricably connected even if only by the timing. If the manner of Becky's death and Maxie's fall had any correlation was yet to be seen.

As far as anyone knew for sure, there were only three people in the mansion when Max Shacknai went over the second-story railing: Max, Becky, and her sister Zaré. Becky had been in one bathroom washing her hair, and Zaré was taking a bath in another bathroom. Max wasn't a toddler, and it wasn't unusual for him to be out of sight and earshot for fifteen or twenty minutes. There were corners and dead spots in the huge mansion where sound didn't carry well.

But Max's accident was loud enough to wake the dead, an eerie expression in this case. Becky and Zaré were horrified when they heard the loud crash of the chandelier that hung over the circular front entry. While Becky rushed to kneel beside the little boy and do what she could to help him, she shouted to Zaré to call 911.

Zaré was so upset that the operator misunderstood her. A tape of her call shows that the 911 dispatcher thought Zaré was calling about her *mother* who had fallen down and injured herself. Zaré's voice was so full of sobs that it was hard to figure out what had happened. Frustrated, Zaré finally just gave up trying to explain; all that mattered was that the operator said that paramedics had been dispatched and were on their way.

Nobody knew why Max had gone over the rail. He was a very active little boy and he had a Razor scooter that he zipped wildly on through the halls of the huge home. It was beside him on the floor of the entryway, along with a soccer ball and a deep red stain of blood.

Of course, Rebecca Zahau was horrified to find him barely conscious under the chandelier. So was Zaré. Becky loved Max and photos of them together certainly validated that.

Some people believed that Max had Asperger's syndrome, a much milder form of autism. Recently, experts in child behavior have said that Asperger's has become a convenient catchall diagnosis for very active children. If, indeed, Maxie had Asperger's symptoms they were slight.

And anyone who has parented little boys knows how lively they can be, seemingly indefatigable.

Maxie Shacknai was bright and full of joy, a charismatic, elfin child who loved to play sports—especially when his father was there to watch him make soccer goals. Now he was silent in the intensive care unit. After his fall, he had gasped only one word out; it sounded like "Ocean," his dog's name.

Monday had been a blur for all of them, with Jonah at the hospital with Max, and Rebecca staying home and taking care of whatever needed to be done there. She felt that Maxie's birth mother, Dina, should be there with Jonah, watching over their son. As much as she longed to be at the hospital, Becky stayed away.

She knew that Zaré was distressed and disappointed, but the only reasonable thing to do was to send her little sister home. The aftermath of Max's fall and the desperate wait for some word about him had destroyed all possibility of Zaré having the fun vacation she had looked forward to. Hopefully, Max would recover and Zaré could come to Coronado or Arizona another time.

So Zaré was scheduled to fly home late on the afternoon of July 12. Rebecca's sister Mary would meet her plane.

Another time, Rebecca promised Zaré. She had even managed to hide her own desperate concern about Jonah's son, stretching the truth as she assured Zaré in text messages that Maxie seemed to be doing better, that he wasn't in as deep a coma as he had been.

Rebecca kept texting Zaré until just before the teenager's plane took off.

7/12/2011, 4:08 P.M.: "Bye miss Zaré, I love u very much let me know when y r on the plane ok . . . remember u r gate 4."

4:14 P.M.: "Do I just wait here until my flight?"

4:37 P.M.: "Ugh!!! I have to wait an hour!!! A whole full hour!!!"

It was 8:39 P.M. when Rebecca could call Zaré back, and she learned Zaré was waiting in another city for her connecting flight. "So sorry, my dear. Please call Mary when u land ok I miss u so much already and I am so very sorry that u had to leave. Max is doing much better now but please keep praying . . . ok love u very much."

"Yeah . . . don't be sorry. Just make sure that u and Jonah get at least a little bit of sleep."

That was the last communication between Rebecca and Zaré. Rebecca's family knew by noon the next day that their beloved daughter, sister, and aunt Becky was dead.

At 3:17 the next afternoon, thirteen-year-old Zaré wrote a text message, even though she knew that Rebecca would never read it. She knew her beloved big sister was dead, but she was pretending it was all a bad nightmare.

"becky I don't believe it com back!!!!! Im not gonna live without u!!!! I love u becky. Come back nothing is your fault."

What did Zaré mean by that? Probably she knew that Becky would be feeling guilty because she had taken her eyes off Maxie long enough for him to fall.

Although Rebecca Zahau and Jonah Shacknai might have seemed a mismatched couple in terms of age and ethnic background, they were probably happier together than most couples experts would assume. Jonah was brilliant, an entrepreneur who had maintained his huge success for many years. Rebecca was also extremely intelligent, and her surgical assistant training let her understand the intricacies of Medicis, Jonah's corporation.

None of Jonah's and Rebecca's differences concerned them. They were attracted to each other from the beginning when they met in 2009 in Scottsdale, Arizona, at the offices of the laser surgeon where Rebecca worked as an assistant.

Becky was married, but estranged from her first and only husband. Jonah and Dina's marriage was nearing an end.

On September 13, 2008, Jonah Shacknai's marriage to Dina Romano Shacknai imploded. They were living in Paradise Valley, Arizona, when Jonah went to the local police station to report that Dina and he had had an argument. He said she had become very angry and abusive with him. Jonah had an attack-trained German shepherd at the time and the dog became agitated to see his master threatened. According to Jonah, he quickly got between his dog and Dina, and that had given Jonah a chance to leave before the situation grew worse. He didn't want to make a formal police complaint, but he did want to have the incident on record.

A short time later, Dina, too, filed a complaint. She phoned the police station to report that she had been bitten by Jonah's dog during an argument. Asked if she needed medical help, she said that wasn't necessary—but she, too, wanted a record of the situation on file.

Dina, however, did not let the incident go; she came

into the Paradise Valley Police Department the next day, bringing with her a computer disc containing sixteen photographs of bruises on her body that she said had been caused by the dog.

While Dina Shacknai would not say that Jonah had ordered their dog to attack her, she said he was in no hurry to call the dog off. She insisted she had never tried to hurt Jonah; she had only raised her arm to get some space between them when he came at her "nose-to-nose."

No charges of domestic violence were brought. Paradise Valley investigators did talk to a marriage counselor who Dina said would vouch for her fear that she would lose custody of her son with Jonah if she fought back. The therapist confirmed that, but he said Dina had never said Jonah was physically aggressive toward her.

They were divorced shortly thereafter and agreed to share custody of Maxie.

So when Jonah Shacknai met Rebecca Zahau Solanev, they were both essentially alone, perhaps hoping for a new relationship. Not only was Rebecca astoundingly beautiful and intelligent, but she had a cool head and was not easily upset or angered. After his two somewhat hectic marriages, Jonah Shacknai wasn't eager to marry for a third time. But he was entranced with Becky, and comfortable in what quickly became a completely loving and noncombative relationship.

One thing the two had in common was a need for close family connections.

Chapter Seven

Even with major advances in forensic technology, some of the oldest methods in crime solving cannot be duplicated by electronic devices. Detectives call it "hitting the bricks," or "heel-and-toeing." Those San Diego sheriff's investigators who weren't on the Shacknai property gathering evidence or diagramming the crime scene set out in two-person teams to question the neighbors along Ocean Boulevard.

Most of those residents dwelling along the beach road were at least millionaires, and their homes were far grander than the ones where detectives usually knocked on doors, and showed their badges and ID.

But that was the only difference. All of the people who came to the door were both curious and frightened.

Detectives Todd Norton of San Diego County and Angel Sadanjo of the Coronado Police Department, and Special Agent Sonia Ramos of the California Department of Justice moved along the street.

Two doors northwest of the Spreckels Mansion, a middle-aged woman welcomed them and introduced her daughter, her niece, and several children, all of whom looked to be under six years old. The adults remembered the police and ambulance coming to get Max Monday morning.

"We saw him being brought out on a stretcher and then the ambulance took off," the homeowner recalled.

"Do you know the woman who lived there?"

"We know Jonah Shacknai—he bought the mansion in 2009," the older woman said. "And I saw him at the sports club at the Hotel del Coronado. He was with a voluptuous, young Asian woman. That would have been the day after the Fourth of July. But I don't really know her."

During the forty-eight hours between Max being carried out and the second arrival of emergency vehicles, however, none of these possible witnesses had seen or heard anything worrisome.

"You might ask at the house that's two doors on the other side of the Shacknai place," the woman offered. "I know the couple who live there have teenagers who seem to be friends of the teenage girl who often visits at the mansion. I think she's Jonah's daughter. They're likely to know a lot more than we do."

Although all the estates along Ocean Boulevard were "next door" to each other, they weren't nearly as close as in middle-class neighborhoods. It wouldn't be at all unusual for neighbors to fail to hear cries for help or sounds of a struggle.

In the aftermath of double tragedies, a number of the nearby residents had gone to their balconies, roofs, or upper stories of their huge homes, or found another view-point from which they could see Becky Zahau's body and the police and fire EMTs' activity below.

Next door to the first estate, the residents were an older couple who lived on Ocean Boulevard year-round. They said that the Spreckels Mansion was very quiet and dark when they got home around 8 P.M. on Tuesday. That was probably within an hour, give or take, of when Becky and Adam Shacknai had driven home after dropping Jonah off at the Ronald McDonald House.

"There were no lights on at Jonah's house, and I saw just one light in the guesthouse. I'm quite sure there was no body lying there then," the woman told the investigative trio. "I saw the woman's body at about a quarter to nine this morning—she looked like a mannequin. And I remember seeing a woman who looked similar getting out of a taxi about a month ago."

"Have you seen people coming or going to the Shacknai estate?" Sonia Ramos asked.

The wife shook her head. "No, there weren't many people there. The ones who visited were mostly younger—kids from about eight to sixteen. Usually, there's a young couple who live there in an apartment over the garage—but I haven't seen them lately. They were caretakers of the estate, I think. I know the husband is a chef. I can't think of their names right now."

"How well do you know Jonah Shacknai?"

"We don't know him well—just well enough to say 'Hi' when we ran into each other. We'd meet him at City

Hall when there were meetings about changes in the building codes. He owned a few other homes in Coronado that he was fixing up for resale.

"At Easter, I saw Jonah playing football with his kids on the lawn."

There were parts of the case that the detectives didn't want revealed to the general public yet, and they asked all the neighbors not to tell anyone that the victim was naked—and not to say if it was a male or female—not yet. They wouldn't be able to keep this information secret for long, but perhaps they could keep it on the down-low for a few hours.

The husband said they had been away from home all day on Tuesday. "We left about ten A.M., and got home at eight thirty P.M.," he said. "We didn't hear anything unusual during the night."

The husband rose as usual at 5 A.M., and his wife said she had heard a dog barking next door around seven.

The next homeowners had more to say, giving the detectives a glimmer of hope that there might be witnesses who could help them determine what had happened to Becky Zahau.

The husband had gone to his room before 11 P.M., but his wife was in the other part of their mansion where she was watching a favorite television show that came on at 11:30. She rarely missed it.

"It was a warm night and our front windows were open," she said. "I heard kids—teenagers—hollering from the beach side of the street. We're used to that. But it was ten minutes later—about twenty minutes to twelve—when

I heard a woman screaming. It came from the direction of Jonah's house."

"It wasn't the kids yelling again?"

"No." She shook her head sharply. "This was a grown woman—maybe in her late twenties or early thirties. There's a difference. I heard a scream, and then another scream, and then 'Help! Help!' I turned the TV down to listen."

"Was it from the beach?"

"No. She was screaming from this side of the street."

While the neighbor listened, the cries for help subsided and then stopped. The witness said she couldn't decide what to do: wake her husband or perhaps call the police. She waited to see if there were more cries in the night.

But she had heard only the teenagers again. They were definitely down on the beach, and those shouts and laughter were not what she had heard a few minutes earlier. The woman's screams had come from the witness's own front yard or possibly over in Jonah Shacknai's yard.

And then there were no sounds at all. In the end, the woman hadn't told anyone about the screams. Not her husband. Not the police.

Another neighbor told the detectives that she had met Jonah Shacknai's girlfriend—but only briefly. Becky, wearing a bikini bathing suit, was riding a bicycle on Ocean Boulevard and stopped to introduce herself, saying she and Jonah would be living in his estate for the summer.

But that was weeks before Rebecca died.

Becky Zahau loved Jonah Shacknai and was happy to live wherever he lived, but she didn't seem to have any friends in the posh California neighborhood on Ocean Boulevard and she was probably lonesome. Women as beautiful as Becky was often have a difficult time finding female friends.

If someone had called 911 during the shadowy hours of Tuesday night, was it possible that Becky Zahau could have been saved? It didn't seem likely that a would-be suicide would scream for help—or could scream at all if she had a noose around her neck. But a woman in peril might well call out desperately if she was running from an attacker. If she had cried out for help from someone who overpowered her, strangled her, and then hung her from a rope to make her death look like a suicide, no one else had heard her.

Hank Bowden,* who was vacationing in Coronado with his family, contacted the San Diego County and Coronado detectives, saying he might have information that would help their probe.

The Web designer said that he and his family were riding bicycles from a grocery store back to their vacation home shortly before 10 P.M. on July 12.

His children had spotted a possum waddling beside the road and stopped to watch it. He happened to stop his bike right in front of the Spreckels Mansion, where he waited for them to catch up with him. He had glanced up at the Shacknai residence and noticed some movement at the front door. He could see that it was a woman, and he watched her. She checked the door but didn't go in.

She was nervously turning around, and walking back and forth—as if she was "trying to decide whether to go in."

Then she came down from the porch, walked back and forth some more, hesitated, and started pacing again. Finally she walked along some grass that adjoined the driveway and disappeared.

The informant told detectives he thought she was behaving in a peculiar way, but at that point his kids and wife had caught up with him. His wife had also seen the indecisive woman walking toward the back of Shacknai's estate on the driveway and then into the shadows beyond. They both wondered about her, but she didn't exactly look like a home invasion robbery suspect, so they rode on home, arriving at about 11:25 P.M.

The bicyclist said he'd wakened to the sound of sirens early the next morning, and he followed them to the Spreckels Mansion, where he learned a woman had been found dead.

Two detectives took him into the mobile crime scene office. He described the woman he'd seen. They nodded but gave him no information about who it could have been.

Curious, he'd checked the name "Shacknai" on his computer and come across a photograph of Dina Shacknai. He was positive that *she* was the woman he had seen at 1043 Ocean Boulevard, so he returned to the mobile office and told the detectives. They interviewed him again, and showed him a lay-down of six photographs. One woman looked like the mystery woman, but she had light hair.

When he heard later that it was Dina's twin—Nina—who said she was at the mansion, he could not agree with that. He insisted it was Dina, Max's mother, he had seen and she had dark hair.

The bicyclist must have been mistaken. Numerous witnesses place Dina in the hospital at Max's bedside throughout Tuesday night.

He also looked at photographs of Becky Zahau. The woman pacing around the entrance to the mansion had looked nothing at all like the dead woman.

"Did you see her go inside?" a detective asked.

"No," he said. "This woman didn't appear to go into the Spreckels Mansion—she only walked back and forth from the front porch to the driveway several times in a way that made her look distressed—but not terrified."

Was this another suspect in a case that was growing stranger by the hour? Or could it have been Becky herself, wandering the darkened grounds of her lover's estate, beside herself with grief over Max? Or so upset with something or someone inside the estate that she was afraid to go back inside?

Everyone looks different in the dark.

There was one thing no one but a very few people knew: the back door of the mansion was never locked! Jonah, Adam, Becky, and Dina—who had once lived there—knew that. Possibly Nina did, too.

There may have been others aware of the unlocked door—deliverymen, employees who worked around the estate. It was hard to know how many—if any.

Chapter Eight

Becky Zahau's autopsy began at 10:18 on the morning of July 14. Aside from Dr. Lucas and his assistants, there were many witnesses. From the San Diego Sheriff's Department came detective Mark Palmer and forensic evidence technicians John Farrell and Brande Silverthorn. Detective Keith James represented the Coronado Police Department. Deputy district attorney William LaFond was there, along with forensic autopsy specialist Steve Hannum.

Rebecca was nude except for a "Power Balance" band on her right wrist, and a black "Bionic Band" and yellow "Live Strong" band on her left. She had clearly been a believer in exercise and a healthy lifestyle.

And her autopsy would show that she *had* been in perfect shape. All of her organs, including her heart and lungs, demonstrated how careful she had been about her health. Although she was petite, she had strong muscles. If she had been attacked by someone who choked her and then hung her, and if she had any warning, she would have fought hard to survive.

Perhaps she had no warning at all.

Rebecca was very well groomed, with permanently tattooed eyebrows and eyeliner, and her very long black hair was clean and shiny. She had medium-sized breast implants, a taut body, and neatly trimmed fingernails painted a bright orange.

The thick, reddish-orange towrope had been used to bind Rebecca's hands behind her back and tie her ankles together. There were five loops around her right wrist and six around her left. At their narrowest point, it was possible to separate her wrists about two and a half inches. The rope was eighty-four inches long and extended from the slipknot on her left wrist, exiting between her right index and middle finger. The shorter segment of the same rope extended from a fixed knot on her right wrist. The segments of rope were haphazardly arranged in a figure-eight pattern.

Dr. Lucas noticed a small amount of what appeared to be black paint on one of the loops around her left wrist. He had noted black paint dabs on her breasts the evening before.

He found that Rebecca's right hand could be slipped out of the binding with mild pressure, and when he took up slack on the right side, her left hand could be removed. Her ankles were bound much the same way as her wrists were.

There is, of course, an immediate question that begged an answer. Why would someone intent upon hanging herself even bother to tie her hands and feet? How could she have managed to get up on the balcony's railing and drop off—without the use of either her hands or legs? And she surely could not have slipped her hands out once she dropped at the end of a noose.

Another segment of the towrope was around Rebecca's neck, and it had left deep furrows and petechiae (pinpoint hemorrhages) before it reached its apex behind her right ear. Her neck was not broken, but there was a good deal of hemorrhaging in the sternocleidomastoid and strap muscles there. The pathologist felt this had occurred when she had dropped the nine feet, two inches from the balcony.

Perhaps.

There were many petechiae in Becky's eyes, face, and mouth, and coarser petechiae above the furrow left by the rope in her neck. These small explosions of blood occur during strangulation—whether by human hands, ligature or garrote, or hanging. Her hyoid bone (at the far back of her tongue) was fractured, something that often happens when a victim is manually strangled.

A detail that most women might notice—but men wouldn't—was that Becky's long hair was *beneath* the rope around her neck. Women whose hair extends below their necks invariably lift it when they put on coats or other garments that might bind it in. If Rebecca Zahau had intended to hang herself, it would seem logical that she would lift her hair free of the rope, if only to get a tight fit around her neck.

When Dr. Lucas had initially examined her body around 7:30 the night before, he had found rigor mortis was marked in her upper and lower extremities (arms and legs), and in her neck and her jaw. By then she had lain on the grass all day and into the evening. The purplish lividity pattern in her body was along her back and the back of her legs, and it was fixed. If she had hung for hours during the night before being discovered, gravity would have dropped the deepest purple-red stains to her feet and lower legs.

The towrope was seven-sixteenths of an inch thick, and the handle had a warning that read, "Intended only for towing up to a maximum of two people or 340 pounds on an inflatable tube."

The manner in which the rope was knotted and tied was extremely complicated, done by someone accomplished and familiar with such knots. A Boy Scout or a sailor would surely know more about tying ropes than Rebecca would.

Some of the findings were problematic. Becky had blood in her vaginal vault, and dried blood along her perineum, trickling down the inside of her thigh, but it didn't appear that she had been raped. She had possibly been menstruating at the time of her death.

There were no contusions on her vulva or inside her vagina. A birth control device was still in place in her uterus.

But it was possible that she had struggled for her life. She had a group of three linear abrasions on the center of her forehead. The scratches ranged in length from one inch to one and three-fourths inches. There was a scratch on her upper right forehead, almost hidden by her hair-line.

How had those gotten there? More puzzling were the four hemorrhages *beneath* the right front part of her scalp.

This blood was trapped between the bony part of the skull and the scalp, in what is called the subgaleal area. It is a problem found most often in newborns after a tough delivery, but it can also be caused by blows to the head in adults.

It was fairly easy to attribute some of the scratches on her body to bramble bushes beneath the balcony where Rebecca had allegedly been hanging. Moreover, if she had run for her life in the dark, she could have sustained similar cuts. Most of the scratches, small cuts, punctures, and bruises were on her back extending from her neck to the middle of her buttocks.

On the back of Rebecca's right hand, Lucas saw four red scratches, and there was a deeper abrasion between her third and fourth finger with skin tags that had been torn free at the edges of the wound.

Her feet were caked with mud.

If there were questions about what the investigators found outside the Spreckels Mansion, there were even more about what was *inside.* Detective Angela Tsuida, who was directing the murder probe, wrote a report about what she found on the second floor of the main house. Rebecca's room was at the east end of the second level of the residence. Detective Tsuida noted a white and green towel in the hallway just outside that bedroom, along with drops of what looked like dried blood.

It could also have been black paint.

More chilling, however, was a crudely painted message on one panel on the hall side of the door. Someone had used black paint as a medium to print the words, all in caps:

**SHE SAVED HIM
CAN YOU SAVE HER**

What on earth did that signify? The meaning behind these seven words has eluded almost everyone who has heard about them. There have been myriad opinions on who "SHE" was and who "HIM" and "HER" were. If this was a code, it certainly wasn't going to be easy to decipher.

Early on, the sheriff's office chose to keep what was painted on the door a secret. It could have become one of the unknown bits of evidence that might distinguish a chronic confessor from a real murderer.

Just inside Rebecca's room, Tsuida found two paint-brushes. One had black paint on its bristles. There were also two knives—one with a four-and-a-half-inch blade, and the other with an eight-inch blade—a white plastic bag, and, closer to the bed, a tube of black paint. She also saw the now-familiar red towrope.

Although the connections among these items of possible vital physical evidence were obscure at this point, it might all come clear as the investigation proceeded.

And then again, some of these items might never be explained adequately.

Farther inside the room, there was a brass and white

metal full-sized bed, a desk, chair, bedside tables with matching lamps, shelving, and a bookcase.

Rather than a woman's bedroom, it appeared to have been used as an office. There were two computers there, but the furnishings were not particularly feminine or expensive. Tsuida noted things that might indicate a struggle had taken place here. The desk chair had been knocked over from where its original position probably was—squarely in front of the desk.

The bed was formed into a delicate design, the brass posts highly polished and the white portion shaped into narrow filigrees, circles, and carved rose shapes.

The room was fairly neat except for the out-of-place furnishings. The bed's frame was pulled ten to twelve inches away from the wall. One end of the red rope was still tied to the left bottom leg of the bed with the same complicated knots that bound Becky Zahau's ankles and wrists. From there, the towrope crossed the room, went through the door out onto the balcony, and, finally, over the rail, where it descended to the point where Adam Shacknai said he had cut it to get the dead woman down.

The French doors to the balcony were almost closed when the police arrived, and the door on the right was latched.

The wrought iron railing around the small balcony looked to be about thirty-six to forty-two inches high, high enough so that a woman, even one intent on suicide—and who was just over five feet tall—might well have difficulty tumbling over it. With her ankles and wrists bound behind her, she would have had to *hop* to the railing, and somehow hoist herself up and over, more than likely headfirst.

The balcony was dusty, and there was one complete set of footprints etched in the dust. When they were left there was impossible to determine. Two small feet, pointed outward so that their separation formed a V, had left their impression. There was another print—only half of one booted foot. The criminalists working the case would try to find just who had left the boot print.

According to Adam Shacknai, Becky had also had a T-shirt wound around her neck and then stuck down her throat. If she *had* intended to commit suicide, why would she have handicapped herself to such a degree? All her limbs restrained and a T-shirt down her throat?

To be sure she wouldn't—couldn't—change her mind and grab on to something? To keep herself from scream-ing out?

Angela Tsuida and members of her unit were trying to figure that out.

Tsuida assigned Forensic Evidence Technician Denys Williams to lift as many finger and palm prints as she could in Becky's office/bedroom, the balcony, doors, the bathroom there, and any other likely spot in the mansion where the dead woman might have been on the last night of her life. Moreover, Williams was asked to use moist-ened swabs and other methods to retrieve any blood or bodily fluids she might come across.

Williams had requested that Forensic Evidence Technician John Farrell take photographs, both during the dead woman's postmortem exam and at the death site.

The list of evidence items and photos grew longer and longer.

Becky's finger and hand prints were expected to be in her room. Denys Williams hoped to isolate those prints. That would allow her to identify any other prints that were *not* expected to show up in the dead woman's office/ bedroom.

Since Adam Shacknai was the only other person staying in his brother's estate on Tuesday night, his room in the guesthouse was also photographed and searched for any possible evidence.

And so was the master bedroom that Rebecca had reportedly shared with Jonah. It was much more lushly furnished than the small room with the balcony. In this master bedroom, small-sized women's clothing—a pair of blue jeans, a white undershirt, and a black, long-sleeved top—were folded neatly on the bed.

Williams bagged and labeled the clothing. She also removed a clump of black hair that clung to the wall of the shower in the en suite master bathroom, and collected samples from trickles of red fluid on the shower floor.

Moving to the guesthouse, Williams took men's clothing from the floor of the south master bedroom there: blue jeans, boxer briefs, a black T-shirt, and black socks. She found and saved for evidence a long strand of dark hair in the bathroom attached to this bedroom.

The evidence tech worked steadily, saving and marking

anything that might prove to be of vital evidentiary value: tissue with red stains from a child's bedroom, a candle from the grass north of where Becky had lain, a bottle of water from the north master bedroom of the guesthouse where Adam spent the previous night, two red plastic cups from the same room, and, curiously, a pair of women's panties that were pink, purple, and white, found in a wastebasket there.

What would prove to be important and what was only mundane and expected to be where it was found? The pink bedding in the master bedroom Rebecca had shared with Jonah? The knives—one on the brick walkway near where the body lay and others from the floor of the bedroom with the balcony? The Samsung cell phone with a dead battery just outside that room? The two paintbrushes there—one with black paint on its bristles, another with green paint?

The white door to that room, with the cryptic question scrawled in black paint, was removed from its hinges and moved carefully to the crime lab.

The San Diego detectives and criminalists gathered masses of evidence, but it would be a herculean task to adequately search every corner of the Spreckels Mansion, and, unfortunately, they didn't. Nor was every item they *had* gathered tested in the crime lab.

Chapter Nine

San Diego County sheriff's investigators had a massive probe ahead of them. Not only would they have to match what physical evidence they had to a suicide *or* to an as-yet-unknown killer, but they needed to explore the complicated personal relationship between Jonah Shacknai and Becky Zahau. They also had to expand their search to include both Jonah's and Becky's families and others whose lives interacted with theirs.

Jonah was spending most of his time at Max's bedside, hoping against hope that his small son would defy the odds and waken from the deliberately induced drug coma that might help him heal. Jonah was as cooperative with detectives as he could be. Rebecca's relatives were grieving deeply and preparing to bury their beloved daughter and sister, while they questioned how she had died. They knew she had been found hanging, but they simply could not reconcile the Becky they knew with someone who could commit suicide.

Becky Zahau's religious beliefs were strong, and she was a woman full of life and hope for her future. In her last conversations with her sisters Mary and Zaré, there had been no hint that she was considering such a thing. As sad as she was about Max's terrible accident and Jonah's grief, she had reacted as she always did, putting her own needs aside and trying to help her lover, his family, even his former wife Dina, as much as she could.

Sometimes, however, Rebecca had to face the problems that most women have when in love with a man who has prior wives and children. It's natural for loving fathers who share custody to want to spend time with children who come from a broken home. They also tend to spoil them—perhaps feeling guilty about their divorces. Jonah Shacknai had his two children from his first marriage to Kim, and Max from his marriage to Dina, and he tried to arrange his time so that none of them felt left out.

Becky adored Max and he felt the same way about her, but his older children kept their distance. In trying to juggle her relationships with Jonah and his teenage children, Rebecca found her life was not without problems.

One of the thorns in her side that hurt her the most was the way Jonah's daughter, Cameron, seemed to resent her. That was hardly unusual. A teenage girl almost always resents a new woman in her father's life, and Cameron didn't like this woman who wasn't even her stepmother.

Becky was crushed again and again by Cameron's disdain for her. Several months before her death, Becky wrote a letter in her journal to Jonah, a letter she never intended to send. She was trying to deal with her feelings. Becky may even have been "practicing" for a time when she could be totally open with Jonah.

She had initially declined to attend a dinner with Jonah and his children after she was humiliated at a similar function just two days earlier. Jonah had been impatient with her about her timidity.

"My decision to not attend dinner should never be seen as 'losing,' " she wrote. "Cameron and I are not in a war that will end up with winning or losing.

"If roles were reversed I would have dealt with it on my own without the need to even mention it to you, let alone place you in such a situation. You did not consider to ask me or understand how uncomfortable I would be. However, the requests that pile on me to basically get out of Cameron's way because my presence makes her uncomfortable have been a non-issue. Now, I have to consider your situation and how unfair it would be to put you in an awkward situation if I did not attend. Once again, I place my feelings and hurt on the shelf for those of yours and your family's.

"I am hurt by your comment that if I did not attend, you will take it as 'an interesting signal,' as if none of my other actions have not been interesting enough to show I care, that I love you, that I have tried with everything I know to be open and available to your kids.

"So, yes, I will be present at dinner. I am sure Cameron will put on her best behavior."

Rebecca loved Jonah a great deal, but there were many times when she wanted more from him than he was prepared to give, an emotional tug-of-war that occurs in most complicated romances. In her secret journal, she wrote a poetic essay on her feelings.

"There is a fire within my heart that rages with such burning desire . . . to be looked upon with eyes [so] full of love that I would be lost in them like a seaman in the vast ocean . . . to have my face cupped in loving hands as if they were cradling a fragile egg, lest it would crack under the slightest pressure . . . to have my hands held in two loving hands as I am told how much I am loved . . . that things are going to be o.k. . . . to know that I'm always number 1 no matter what may be . . . to be held like a piece of art, a rarity . . . someone so special . . . alas . . . these will never come true as long as I'm with him. Is this my curse for leaving Evan? That I have finally found someone that I love more than they love me so I would finally feel the pain of constantly giving more than what I thought I ever could, then hoping the same in return . . . in vain? I know he loves me and believe he is as emotionally involved as he knows best, but sometimes it is not enough for me. Is that why I feel this incredible emptiness?

"Am I just too much of a coward to face the truth that I'm settling for the hope of a few happy years??? Which may never even come?? Am I pretending that I will be content without ever having a child???? Am I sacrificing my true happiness because of momentary comfort??? It seems like I have the perfect life to my friends and those who watch from the outside—living in a mansion, a car that was paid for, no job, access to credit cards—so why does it not seem that way?"

Rebecca hastened to write that money was never a consideration for her. "If it had been, I would have bid farewell by now." She wrote of being harassed and hated by "2 ex-wives" and of her loneliness at being essentially cut off from her family, and of having no one to talk to.

"My reward must be his love, whatever the dose may be, remembering the rare sweet times that we get to share, remembering that he is indeed a good man at heart, and things that he does [or rather, doesn't] do, he does with ignorance. If only he knew I deeply I care for him, and how much I have sacrificed for our relationship . . . and how much I hold in so he does not need to be bothered."

Becky finished the long journal entry by pledging to do what she could to help Jonah "in pursuit of our happy life." She prayed to God for guidance in being the "best girlfriend" and the "best caretaker" of Jonah's three children. She wrote that she had no idea when she and Jonah would be engaged, "let alone get married."

Still, even though Rebecca Zahau was having a difficult time on that day so many months before she died, she was not about to give up. She was usually content with the role she played in Jonah Shacknai's life, and hopeful that, in time, they *would* marry and be together forever.

Her journal entries could be very dramatic. It's likely she never intended for anyone else to read them. She felt guilt over divorcing her ex-husband, even though theirs was basically an arranged marriage. She had gone back to him a number of times because she *did* feel guilty. Some members of her family had wanted her to make her first and only marriage work—but she didn't love him; she wondered if she had ever loved him.

*   *   *

While Rebecca's family made arrangements with the Meierhoffer Funeral Home in St. Joseph, Missouri, for her memorial service and burial, Jonah Shacknai spent his time at Max's bedside. Max had never awakened from the medically induced coma that had seemed his only chance to recover. His doctors shook their heads sadly as his mother and father asked for some sign of improvement. In truth, Maxie was brain dead, and probably had been since shortly after he fell. It was finally evident that the little boy was drifting away more each day. On Friday, July 15, 2011, Max Shacknai died.

On July 17, Jonah released a statement to the media.

"With great sadness," he wrote, "Dina and I convey the tragic passing of our beloved son, Max. Despite heroic efforts on the part of the paramedics and hospital staff, he was unable to recover from the injuries that he suffered last week."

In the space of only five days, the idyllic life on Ocean Boulevard had come crashing down. And it seemed almost impossible to adequately explain either Max's or Becky's violent deaths.

KZ, the medical expert, examined Max's autopsy report carefully and posted once more to "The Hinky Meter." The autopsy report said that Max's death had probably been caused by the hyperextension of his spinal cord during his plunge from an upper floor of the mansion. It had been so severe that his spine was virtually "unplugged" from his brain stem. There would have been no way for ER physicians to save Max at that point; his spinal cord was "shredded."

Why hadn't the doctors treating Max told Jonah and Dina the truth from the beginning? For all intents and purposes,

Max died at the bottom of the stairs. Being brutally candid is difficult for physicians; they try not to destroy all hope.

And so the six-year-old's parents had held on to the slim possibility that he might recover for at least two more days. Neither of them was a novice in their medically connected fields; somehow they must have known that there was no way for Maxie to come back.

Maxie's vital organs were donated to children who desperately needed them. All but his heart; it was too badly damaged from a half hour without respiration or pulse.

Everywhere those who loved Max and Becky looked, there was death and despair.

Max was buried in Arizona. Jonah paid for all the costs of Rebecca's funeral, and he flew back to Missouri to attend it, bringing with him two men who may have been bodyguards or simply business associates.

Soon he put the Spreckels Mansion on the market. The property held nothing but heartbreaking memories now.

The public—first in Southern California and the Phoenix, Arizona, area—was anxious to know what had really happened. Within twenty-four hours of Becky's death, the news about the mystery of the two deaths in Coronado spread across America and overseas. The way it had played out was so incredibly bizarre.

The law enforcement agencies involved were as baffled as laymen, and they were playing their cards very close to their vests. The results of Becky's autopsy were sealed, and they would not name any suspects, saying only that they had talked to many people, whom they referred to only as "witnesses."

Actually, they had no *true* witnesses to either Max's fall or Becky's hanging. Or, rather, they had no one who would admit that they personally saw either event. Adam Shacknai was the closest thing to a witness and he continued to insist that he had cut Becky's body down. He was allowed to leave California to return home to Memphis. If San Diego investigators had more questions for him, they knew where to find him.

Back in Missouri, the Zahau family was at a loss, grieving for Becky, wondering what could have happened. They had little money to hire attorneys or private investigators, but beginning with Mary Loehner—who probably knew Becky better than anyone—the Zahau family demanded answers.

Mary was the most outspoken. She gave an interview to the *Phoenix New Times* on July 21, 2011: "Obviously the investigation is not complete yet, but as far as I know about my sister, my sister did *not* commit a suicide," Mary said vehemently. "My sister was not depressed, my sister was not frantic, my sister was planning on calling my parents the next day."

Mary Loehner would never change her mind about that, nor would the rest of Becky's family.

The San Diego County sheriff's detectives widened their probe. Now they picked up the threads of Becky Zahau's life before she fell in love with Jonah Shacknai, hoping they might find a key to the mystery behind two deaths.

Chapter Ten

I have always been interested in following the paths of lovers who had only a minuscule chance of ever meeting. And yet some of the great romances of all times have begun by unbelievable synchronicity. Jonah Shacknai and Rebecca Zahau had that. But, before Jonah, there was Evan. Evan Solanev, Becky's ex-husband.

Rebecca was attending the Calvary Bible College in Germany when she signed up for her church's "Summer Service," a religious outreach program. Her assignment was to go to Austria in the summer of 2001. She was twenty-two years old then and quite naïve, having been sheltered by her strict parents and loving siblings.

While in Austria she met a young man named Evan Solanev; he had come from America to attend the program. They didn't spend much time together, since Evan left for Kosovo shortly after they met. His avid courtship consisted only of a flurry of emails over the next four months.

Evan quickly idolized Becky, describing her as "this Burmese princess—sincere, sweet, God loving girl. This was one of the most beautiful girls I'd ever met!"

Solanev was twenty-five, three years older than Becky, and he seemed set on marrying her. "We were friends at first," he recalled. "But then we did email and we fell in love that way."

He proposed to her in October 2001. It appears that their parents approved of the match. Evan went to Germany to ask her father for permission to marry her. He took his mother to meet her family at Christmastime that same year.

In the meantime, Becky stayed in Austria. She had no citizenship rights at all yet in America. Evan returned to the United States and got a job in security on Long Island.

After immigrating to America, several members of the Zahau family had settled near St. Joseph, Missouri. Becky's older sister, Mary, stayed in Missouri and married a police officer on the St. Joseph force. Her sister Snowem married her husband, David,* and they chose to live in Germany.

Becky's other two siblings were much younger than she was. Besides Zaré, she had a younger brother, James.* Mary and her husband, Doug, were raising the two younger children since her father was quite elderly and her mother middle-aged when they were born.

At Evan Solanev's urging, Becky came to America in April 2002, and she married him very soon after. She felt sometimes that she had been caught up in a whirlwind without time to ponder whether she really wanted to be Evan's bride. Evan explained that there were pragmatic reasons for the rush.

"We had to be married by May 1 because Becky only had a temporary permit to be in America," he explained.

Was she rushed into marriage? Probably. She had known Evan for about nine months but had spent precious little actual time with him. Most of their communication had continued to be through email. Still, Becky wanted to make their marriage work.

They both remained heavily involved with their church, and they left New York on May 6, headed for Temecula, California, a baking hot desert town. Evan was to be the youth pastor at the Calvary Chapel Bible College in nearby Murrieta. They were soon working hard to help build the congregation, and especially in overseeing youth groups.

The church was mission focused, and, according to Evan, they had high hopes.

But there were roadblocks that quashed much of their enthusiasm. Apparently the main pastor at the Murrieta church and Evan didn't see eye to eye. Evan resigned and he and Becky moved to Portland, Oregon, where his brother, an agent in the Drug Enforcement Administration, lived.

"We always thought we could start over," Evan said to detectives who interviewed him years later. They noted that he spoke as if his ex-wife had been of the same mind he was. In fact, she wasn't. She believed in her church, but she wondered why it was so difficult for Evan to get along with people.

Things didn't get better in Portland. Becky suffered

a miscarriage, and the couple continued to grow apart. She was so young when she married and everything had happened too fast. Becky never wanted to hurt anyone's feelings and everyone around her had seemed to be urging her to marry Evan. Although it wasn't easy, she tried her best to keep believing in him as he hopped from job to job.

Although Becky lost her baby, her sister Mary delivered a boy, Matthew,* in April 2005. Becky told Evan that she needed to go to Missouri to help with the new baby, and he insisted he would drive her there. She demurred at first, but finally agreed that they would drive back east together. He left her with Mary and Doug Loehner and her parents and drove back to Oregon.

It wasn't long before Becky called Evan, and she was crying. She told him that they should just "let their marriage be."

But Evan wasn't ready to let her go. He got another low-wage security job, this time at a retirement residence in Oregon. He told Becky he was hoping to become a police officer. With his brother an often-promoted DEA agent, the idea of a job in law enforcement appealed to him.

Evan managed to persuade Becky to come home and try again. He even drove all the way back to St. Joseph and picked her up. They returned to Oregon but stayed only a short time. They moved next to Philadelphia.

No one can ask Becky Zahau how she felt about their frequent moves because she is gone forever. Her sister Mary knew that Becky didn't want to hurt Evan, but that she wasn't happy with him.

Six years later, Evan told detectives he thought that

things were "okay" between Becky and himself, but that he'd suspected Becky had begun seeing another man.

"After a month," Solanev said, "I said I was done. I moved to Colorado Springs, got a job at the Air Force Academy, and I started dating a girl there."

When California investigators asked him how Becky had felt about that, Evan Solanev said that she found out he was with another woman and phoned him. "She said she knew how I must have felt when I found out she was dating someone else. She asked me if she could come back to me and we'd try one more time," he recalled.

Perhaps she did. He may have been the one who suggested a reconciliation. At any rate, she did come to Colorado Springs, and they stayed together for another two and a half years.

In March 2008, the couple moved once more—this time to Scottsdale, Arizona. Becky got her job working as a nurse/surgery assistant for a laser eye surgeon there. Evan applied to become a police officer in Phoenix, but he wasn't hired. He decided to go back to school and aim for a career in health care. He thought he might become a registered nurse.

Becky bought a modest house in October 2009 in her own name. Solanev would recall that he believed his wife was again seeing someone else. She may have been. Becky had stayed with Evan for seven years, a period where they lived a peripatetic lifestyle across America. She was a trained surgical assistant, but his career goals changed continually, and their frequent moves gave them no sense of roots at all.

She was also far away from her family in Missouri.

Some people who knew them whispered that she had married Evan to obtain her citizenship papers, although her family doesn't believe that. It did not, however, seem to be a happy union. Becky had given in to Evan's pleas to come back to him so many times, but things had never changed. They were still unsettled. Evan had suggested that they buy the house, but she paid for it. He wanted to give her a reason to believe they had finally made a permanent commitment.

But it wasn't enough. And it was too late. Becky was the one with the steady job and the one who had to make the mortgage payments.

As much as she had tried to keep her marriage together, Becky *was* attracted to other men—older men, more exciting men who seemed to have their lives in order and were actively achieving their goals. She was still very young, and very beautiful. As he turned thirty, Evan was a perpetual student, working at mostly minimum wage jobs.

As he talked to the San Diego detectives, Evan recalled becoming "a Christian" in April 2009, and giving up alcohol, cigarettes, and any drug use. Since he had been so connected to the church more than five years earlier and even a "youth minister," his acceptance of Christianity in 2009 seemed strangely after the fact.

It was inevitable that Becky and Evan Solanev would separate. That happened in Arizona. He began nursing school in January 2010, and they no longer lived together.

"She didn't file for divorce," he said, "so I did—in 2010."

Nevertheless, Evan said that he and Becky stayed in close contact. Their divorce was final in February 2011. Becky took Ocean, their Weimaraner, with her.

"Ocean was really my dog," Evan said.

After they were divorced, Becky lived for a short time with a man she met in Scottsdale. But then she met Jonah Shacknai. He was everything that her ex-husband was not. Jonah Shacknai was handsome, rich, and dynamic.

Evan recalled one incident where he encountered another man at Becky's Arizona home and the police were called. He did not give the man's name. It might have been Jonah; it could have been the man Becky dated before Jonah. Evan wasn't sure.

"She came outside and told them [the police] there was some contention between us, but it was only yelling— no physical assaults or anything like that," Evan said calmly.

"Do you know Jonah?" a San Diego investigator asked in the summer of 2011.

It was clear that Becky's ex-husband didn't like Jonah.

"I know him," Evan said evenly. "My stepmother worked for him in Scottsdale. He's rich. I suspected when Becky went out on her 'girls' night out' evenings, she was really with him. She just didn't want to tell me. It made me angry."

"Do you *hate* Jonah?"

"No," Evan said. "But I read where his ex-wife sold their house in Arizona for the highest price in Scottsdale history. I wanted to know how rich he was. I knew then I could never get her back. She wouldn't give me her address. I knew she'd quit work, so how could she get by and pay for her place?"

Evan Solanev was just shy of becoming "a person of interest." He had lost Becky to Jonah Shacknai and he certainly sounded jealous of Jonah. But Evan insisted he had never been to Coronado, and he had witnesses who saw him at his gym in Arizona on the early morning of July 13, 2011.

"I didn't even know Becky was dead until somebody from CBS called me on Thursday—July 14. Then the media called me all day. They even called my father and my aunt. When I heard, I basically had a panic attack."

Solanev said he had no idea where Becky and Jonah lived in California; when CBS called him with the news of her death, he said he thought that she'd died in Scottsdale.

"What do you think happened to Becky?" San Diego sheriff's detective Todd Norton asked.

"I've heard the news. Adrian from CBS told me that she was found in a common area—that she was bound and hanging—"

He hadn't really answered the question, and Norton pressed further. Was it possible that Becky had committed suicide, he asked?

"No!" Solanev said that there no way his ex-wife would have taken her own life. "We've been through a lot—and she's had a lot of pain in her life. She dealt with it. She loved life. She would never commit suicide. I've always felt she would come back to me if she needed to."

"Was she too naïve for this world—too trusting? What if she lost everything, the money—whatever—?"

"She'd dust herself off and get a job. She had family! She always had me!"

The investigators told Solanev straight out that he was on the "suspect board" of six people. They had already cleared other possible suspects, and they reminded him that he had had an eight-hour "window to commit murder" between his classes at Scottsdale Community College and the time he was seen in the gym the next morning. It was *possible* for him to have caught a flight, confronted Becky, strangled her, and managed to be back in Scottsdale by early the next morning.

But not likely.

"Any reason you'd want to hurt Rebecca?"

Evan shook his head and began to sob at the possibility that she would have killed herself.

"Do you think you were obsessed with her?"

Evan shook his head. "I don't think so. Yeah, I know I put her on a pedestal. She was the greatest thing there ever was. Even with the divorce, I didn't think she'd *never* come back to me."

In the end, although Evan Solanev may well have been obsessed with Becky Zahau, further investigation strained credulity to find him jealous enough to have flown to Coronado to kill her, and then manage to get back to Arizona in time to work out at his gym at 5 A.M.

Every connection would have had to mesh like clockwork. A flight delay. Bad weather. Headwinds. Tailwinds. *Anything* could have messed up such a plan.

*   *   *

All of the likely suspects were being eliminated. Or *almost* eliminated. San Diego area newspapers, television news shows, radio talk shows, and online outlets continued to be peppered with comments from the general public who demanded answers. Some of the calls, letters to the editors, and posts sounded ridiculous, as if they emanated from "crime experts" who hadn't thought things out. Some were comments from citizens heartsick at the tragedy of two deaths. There were also views from people who seemed to be on the "inside," either because they knew the principals or because they were employed as psychiatrists, psychologists, or law enforcement professionals, comments obviously written by experts in forensic science, murder, suicide, and human behavior.

No one seemed disinterested in what had happened to Max Shacknai and Rebecca Zahau.

Some were sympathetic to Becky, some to Jonah, and some were full of the kind of heedless sarcasm employed by those who hide behind anonymous screen names.

Most Internet posters doubted that Becky Zahau was a suicide. Many of their posts and questions were similar. One wrote:

Three criteria: motive, opportunity, and ability, are considered about suspects in any criminal investigation.

Who had the desire to injure or kill Ms. Zahau?

Who had the opportunity to get close enough to actually cause her harm?

Who had the ability [physical] to actually cause her harm and hang her?

The truth was that no one, except an actual killer—if, indeed, there was one—knew what had happened. But the eager Internet posters of San Diego County were consumed by the possibilities.

One thing was certain: everyone in the San Diego area had questions and opinions. Ironically, the sheriff's investigators were asking themselves the same questions.

Nothing fit.

Several citizens commented on how hard the San Diego detectives were working. And that was true. They were losing sleep and time with their families, only to find themselves at yet another dead end.

And then, on September 2, just seven weeks after Becky died, Sheriff Bill Gore announced a press conference. He told the mass of reporters who gathered that his department was closing the Rebecca Zahau investigation because they had determined she was, indeed, a suicide.

Many people were shocked, the Zahau family most of all. Giving several interviews to the media, they made it clear that they would not stop in their quest to find out the manner of Becky's death. A few weeks later, on September 16, 2011, Jonah Shacknai publicly agreed that the case was nowhere near over, and he, too, called for further investigation. He was still reeling over the loss of his "golden son," and concerned about his girlfriend's death.

Chapter Eleven

In desperation, Becky Zahau's family contacted Anne Bremner in Seattle.

After she was approached by Becky Zahau's sister Mary in the fall of 2011, Anne did some initial research on Becky's alleged hanging death. Now she agreed to donate her legal experience and education to help the Zahau family find out just what had happened to Becky during the dark hours of July 13.

Another familiar name in the justice system stepped up to offer his services on the strange death in Coronado. Chicago private investigator Paul Ciolino is a legend. Dan Rather once called Ciolino "one of America's top five investigators." Ciolino, who looks like a man that Central Casting would suggest for the role of a tough cop, has received dozens of awards for his expertise, including International Investigator of the Year. He lectures to prestigious universities from Yale to Northwestern to Columbia.

His topics include investigative ethics, debunking "experts," child homicide, sexual abuse, repressed memories, and death penalty investigations.

Most impressive, perhaps, is the fact that Ciolino has helped free five innocent men from death row. He also obtained a shocking videotaped confession from a double murder suspect.

Like Anne Bremner, Paul Ciolino has worked many infamous cases, including the heartbreaking murder of two-year-old Caylee Anthony in Florida. Ciolino, too, was doubtful about the San Diego County Sheriff's Department's official decision to close the investigation into the manner of Rebecca Zahau's death so soon. He joined the team dedicated to find answers to what most people felt was a continuing and tragic puzzle.

Although the postmortem exam of Becky's body had been remarkably thorough and detailed, Paul Ciolino and Anne Bremner studied Dr. Jonathan Lucas's report and questioned some of his conclusions. Becky had had many scratches, cuts, and contusions, and the pattern of lividity on her back rather than on her lower legs seemed odd.

Fortuitously, Becky's body had not been cremated; she was buried in St. Joseph, Missouri, near her family. Although it was excruciatingly painful for them, they agreed to consider having her body exhumed for a second autopsy. For Mary Loehner, the answer came with her belief that her sister Becky had *never* really rested in her grave, and never would rest if she wasn't vindicated.

Not much time had passed—only a few months—and she had been embalmed. There was a fairly good chance that Rebecca Zahau's body was in essentially the same condition that it had been when she was buried.

There are only a handful of esteemed forensic pathologists in the United States, and they are much sought-after by those dealing with seemingly unfathomable cases. Dr. Michael Baden is one. Baden is the former chief medical examiner of New York City and now works for the New York State Police. As a board-certified forensic pathologist for forty-eight years, he has worked on or testified in a number of headline death cases, including David Carradine, Chandra Levy, Sunny von Bülow, and Caylee Anthony.

Perhaps the most experienced of all is Dr. Cyril H. Wecht, who has been a board-certified forensic pathologist for more than fifty years. He has personally conducted more than 17,000 autopsies and consulted on another 37,000 death cases. He, too, has testified as an expert witness in trials all over the world.

Wecht is a past president of the American Academy of Forensic Sciences, is on the board of directors of the National Association of Medical Examiners, and, among many other boards dealing with questions of mortality, is a chartered diplomate of the American Board of Disaster Medicine. He is also an attorney in his home state of Pennsylvania.

Along with his coauthor, Dawna Kaufmann, Dr. Wecht has written several bestselling books on both unknown mystery deaths and those of deceased celebrities such as President John F. Kennedy, Anna Nicole Smith, Sharon Tate, and JonBenét Ramsey.

Either Dr. Baden or Dr. Wecht could make a powerful advocate for a death other than suicide in Rebecca Zahau's case—*if* they disagreed with Dr. Lucas's conclusions. Anne Bremner had worked with Cyril Wecht before, however, and she approached him about performing the second postmortem exam of Becky Zahau.

Her family would find it difficult to pay for this procedure, but providentially, Dr. Wecht chose to do this autopsy for no charge—if Becky's family agreed to have her body exhumed and sent to his offices in Pittsburgh. Dr. Phil McGraw of television fame was also puzzled about the facts behind Becky's death, and he stepped in to pay for the exhumation and transportation.

As a death investigator, Wecht was most concerned with the scientific findings at autopsy, but he always sought to find out the circumstances surrounding the demise of his subjects. By weighing the two views, one medical and one anecdotal, he found he could get a fully dimensional grasp of what could have happened.

In November 2011, four months after Rebecca Zahau died, Dr. Wecht performed a postmortem exam. There were certain things he would not be able to do because her body had been embalmed. But the first autopsy, performed by Dr. Lucas, had included tests to determine if she had any alcohol or drugs in her system at the time of her death. And, of course, lab reports came back that she had neither. As a health fanatic, Becky had eschewed both.

After he finished the postmortem exam of Becky

Zahau, Dr. Wecht was asked if he thought Becky had died from strangulation caused by the blue T-shirt that had been wrapped around her neck three times, or in some other fashion that differed from the hanging diagnosis.

"My reply is that when there is so much internal damage to the neck structures, it's not always possible to differentiate a pre-hanging strangulation from a staged hanging. Ms. Zahau's body showed substantial damage to her neck. Her hyoid bone—the small U-shaped cartilage beneath the jawbone—was broken, but there were also hemorrhages in the underlying muscles down to the fractured cricoid cartilage, the first cartilaginous ring beneath the Adam's apple. Yet, the rope was *above* that level. These are the kinds of injuries that can be attained from a forcible, manual strangulation.

"There was a total absence of *any* injury posteriorly," Wecht continued. "The cervical vertebrae—the first seven vertebrae in our spinal column beginning at the base of the skull—showed *no* damage, either by way of fracture or dislocation. Also, there was no damage to the delicate muscles, ligaments, and tendons that lie on the front, back, and sides of the vertebral column. There was all that damage and force in the front of her neck, and not even one drop of blood or tear or disruption of any soft tissues in the rear.

"Dr. Jonathan Lucas noted four separate subgaleal hemorrhages on Ms. Zahau—in the area beneath her scalp but over her skull, I confirmed them on Rebecca's second autopsy," Wecht noted. "But nobody has provided an explanation as to how the top of her head got those bright red, fresh injuries, which only could have come from something hitting her on the head—or her head hitting something—four times."

Wecht said that no one knew just what object had struck her. "It could have been a fist, or anything with a reasonable amount of firmness that would not perforate, lacerate, or abrade the scalp [itself] in any way. Crime scene photos show a plastic red toy dog bone in the room by the balcony; that could have easily been the weapon."

Dr. Wecht pointed out that there is no soft tissue between the scalp and the bony skull. Although the four injuries were not strong enough to fracture Becky's skull, they definitely had occurred very shortly before her death. How had these wounds happened?

"In order to get four separate, distinct hemorrhages," Wecht wrote, "you have to have four points of impact—not so hard as to fracture the skull or lacerate the scalp, or cause death on their own—but sufficient to produce the hemorrhages. And the bright red color of these injuries shows they were acute—meaning *immediate* to her demise, not from bumping her head on something days—or even hours—earlier."

Had Becky's head hit some tree branches as she dropped from the balcony? The San Diego detectives thought so. Or could she have struck her head on some outcropping from the balcony? No—there *was* no outcropping of stucco, wood, or metal.

Becky had allegedly been hanging from a taut, nautical rope, not something like a bungee cord that would have made it possible for her body to bounce upward several times and cause the four impact injuries.

Dr. Wecht also wondered about the many scratches, punctures, and bruises on her back. "If they came from her dangling on the rope and coming into contact with foliage, as investigators assert, why weren't there similar abrasions to her arms, which were tied behind her back? Her arms should have been the first point of contact if those abrasions came from hitting foliage while swinging on a rope, and her arms should have shown more abrasions than were on her back."

The renowned forensic pathologist felt if there had been enough momentum for Becky to rotate while hanging, or to allow her to hit the balcony on her way down, one should expect to find injuries to her nose and the front of her face.

There were none.

Dr. Lucas's autopsy summation had attributed the four mystery red areas as something that had happened when Adam Shacknai cut her down. Dr. Wecht didn't concur.

"Without knowing how she got those marks, we cannot eliminate the possibility that someone assaulted her and caused her to have a cerebral concussion and become momentarily unconscious—and that suggests the application of some degree of force against her and a possible murder scenario. Authorities maintain that there was no evidence of a struggle—but when someone has had a cerebral contusion and unconsciousness [however brief], he or she is not going to struggle."

Dr. Lucas had noted three rectangles of what appeared

to be tape residue on Becky's lower right leg but hadn't found this particularly relevant.

"Are we to think," Dr. Wecht asked, "she first bound her legs with duct tape, but took it off and used rope instead? If so, where is the roll of tape from which the tape was cut, and the wadded up bits she decided not to use?"

All in all, Cyril Wecht found the mystery of Becky's death inexplicable. "I have never experienced the same set of circumstances that I see in this case. Any scenario I try to come up with to explain the physical circumstances in which Rebecca was found defies my imagination.

"The knots around Ms. Zahau's wrists enabled her, apparently to put her hands in and out of the bindings."

Dr. Wecht wrote that he had appeared on a television show with a "well-respected" rope knot expert and discussed the way Becky was bound up with him.

"He stated that he didn't see how *anybody* could have accomplished what Rebecca was alleged to have done."

Even though the San Diego investigators had re-created the hanging of Becky to counter criticism from the public, showing that "Rebecca fastened the bindings in front of her, then pulled her right hand out of a sophisticated slip-knot, repositioned the rope behind her back, and put her right hand back in the binding," Wecht wrote, "I contend that it is no great surprise that they could instruct someone to do the act for a re-creation. Harry Houdini did this 70 years ago. What I want to know is how Ms. Zahau learned to fashion these kinds of knots that were around her neck, wrists, and ankles, and tied to the bed leg. Where did she acquire this special skill?"

Cyril Wecht is at an age and with enough experience under his belt that he doesn't soften his conclusions. He criticized the investigators for failing do a "proper and meaningful" re-creation. Rather than use a newly hired policewoman as a subject to represent Becky, he felt the sheriff's investigators should have used a dummy of *exactly* the same weight and size of Becky, and videotaped how her fall might have occurred. It wasn't enough in his opinion to re-create the "hanging" with a female police officer who was only approximately Becky's size.

Wecht wondered just how Becky had suffered the marks on her body that were apparent on autopsy. And why was the bed frame in her office/bedroom moved so little? He felt that the iron bed should have moved more when the sudden weight of a plunging body pulled it. In the photos of the floor in Becky's office/bedroom, there were no drag marks—no furrows on the rug. Indeed, it looked more as if it had been lifted and then moved to the position in which it was found.

Dr. Wecht also determined that there should have been acoustic tests in the mansion. Had the screams neighbors heard come from *inside* the Spreckels Mansion?

Or from outside?

Dr. Cyril Wecht believed that Becky Zahau had not perished from hanging herself. He, Anne Bremner, Paul Ciolino, and Becky's sister and brother-in-law, Mary and Doug Loehner, appeared on the *Dr. Phil* show and presented their conclusions on the manner of her death.

Although Sheriff Bill Gore, a former FBI special agent, was a good friend of Adam Shacknai's attorney, Paul

Pfingst, there was no ulterior reason that Gore had opted to close the death investigation prematurely. There seemed to be just as much circumstantial evidence on either side of the dilemma, and there was no question that everyone involved sincerely wanted to find the manner of Becky Zahau's death. Of course, her demise garnered more headlines than if she had been the girlfriend of an average "Joe the Plumber" type of man. Instead she had been the love of a world-famous pharmaceutical billionaire.

And the fact that Becky and Maxie had allegedly plunged to their deaths within forty-eight hours could not be ignored.

Was there any way to winnow out what really happened?

Private investigator Paul Ciolino flew to California and looked around the grounds of the Shacknai estate, studying the balcony where Becky Zahau had reportedly hung herself and estimating the distance from Ocean Boulevard to the front door, where Hank Bowden, the bicycling tourist, still insisted he had seen Dina—not Nina—on the night before Becky died. He knocked on doors along the street, and reinterviewed many of Jonah and Becky's neighbors.

Ciolino located a second resident who had heard a woman's frightened screams in the night.

"That's 'Homicide 101,' " Ciolino would later state on the *Dr. Phil* show. He'd read the Zahau case files, talked to witnesses, and visited the death scene and the surrounding area for himself. He was not allowed to go inside the mansion or the guesthouse. (Nor was Seattle attorney Anne Bremner when she sought permission to go inside.) Ciolino wondered why the case had been closed so prematurely. Something wasn't right.

"It didn't pass the 'smell test,' " he said bluntly. "It stinks."

Ciolino went to Dr. Mark Kalish, a board-certified psychiatrist, and laid the troubling case out for him. At length, Dr. Kalish shook his head. "This was no suicide," he said. "It doesn't make sense."

Sometime later, when Dr. Phil asked him why someone would tie a victim up so elaborately to make it look like suicide, the PI from Chicago flatly replied, "Killers are stupid."

Paul Ciolino criticized the San Diego investigators. "I've seen it before," he said. "I call it 'confirmation bias.' The detectives draw their original conclusions—and then they look for clues and evidence to support them. When they do that, they miss details that might point in an entirely different direction."

Jonah had put the Coronado mansion up for sale—not surprising. There were too many memories of despair and loss there now. But Paul Ciolino worried about the dozens of prospective buyers who were "constantly contaminating" the scene more and more. If there was evidence there—and there probably was—visitors were probably taking some of it away with them—no matter how small—

and they were tracking in stuff from wherever they had been, leaving their fingerprints as they moved from room to room.

Moreover, Anne Bremner, California attorneys David Fleck and Martin Rudoy, who also represented the Zahau family, along with Ciolino, were convinced the sheriff's department still had possible vital evidence that had never been tested, statements that had never been followed up. Jonah Shacknai joined them in asking that more investigation be done. Although not as vociferous in his plea as the others were, he seemed to feel that not enough had been done to find out what really happened to Becky.

Seven weeks just hadn't been long enough to thoroughly work such a tangled case—actually *two* tangled cases.

Chapter Twelve

But when 2012 arrived, nothing had changed. Rebecca Zahau's family mourned the daughter and sister they loved so much, but there were no answers to their questions. The investigation into her death was closed. The world went on without Becky and without Maxie. For the thousands of people who had followed their cases avidly, it seemed impossible to let go of wondering. The websites were still filled with queries, opinions, theories—both from those who were highly educated in medicine, psychology, and criminal justice and those whose gut instincts and empathy drove them to keep tabs on what was now a closed murder probe.

On January 6, 2012, the Zahau family's legal team—law partners David Fleck and Marty Rudoy in California, along with Anne Bremner in Seattle—drafted an eighteen-page-letter to Julie Garland, the senior supervising deputy attorney general in the California Department of Justice. The department's office had earlier declined to review the San Diego County Sheriff's Department and Coronado Police Department's handling of the Rebecca Zahau case.

There were very narrow criteria for such a review. The state of California had scarce financial resources and their policy was that they could only review cases where a clear conflict of interest existed, where local authorities' resources had been exhausted and they had asked for help from the state, or when there were allegations of gross malfeasance by a local law enforcement agency or agencies.

The Zahaus' attorneys felt they had a case that fit within the DOJ's requirements. The letter was a bold move—and quite probably the final chance to see Becky's death satisfactorily investigated.

Fleck, Rudoy, and Bremner mentioned the "blue ribbon" panel of experts who had joined them in their disbelief that Becky had been a suicide: forensic pathologist Cyril Wecht; retired Los Angeles homicide detective Steven Fisk, with five hundred homicide, suicide, and suspicious death investigations under his belt; private investigator Paul Ciolino; and several expert instructors from the FBI Academy in Quantico, Virginia.

They felt there was a clear conflict of interest in the close relationship between Sheriff Gore's office and Adam Shacknai's attorney, Paul Pfingst, the former two-time district attorney of San Diego County. Attached to this letter was the photograph of Pfingst at Becky's death site *inside* the yellow crime scene tape even before the arrival of the deputy medical examiner. One of the detectives clearly had his arm around the former DA's shoulder.

"Paul Pfingst used a non-published phone number to reach the police," the legal trio noted, "to tell them not to give his client (Adam) a polygraph. In this recorded call, Pfingst referred to the incident as a 'homicide.' "

"We know from experience," David Fleck wrote, "that homicide detectives do not hobnob with a prime suspect's defense attorney during an active investigation, and it is highly unusual for a defense attorney to be at a [working] crime scene. At a minimum, it creates a disconcerting appearance of impropriety."

Fleck, Rudoy, and Bremner listed again the circumstances when Becky Zahau perished. They could, of course, recite the details in their sleep—but they wanted to be sure the California Department of Justice was fully aware of them.

"According to Adam Shacknai, a tugboat captain from Memphis, he found Rebecca hanging and he cut her down. She was naked. Her feet were filthy with dried mud. Her hands were bound behind her with sophisticated knots. Her ankles were bound with sophisticated knots. The noose around her neck was applied *over* her hair. There was a T-shirt wrapped around her neck three times and stuffed into her mouth as a gag. The blood had pooled in her back—not in her feet or legs. Painted on the door to the bedroom where the rope was anchored to a bedpost was the message: 'She saved him. Can you save her.' It was not a suicide note; she left no suicide note.

"Detectives concluded that Rebecca tied herself up, made her way onto the balcony [with feet bound] and threw herself over, leaving minimal footprints. They admitted there was no suicide note, and made no attempt to explain the message on the door."

The orange-red towropes that bound Becky Zahau's ankles and wrists, twisting her into what everyday people might call a "hog-tied" position, were fashioned in a complicated pattern. Her family's attorneys had conferred with rope experts, and they'd learned about a Japanese "art" and/or "sexual sadomasochistic" practice of tying ropes around human beings. It is called *Shibari*.

Sometimes, *Shibari* can be as innocuous as a delicate art of wrapping perfect packages. At other times, it is a sexual practice or fetish, one that few have heard of. Currently trendy in the Orient and Europe, the intricate machinations of what can only be termed "rope sex" demand the winding, knotting, and rewinding of ropes around the limbs and other body parts of sexual partners or those who pose in bondage positions. It can be very, very, dangerous, particularly when precise balance must be maintained between more than one person. One wrong tilt and participants can—and have—died. An Italian case involved three people, all balanced precariously. One woman, new to *Shibari*, fainted and her full weight shifted. It is just one instance where this extreme fetish, which requires total control, ended in the fatal strangulations of two of the participants.

"These were nautical knots, likely tied by someone right-handed, according to our experts' reports," David Fleck's letter to Garland continued as he spoke of those that bound Becky Zahau. "They are not the safe knots used in conventional bondage. There are two styles of knots [employed;] some are utilitarian and nautical—others are reminiscent of *Shibari*-type bondage. It would have been unlikely for Rebecca to have tied these knots because of their complexity. Less sophisticated knots would have done the trick. Unless there was an intent to make a display, there's no reason to use such an elaborate knot."

Dr. Cyril Wecht had come to the same conclusion. Becky Zahau simply didn't have the knowledge or even the dexterity to bind herself in the position in which she was found, much less be able to get to the balcony railing in one hop and plunge over.

There had been one set of her tiptoe footprints, hampered by being tightly bound, and a half print of one of a man's boots in the dust—which was believed to have been left by a police officer. These, admittedly, were some of the most troubling pieces of physical evidence that seemed to indicate she had committed suicide.

Where and how, then, had Becky's feet been caked with mud?

Step by step, the all-encompassing letter asked Julie Garland for further investigation and brought up things that they felt had not been efficiently explored: the four hemorrhages on Becky's skull; the multiple abrasions; the unexplained duct tape residue on her ankles, when detectives had found no such tape in the mansion; the injuries to her neck, throat, and back, with no broken vertebrae, and no damage to the *back* of her neck, making it look as if the manner of death was manual strangulation—not hanging.

Retired homicide detective Steve Fisk was concerned by the substantial percentage of the fingerprints that were dusted and lifted only to be termed "unusable."

"They might not have been clear enough for use in a court of law—but they could have been used to see if there were points that matched known persons of interest," he commented.

Some DNA had been collected and evaluated, but there were no DNA exemplars from Dina Shacknai, and no fingerprints from her, either.

Just as they had wondered about why Becky's long hair had been tucked *under* the blue shirt and the orange-red noose, Anne Bremner and her assistant, Misty Scott, also noted that hanging is an unusual way for females to kill themselves. Sometimes only women understand what women are likely to do. Bremner and Scott have sensitive antennas that catch subtleties males might not recognize.

The National Institute of Mental Health did a study on the most common methods women use in suicides, and number one, by far, was poisoning (including sleeping pills). Number two is a gun—although women rarely shoot themselves in the head or face.

Detective Fisk, with all his many years of experience, had never seen—or heard—of a woman who hung herself naked. Becky Zahau would have been aware that her nude and twisted body would be visible to the public—including her neighbors on Ocean Boulevard. One cannot be "embarrassed" after they are dead, but Fisk knew the vast majority of female suicides attempt to look attractive—even in death.

The three attorneys suggested that the San Diego County medical examiner and the San Diego County Sheriff's Department had jointly ruled Becky Zahau's death a suicide, "relying primarily on each other's flawed analysis of the situation, and ignoring compelling evidence of murder," with circular logic going virtually nowhere.

The Zahaus' legal team was concerned that there were other individuals who might have wanted Becky dead, although only Adam Shacknai had been questioned intensely. Whether any one of them had reason to really kill her, however, was a big question.

There was no love lost between Dina Shacknai and Becky Zahau. Even though Dina had seemed eager to divorce Jonah and benefited handsomely from their divorce settlement, she must have resented the woman who had replaced her. Witnesses had told detectives that their relationship had been "on the edge of civil."

The wife of the couple who took care of the Shacknai mansion had told detectives about a public event in February 2011, when Dina and Becky had a confrontation.

"The black paint on the bedroom door matched the black paint on Rebecca's body. But she was an artist," Fleck wrote. "She wasn't likely to smear paint on herself. Our handwriting expert expresses concern over the conclusion that Rebecca painted the message on the door, based on a number of factors.

"The San Diego Sheriff's Office relied on a recent receipt for painting supplies purchased by Rebecca as proof of intent to commit suicide. However, my partner, Marty Rudoy, spoke with Mike, the salesperson/manager at Coronado Hardware. Mike confirms that none of the supplies purchased on that receipt were artistic brushes, nor was any of the paint [artists'] 'tube' paint. The painting supplies that were purchased were the type for painting a room, including large brushes and gallons of paint. None of the supplies listed on the receipt found in the car were used in this crime. The receipt is a red herring."

Attorney David Fleck wrote that there were many things that he felt flawed the sheriff's investigation, far more than he could list, even in an eighteen-page letter.

He asked for myriad specific actions the San Diego sheriff's investigators could take that would help to unlock the *real* events of the night of July 12–13, 2011.

"Despite the length of this report," Fleck wrote, "it just scratches the surface of what we have found. For example, there are two witnesses who need to be interrogated by law enforcement as they have reported new, unverified, information regarding several of the individuals discussed herein. [We can discuss this with you in person, but the information is so sensitive that we do not feel comfortable sharing it with San Diego County law enforcement at this time.]"

But Fleck agreed that there were steps that could only be accomplished effectively by law enforcement.

He listed a number of witnesses whose identities remain confidential and asked that witnesses to Dina's altercation with Becky be interviewed.

Although stacks of police files had been turned over to Rudoy, Bremner, and Fleck, there were many they still did not have. Fleck asked that the sheriff's office obtain records from the local cable company, Verizon, Yahoo, ADT, Adam's iPhone, and Dina's cell phone for forensic analysis. He also asked for receipts of specific customer records (currently preserved under the Demand for Preservation of Evidence). The Zahaus' attorneys could not obtain any of these without notifying the consumer(s). Fleck noted that he knew that some of the records might be out of state and beyond subpoena.

Moreover, the three attorneys were looking for Becky's email records, contact list, video records, photos, instant messages, and browsing history. Under federal law, only law enforcement could obtain those.

Solving cases where the manner of death is undetermined has certainly changed with the advent of the Internet and cell phones. Knowing that much of what they sought to examine was beyond their reach, Bremner, Fleck, and Rudoy nevertheless tried to find it.

And yet even as they drafted this letter, they worried that a lot of the evidence of the last moments of Becky Zahau's life was disappearing and being obliterated. There had been potential buyers moving through the Shacknai estate. Those who did ultimately buy the property said they would tear down the balcony first, and they wanted to begin immediately. They would excavate for a pool where Becky's body had lain.

Neither Jonah Shacknai nor the group that had purchased the Spreckels Mansion would consent to letting Fleck, Rudoy, Bremner, or Ciolino on the property unless they were supervised by officers from the Coronado Police Department or the San Diego County Sheriff's Department. They had been asking for a month, and been told a flat "no" three times.

The first forty-eight hours of a death investigation are

the most important in terms of obtaining and testing possible evidence. After that, the possibilities of finding it diminish in direct proportion to the time that elapses.

And that time had long passed.

David Fleck wrote that they were intensely interested in what pornography sites were allegedly accessed on July 12–13. And, of course, by whom? These were on the computer in the room where the "hanging" balcony was. Who had access to it during that night?

He listed other requests as he moved on to the last page of his letter.

1. Obtain Nina's cell phone for forensic analysis.
2. Test hair from shower [master bathroom].
3. Test knife used to cut Rebecca down for Adam's fingerprints.
4. Conduct a second polygraph of Adam, asking more appropriate questions.
5. Conduct a psychiatric autopsy of Rebecca.
6. Compare fingerprints and DNA from Jonah and Dina to exclude them from evidence found at the crime scene.
7. Test the panties found in the guesthouse. Identify who they belonged to.
8. Supervise our efforts to inspect the mansion, photograph and videotape it in its present condition, and do non-destructive testing.
9. "We are unlikely to receive GBS data, text and email data in a condition with usable data," Fleck said, "but law enforcement can."

David Fleck concluded, "The evidence of foul play is overwhelming and the bases of the suicide conclusion are weak at best. We don't know why Rebecca's investigation was cut short. There are discomfiting appearances of impropriety regarding the relationship the Sheriff has with the Defense, but anything beyond that would be speculation. Nonetheless, it is painfully obvious to all of the experts who have looked at this case that more investigation is called for. Justice demands it. The value of a poor girl's life must be the same as that of a billionaire and his family. At a bare minimum, fair play requires that actual evidence of suicide must be found before this case has closed."

Chapter Thirteen

Detective Angela Tsuida and dozens of other investigators from both the Coronado Police Department and the San Diego County Sheriff's Department worked countless hours on the case of the death of Rebecca Zahau. It's difficult to fault them, and I suspect many of these detectives must feel a sense of a job left undone—but don't have the authority to continue working on Becky's case.

Tsuida ended her report with "All indications are that there was no foul play."

There were, of course, many indications of what might very well be construed as foul play, and they have been listed in this book. There were a number of factors that were not addressed, or were not followed through to a satisfactory end. Many forensic lab tests were not completed, or even begun.

The best solution, in my opinion, would have been to risk bringing charges against one or more persons, and to see the circumstances and evidence presented to jurors and let them decide. If an acquittal(s) resulted, then double jeopardy would attach, and any defendants would be protected from ever facing murder charges again.

As it is, the mystery floats in dead air.

On February 21, 2012, Sheriff Bill Gore's special assistant and chief attorney, Robert P. Faigin, sent a letter to one of the Zahau family attorneys, Martin Rudoy.

"This letter serves as formal written follow-up to our meeting on January 27, 2012, and your numerous emails relating to the death of Rebecca Zahau. The meeting was . . . attended by members of the Sheriff's homicide unit and crime lab, as well as members of the County Medical Examiners and the Coronado Police Department.

"At the beginning of the meeting, you and your partner, Mr. Fleck, were advised that the investigation into Rebecca Zahau's death was closed, and that the manner of death was listed as a suicide . . . The purpose of the meeting was to provide you and your partner an opportunity to provide all evidence that you indicated you had. The meeting lasted three hours, with all but a few minutes of the time being utilized by you and your PowerPoint presentation."

Faigin criticized that presentation because he considered it to consist of numerous theories on things that "could" or "might" have happened, but felt there was no actual evidence.

The other titan of forensic pathology in America, Dr. Michael Baden, had read the entire case file and leaned toward the sheriff's interpretation of the manner of Becky's death, and thought it more likely she had taken her own life.

"At the conclusion of the meeting, you and your partner stated unequivocally your belief that Ms. Zahau had been murdered. However, you were unable or unwilling to state who you believed to be the culprit.

"[Your] theories included a 'confidential informant' who befriended Adam Shacknai after the incident in question . . . who allegedly told your investigator in an unrecorded statement that Adam Shacknai confessed to her that he was returning home when he discovered Ms. Zahau's body, as opposed to finding her after he woke up. Without even going into the evidentiary value of the unrecorded, hearsay statement, it does not impact the conclusions in the case. If in fact true, it would exonerate Mr. Shacknai as he would not have been home at the time of Ms. Zahau's death.

"Based on the above, nothing has been brought to light that necessitates reopening the investigation into the suicide of Rebecca Zahau. As a result, the matter will remain closed, and the Department will consider the matter concluded."

Sheriff Gore's name was typed in, but without his signature. Robert Faigin signed the letter.

If Becky Zahau did not commit suicide, and was, indeed, murdered, we are left with other possibilities than those already mentioned. There may very well be suspects and possible motivations not yet considered. No one knows for sure. The following are only questions and not conclusions, but they are questions that beg discussion among those who have followed Becky's and Max's cases and those who may never have heard of their deaths until they read this book.

- Supposedly, only a few family members knew the back door of the mansion was never locked. But Becky Zahau was startlingly beautiful, and very likely to attract attention as she rode her bicycle in her bikini bathing suit. She may have had a stranger-stalker who watched her from the shadows, waiting for his chance, who had somehow known the back door was unlocked. And if such an assailant existed, he may even have known about Max's fall and that Jonah was not at home—but with Max.

- Or had a professional burglar read about Max's condition and figured everyone who lived in the mansion must be in his hospital room, seized an opportunity (as burglars who scan obituaries break into expensive homes during announced funeral services do), and been surprised to find Rebecca there in the mansion?

- There is, of course, the possibility that Becky Zahau *did* commit suicide. She had vowed to be the "best girlfriend" and the "best caretaker" of Jonah's children in her journal entry many months before she died. She hoped to marry Jonah, but she wrote that she was content to stay in the role she played in his life. When she realized that she had not been the best caretaker, could she have plunged into guilt and remorse after Maxie fell? Her family says that isn't possible. But it is one possibility that has to be included in the tragedy of Becky Zahau's life. She once lived for a while in Nepal, where female suicides are a major concern.

Jonah Shacknai never lived in the Spreckels Mansion again. He sold it to investors around Halloween 2011. The sale price was not released, but the new owners said they planned to place it on the market for something over $14 million.

After the investigation into Becky's manner of death was closed in the fall of 2011, Jonah Shacknai issued a statement:

I would like to thank Attorney General Harris for her condolences and consideration of my request to evaluate this matter. I respect and accept the determination of the chief law enforcement authority in the state of California that the circumstances of this investigation do not warrant further review by the attorney general at this time. Given the unusual facts of this tragedy, I understand that Rebecca's family and others continue to have questions. If at any time there is new substantive evidence bearing on this case, it should be presented—not in tabloid form to fuel rumor and innuendo, but rather to appropriate law enforcement authorities who may determine whether further investigation is warranted. I continue to pray Max and Rebecca are now at peace, and that all of us devastated by their losses will be permitted to continue to grieve privately as we struggle to achieve some peace and closure.

During the first two weeks in April 2012, Dina Shacknai announced that she was suing the San Diego County medical examiner's department to obtain Maxie's autopsy photos because she did not believe that he died by falling and hitting his head.

Allegedly, Dina doesn't believe that Max had the strength to grab the crystal chandelier in an attempt to break his fall. It was, of course, found beside him on the foyer's carpet.

Some sources say that the chandelier's chain had been cut; it had broken horizontally in a straight line.

Dina Shacknai also spoke of her plans to sue Rebecca Zahau's estate. That seemed unnecessarily cruel to Becky's family.

As the one-year anniversary of Max's and Becky's deaths approached, Dina Shacknai held a news conference and gave an interview to reporter Craig Outhier for the August issue of *Phoenix Magazine*. The resulting article was very supportive of Dina and portrayed her as a deeply loving, supportive mother as Outhier extolled her intelligence, her volunteer work at the Southwest Autism Research & Resource Center, and her doctoral studies in clinical psychology at Argosy University in Phoenix.

Devastated by Max's death, Dina hadn't spoken out much. She described herself as a "recluse" since losing her only child.

Max's mother revealed in this July 2012 interview that she had hired her own investigators several months earlier because she didn't believe that her six-year-old son's death was an accident, and *her* experts agreed with her suspicions.

Dina said that, as Max's mother, it was her job to find out what had really happened to him, and she vowed she would continue to investigate his death until she found an answer.

"Based on our experts and our findings, we are confident that the scenario put forth is inaccurate on how Maxie's death occurred," Dina's attorney, Angela Hallier, said at the press conference. "Given their cooperation, I think they are going to want to hear from us given what our findings are."

"I want Max back," Dina said. "And I want Rebecca back so I can ask her what happened."

It was very clear that Dina Shacknai blamed Rebecca Zahau for Max's death. She said she had always felt uneasy when he was with Jonah's girlfriend, particularly when Dina felt Becky hadn't given her her legal name, and had, allegedly, been stopped for shoplifting in 2009. After that, Dina said she hadn't wanted Becky to be alone with Max.

Dina announced that she was launching a nonprofit foundation in Max's name to save other children from his fate, and to give her own life "structure and purpose."

Thus far, however, there are no absolute facts and no evidence to substantiate Dina Shacknai's suspicions.

The tragic deaths of Maxfield Shacknai, six, and Rebecca Zahau, thirty-two, in a bleak two-and-a-half-day period in July 2011 may never be solved. They have become part of the lore of Coronado and of the Spreckels Mansion, and will never be forgotten. Although the Shacknais want to move forward, the Zahaus remain filled with grief and the sense of something left unfinished. Of justice ignored.

Perhaps one day the truth will emerge, and hearts can begin to heal.

DOUBLE DEATH
FOR THE KIND
PHILANTHROPISTS

If ever a man deserved to spend his retirement years in peace and comfort, it was eighty-five-year-old Burle D. Bramhall. Certainly the old man was wealthy, and his fifty-five-year marriage to his one sweetheart, Olive, eighty-three, was as idyllic as it had been when they first took their wedding vows. Their sumptuous home in one of Seattle's richest and oldest neighborhoods— Windermere—was just right for them. The Bramhalls lived the kind of retirement that anyone might aspire to.

Nobody who knew Burle Bramhall resented his good fortune, however, for his whole life had been one of service to others and philanthropy.

Almost ninety years ago, Bramhall was a vigorous man in his twenties. During World War I, he worked with the American Red Cross, and he managed to shepherd 783 youngsters out of Siberia for reunions with their families. Like a pied piper, he led the little ones from country to country until they were once again safe in their parents' arms.

In 1973, when they were over eighty, Burle and Olive

were guests of the Soviet Union. There they were reunited with more than two hundred of those children Burle had saved. The "children" had long since grown to late middle age themselves. In the years after that joyous meeting, the Bramhalls' mailbox was always full of letters from these old friends who never forgot what he had done for them. He always found time to write back to those he had rescued, and his small study was crowded with mementoes they sent him.

He and Olive had never been blessed with children of their own, but they felt the children from Siberia who called him "Godfather" were somehow theirs, too.

For all of his long life, Burle Bramhall had been a consummate businessman. His accounting studies at the University of Oregon were interrupted by his Red Cross services in World War I, but, on his return to Seattle, he finished his education and went to work handling investments for the Marine National Bank. There he met the man who would be his partner for more than thirty years in the investment firm of Bramhall & Stein.

During World War II, Bramhall took a leave of absence and went to Paris and London to work with health and welfare agencies geared to serve the survivors of the second great war, and once more he immersed himself in helping displaced persons. He was approaching fifty then, but it didn't matter.

Although his partner retired in 1969, Burle Bramhall never really did. Right up until the end of his life, he was associated with Blyth & Company, rated then as the nation's largest investment house not tied to the New York Stock Exchange.

Burle always tempered a good business head with concern for those who had nothing. He felt grateful that he had been given—and earned—much, and he believed he owed something back.

And Olive felt the same way. The elderly couple were still having a lot of fun in their eighties. Their neighbors in Windermere often chuckled to see them all dressed up and stepping out for the evening. Their age slowed them down a little, but even so, they were considered the "night owls" of the neighborhood, driving out grandly with Burle behind the wheel of his polished 1963 Mercedes. The tall old man was a little stoop-shouldered now, but he still treated the petite Olive with all the courtliness he had used when they were first married.

When the Bramhalls' lights were on late on the warm summer night of Wednesday, August 2, 1978, no one thought anything of it; neighbors figured Burle and Olive were watching television a little later than they usually did.

It was sometime after midnight on August 3 when the 911 emergency line at Seattle police headquarters rang and Operator 63 picked up the receiver. The conversation was terse, but also frightening.

"911 Operator 63."

"Yes . . . I would like to get connected to the police . . ."

"This is the police department."

"Okay . . . there was a murder at 6647."

"When was this?"

"I don't know."

"There was a murder?"

"Yeah . . . two of them."

" . . . 6647 Windermere Way . . ."

"Yes."

Before the operator could ask any further questions, the line went dead. The caller was a man who had no discernible accent, and that was all the operator could say about him. He jotted down the information and passed it to the radio dispatcher.

The first officers dispatched from the Wallingford Precinct in Seattle's north station were Gordon Van Rooy, F. R. Solis, and Dale Eggers, sent to check on a "possible homicide."

They turned into a divided private lane that led to several large homes and pulled up in front of the two-story L-shaped house marked BRAMHALL.

Solis covered the back while Van Rooy and Eggers approached from the front. The front door was standing open while the screen door was closed; the two officers could see the very dim light of a fluorescent grow light over a planter just inside. They could also see that a sliding glass door to what seemed to be a den was standing open, and the TV inside was still on, with only the test pattern on the screen.

Van Rooy and Eggers found no one in the den or in the adjoining bedroom. Beyond that was a hall with three doors—all closed—along it, and another hall just beyond that.

"Nothing out back," Solis commented as he joined them.

The three officers checked the closed doors. One was locked, and the other two led to a second bathroom and another bedroom, both empty. Neither showed signs of a struggle or ransacking.

They kicked open the locked door. There was nothing inside but a laundry room. It was eerie moving through the silent house, not knowing if a murder had, indeed, taken place and, if it had, a killer still waited behind one of the myriad doors.

Solis and Eggers crept down the second hall—which led to the foyer—when suddenly Solis stopped short. "There's a body," he whispered.

And there was. The two patrol officers gazed down at the form of a small and frail woman with white hair. She was prone on the floor between the kitchen and foyer. A large pool of still-wet blood glistened on the kitchen floor tiles.

The patrolmen moved toward a door leading into the garage. That door, too, was locked, but gave with a sharp kick.

There was an old man lying there, crumpled in death beside a parked Mercedes. A copious amount of blood streamed from his head and ran along the floor for approximately eight feet.

In the seventies, there were no shoulder phones, so Van Rooy ran to his patrol car to call radio dispatch and confirm that the report of two homicides was true. Lieutenant

Ivan Beeson, himself a longtime homicide detective sergeant before a recent promotion to the north precinct, left at once to join his men. In the meantime, the dispatcher alerted homicide detective sergeant Craig VandePutte, and detectives Gary Fowler and Dick Reed at home.

It was 2:30 A.M., and none of the detectives would sleep anymore that night.

The homicide investigators parked their vehicles in a paved area just outside the Bramhalls' garage. They were briefed by the officers already at the scene. So far, no one knew who might have attacked the elderly couple. There had been one anonymous call to 911 from a man who would not give his name.

"The den, garage, and kitchen lights were on when we got here," Van Rooy said. "And the sliding door to the den as well as the front door were open. We haven't touched a thing, except for the light switch in the living room."

Sergeant VandePutte took one look at the large house and two separate body sites, and quickly realized they would need more backup. Detective Lieutenant Ernie Bisset and detectives John Boatman and Bill Baughman were also called at home and asked to join the crew in Windermere. They arrived just after 4 A.M.

Gary Fowler photographed the entire home prior to any attempt to remove evidence. The Mercedes was still parked in the garage, but there was space there for a second car, so Dick Reed asked for a check on all vehicles registered to either Burle or Olive Bramhall; it was possible that the killer had left in one of their cars. Word came back from the Department of Motor Vehicles that Olive

Bramhall owned a blue 1976 Oldsmobile Omega. A bulletin was put out at once asking all officers on duty in the city and the county to locate that car.

Detectives studied the pitiful bodies. Burle Bramhall was fully clothed in light slacks and a blue sweater, shoes, and socks. His expensive watch was still on his wrist, but his glasses and hearing aid had been knocked off and lay near the Mercedes. A leather case with keys was almost underneath the car.

The old man's head rested on a board used as a stop for parked vehicles, and it appeared that he had suffered tremendous blows that had literally shattered his skull and knocked his dentures out of his mouth. A half-smoked cigar butt was close by. Was it the victim's? If so, he had apparently been struck unaware—perhaps by someone he trusted. It was bagged and marked as evidence, along with the glasses and keys on the garage floor.

The garage was neatly arranged, with bins for nails, gardening supplies, and tools hung in place, their outlines drawn on a perforated board that lined one wall.

The tiny body of the old woman was dressed in a multicolored dress, nylons, and white high-heeled shoes. She had fallen from the blows to her head so quickly that her hands were caught underneath her body. She, too, had sustained horrendous head injuries. Her wig and glasses had been knocked off by the force of the blows. The back spatter of her blood was medium velocity—indicating that her killer had probably used a blunt instrument of some kind. It had sprayed and splattered the immaculate kitchen as she fell, and then puddled beneath her.

The elderly victims must have been up and awake when their killer arrived. They were completely dressed, and the television was still on. There were no signs at all of forced entry.

Dr. Donald Reay, the King County medical examiner, arrived at 5 A.M. He verified that the cause of death was from head wounds—probably from a blunt object. He checked their body temperatures, and estimated lividity and rigor mortis.

"I think they've been dead about eight hours," he commented. "That would mean that they were killed about nine last night."

As the bodies were removed, Reay said that Burle Bramhall had sustained four blows to the head, almost any one of which would have been fatal to a man of his age. Olive had a wound to the side of her head and one in the back. "It looks like she was hit in the back of the head, fell, and the second wound was administered as she lay on the floor."

It was beginning to get light, and the patrol officers searched the area around the home. Dale Eggers located a large sledgehammer, weighing approximately five pounds, in a vacant lot next door to the victims' home.

It was obviously the murder weapon. There were bloodstains, hair, and what appeared to be brain matter evident on the hammer.

Full daylight dawned as the last of the physical evidence was bagged and labeled. Dick Reed removed the trap from the kitchen sink in the event the killer might have washed his hands there. No one knew about DNA thirty years ago, but if he found blood traces there, they could at least check for blood type, and, if it was different from that of the two victims, they might be able to find the third person—or persons—who had been in the house.

This was a terribly ugly way for two kind old people to die, and inexplicable; although the Bramhalls were wealthy, robbery didn't seem to be the motive. The routine things that thieves take were still in place in the house: televisions, radios, silver, and crystal. Although Olive's car was gone, there were far easier ways to steal a car than to resort to such carnage.

Moreover, both of the Bramhalls still wore expensive jewelry, worth thousands of dollars. It was possible that there were items of great value that had been taken, but they were certainly not obvious.

And no one had broken in. Why would Burle Bramhall willingly admit the killer? They were not paranoid, but they were cautious and it wasn't likely they would let a stranger in after dark.

There were some oddities—a piece of ivy resting on a table in the hall, a blank spot where the poker from the fireplace set was missing. And then it too was found in the vacant lot next door.

At 7:10 in the morning, John Boatman and Bill Baughman talked to the neighbors beyond the vacant lot just to the north of the Bramhall house. The Addison* family members were longtime neighbors of the victims. Cal Addison* and his younger son said they had heard nothing during the night. They had seen that the lights were on in the garage, but that wasn't particularly unusual. As for Mrs. Bramhall's missing car, Addison said that the couple's housekeeper usually drove the car and had permission to take it home when she left for the night after serving dinner.

Now the investigators set out to locate the housekeeper.

The home on the other side of the Bramhalls' house was a mansion that had recently been purchased by the followers of the controversial Reverend Sun Myung Moon, leader of the Unification Church, or "Moonies," a religious cult. Not surprisingly, Windermere residents weren't happy at all to have the "Moonies" in their midst and there had been suits filed against them. None of the neighbors, however, felt that the Bramhalls had had particular difficulties with the oddly dressed Moon followers who came and went from the huge white edifice.

The phone rang in the Bramhall home while the detectives worked and detective Dick Reed answered it. The caller identified himself as the Bramhalls' insurance agent, and he was aghast as Reed told him that both the elderly people were dead.

"I talked to Burle just last week about an insurance policy, and he told me they'd hired a new housekeeper and that she was the best they'd ever had. I called Burle yesterday afternoon and the housekeeper answered, but she said he was outside doing some gardening and that she didn't want to call him in, so I just said I'd call today."

The agent had never seen the housekeeper, and didn't know her name.

Sergeant VandePutte had found a list of emergency numbers in the home, as well as the guest list for a party the victims were planning. One number appeared to be that of the housekeeper, Esme Svenson,* and he checked the reverse phone directory for an address for the woman. An investigator was sent to find her.

Detective Al Gerdes talked to a Windermere resident who reported a peculiar incident he'd observed; sometime around 11:30 A.M. on August 2, he'd looked into the Bramhalls' home and seen a woman he didn't recognize standing between the living room and the kitchen. He thought she was twenty to twenty-four, with long blond hair falling to the middle of her back.

The day shift of homicide detectives arrived at the crime scene. At nine on the morning after the Bramhalls were killed, a roughly dressed man walked up to the Bramhall house, clutching a piece of paper with the home's address printed on it. Bewildered by all the activity, he stammered as he explained that he'd come to do some lawn work.

"They sent me out from the Millionair's Club [a Seattle charity with a deliberately misspelled name that finds jobs for people down on their luck]. I'm supposed to do some cleanup work in the yard."

The man said he'd never been there before, and detectives believed him. He'd simply drawn the wrong time to show up. They took his name and address, checked with the Millionair's Club to verify his story, and sent him on his way.

The detectives checked the basement of the Bramhall residence, but it was obvious no one had been there. Cobwebs still hung, undisturbed, but the blood draining from Olive Bramhall's body *had* leaked through the tiles and then floorboards above and dripped in a macabre pattern over the freezer and on the floor.

At 10:24 A.M., Esme Svenson arrived and learned that her employers were both dead. The stunned woman was asked to look through the house to see if anything had been disturbed or was missing. She agreed to do that at once, dabbing her tear-filled eyes with her handkerchief as she moved through all the rooms.

"Everything's just like it was when I left last night—except for the missing poker by the fireplace."

Esme Svenson gave a formal statement, saying she was apparently the last person to see the Bramhalls alive. *Except for their murderer.* She explained that she had lived in a room in the house for some time, but that she had recently moved to a friend's home in the north part of Seattle. She was obviously the young blond woman the neighbor had seen.

"I've worked for the mister and missus for three or four months. I come to work about ten in the morning, and usually stay until about eight at night," she said.

"When did you leave last night?" Gary Fowler asked.

"It was just about ten minutes to eight," the forty-year-old housekeeper recalled. "I fixed them a nice dinner—steak, salad, and blackberry pie. Then Mr. Bramhall said, like he always does—did, 'Mrs. Bramhall, do you mind if I have my cigar?'

"They went into the den to watch television while I put the dishes in the dishwasher. They were in a good mood because earlier that day, they picked out the cake and flowers for their fifty-fifth wedding anniversary party."

Esme Svenson said that the Bramhalls had a burglar alarm that they always turned on just before they went to bed. "You could hear it all over the neighborhood when it went off. And then there's the security patrol here in Windermere, too."

The housekeeper said that the Bramhalls usually retired about 11:30, after the evening news.

"Have you ever known the alarm to trip?" Fowler asked.

"Only accidentally. Never because there was really a prowler."

"Who else has a key to the house?"

"I do, and I think their nephew in Bellevue does. Nobody else."

Asked to go over the previous day's events step by step, Esme Svenson thought carefully. "I came to work at ten. Mr. Bramhall was in his robe and didn't get dressed until afternoon. I remember they got a registered letter from one of their 'adopted kids.' The mister worked in the garden awhile, and then we ate about seven. I remember because he always watched the six o'clock news first. They would always have their cocktails together in the den, watch the news, and then come to the table."

The woman rubbed her forehead, trying to remember anything unusual about the day before. "Oh, yes. There was a knock at the front door about seven forty-five while we were eating. Mr. Bramhall answered, and I could hear some man asking him if he had a ball-peen hammer. He said he had a small one, and came back in the kitchen and got the hammer out of the closet there and gave it to the fellow at the door."

"Did you see who was at the door?"

"No, I just heard the conversation."

"Did Mr. Bramhall comment on the incident?"

"Yes. He came back in to the table, and said, 'That was so-and-so.' I'm sorry, I think the missus mentioned the name, but I didn't catch it. But I do remember she said, 'He's just been released from a mental institution.' "

"Do you have any idea who they were talking about?"

"Well, I heard them talk before about a boy from next door having some mental troubles. I heard Mrs. Bramhall say that his mother used to have some bad times, and that she would come crying to Mrs. Bramhall and that Mrs. Bramhall helped her the best she could. But the lady killed herself after that."

Esme Svenson stressed that the Bramhalls hadn't been upset in the least on the last night she saw them alive. They'd enjoyed their dinner and then Mr. Bramhall lit the one cigar he allowed himself each evening.

"How about anyone strange in the neighborhood? Anyone you yourself might have seen?"

"Well, there was a knock on the door Tuesday afternoon and I went to the door. A strange man was there, asking for Mr. Bramhall. I told him he'd be back around four thirty. I waited for him to say something, but he just stared at me."

"What did he look like?"

"Young, early twenties, quite tall, casually dressed, with a mustache and a beard."

"Do you know the Addisons next door?"

"I know the couple and the younger son—the one who rides a motorcycle—but I'd never seen this man before."

Esme said she'd cleaned up the kitchen and left, as the elderly couple were watching television in the den. She'd driven home in Olive Bramhall's Oldsmobile. She'd neither seen nor heard anyone outside as she left. She said the garage door closed and locked automatically, and the only time the light was on there was when someone needed to fetch something, since it was dark out there without the overhead light on—even in the daytime.

Detective Dick Reed received a second phone call from the Bramhalls' insurance agent. "I just remembered. Olive Bramhall filed an insurance claim in May sometime for some rare pearl earrings. She thought they'd been stolen by a maid they had back in March."

"Would that be Ms. Svenson?"

"Oh, no. I think it was the woman they had just before her. Mrs. Bramhall felt that the woman was stealing from them and let her go."

That was something to ponder. If Esme Svenson had a key to the Bramhall home, the former housekeeper had probably had one, too, and could have had a copy made. The agent thought the fired housekeeper had moved north to Bellingham.

Detectives Boatman and Baughman talked with Cal Addison next door again, as well as the caretaker and one of the more permanent residents of the Moonie chapter. The Moonies had had a party the evening before and had heard nothing from the Bramhall residence, although they said their relations with the old couple had always been most civil.

Addison said that he, his wife, and his younger son had

been out for most of the evening. The elder son, Rory,* had come home about 5:30 to pick up some clothes and then left their house late with one of his high school friends, Rich Copley.*

Addison admitted readily that Rory, twenty-three, had had many problems since the death of his mother. His first wife had suffered from manic depression. Tragically, after ten years of fighting the chaotic mental disease, she had despaired, and committed suicide in 1975 by jumping from the top floor of a hotel.

Rory had been crushed by his mother's suicide and the brilliant boy had been in and out of mental institutions ever since. Only the day before the double murder of the Addisons' neighbors, August 2, Rory had been released from jail with the stipulation that he undergo "behavior modification" at Western State Hospital.

"His probation officer drove him down there," Cal Addison said, "but I was astounded to get a call from Rory yesterday afternoon about five saying that he hadn't been admitted. He wanted to come home, but I'd been told by therapists that that wouldn't be good for him. I said he could come home and get his things, but he'd have to go to the YMCA, or a hotel. He was here when his stepmother and I left to go out for the evening."

At 5 P.M. on August 3, Rich Copley came into headquarters to talk with detectives Don Strunk and Paul Eblin. Copley said that he had, indeed, spent the previous evening with his old friend Rory Addison.

"He called me about seven thirty and said he wanted to go out. I got there at ten minutes to nine and we went to a restaurant in the University District to have a few drinks. I bought him a hamburger and a milk shake because he was almost broke, and he had to pay for a hotel. Then we just drove around until ten thirty when I took him back to his folks' place."

"How did he seem?" Strunk asked. "Nervous or upset or anything like that?"

Rich Copley shook his head. "Not at all. Rory was in a good mood—better than he's been for a long time. We waited for some of his clothes to get out of the dryer and then we packed up his things and I took him to the Savoy Hotel, where I helped him check in. It's a cheap hotel, and he only had about twelve dollars that his dad had given him."

Copley said that when he first arrived at Rory's home, he saw his friend coming from a trash barrel that was located between the Addison home and the Bramhall residence.

"You were with him all evening?"

"Absolutely. From ten minutes to nine until about midnight. And he even called me a couple of times before I got there wondering what was taking me so long."

The homicide investigators considered the time element. Esme Svenson had seen the Bramhalls alive and well about eight, and Rich Copley came to pick up Rory Addison at ten minutes to nine. At that time, Addison had been cheerful, dressed neatly, and busy cleaning up trash for his family. It hardly seemed possible that he could have committed two such bloody murders, cleaned up, and made several phone calls all in the space of less than an hour.

Add to that the fact that Rory apparently liked the Bramhalls, who had lived next door to him for seventeen years, ever since he was six years old.

Paul Eblin and Don Strunk checked the Savoy Hotel and the desk clerk verified that Rory Addison had checked in at midnight on the second, but was no longer there.

At seven that evening, Rich Copley called again and said he'd heard from Rory and that he was visiting at the apartment of a strictly platonic girlfriend—Sarah Binford.*

"He seemed fine," Copley related. The two detectives attempted to find Rory Addison at the Binford apartment, but found no one at home. They left a card, asking for a call.

They went to the Addison home. They wanted to examine the trousers that Rory was wearing on the night of the murder. They found that the pants were clean and free of any obvious bloodstains. But they realized Rory had been doing his laundry that night, and a cold water wash would have easily obliterated any of the scarlet stains.

Claire Addison,* Rory's stepmother, said she had received information from a friend of the Bramhalls. This was a woman who said she'd talked to the couple at 9:30 P.M. on August 2. This would seem to entirely eliminate Rory Addison as a suspect. He was with Rich Copley at the Blue Moon Tavern at that time. Rory's stepmother gave Don Strunk and Paul Eblin the woman's phone number.

Leads continued to come in to police headquarters from citizens who had read about the murders in stories with banner headlines in both of Seattle's daily papers. One woman reported that she had seen a bearded man carrying what appeared to be a gun walking down the Bramhall driveway on the afternoon of August 2 around 1 P.M.

But many others had seen Olive and Burle alive hours after that. Had the man with the gun returned later? And had she really seen a gun or could it have been a shovel, rake, or other garden tool?

Another informant called to say he had been concerned about two men in a white Volvo he had noticed in Windermere. "They were staring up at the Bramhall house," he said. "Right on that same afternoon of the second."

None of the leads was easy to check out. The second tip, however, was dismissed when the two men themselves called in; they were Realtors viewing the vacant property next door.

Someone—perhaps two someones—had battered the Bramhalls with the five-pound sledgehammer and the fireplace poker. During the postmortem exam, Dr. Reay found that the poker fit exactly into the wounds on Olive Bramhall's skull.

Who could have wanted the kindhearted couple dead? The only logical motive would have been a home-invasion robbery. And yet nothing was missing. The cause behind a double homicide remained inexplicable.

As the days passed, more calls came in to homicide, and there were many new suspects. Detectives traced them to their sources, but none of them panned out.

And who was the man who'd called 911 to report the

murders? He had not come forward. Still, he seemed to be a likely candidate for the "persons of interest" roster.

The probe turned again to twenty-three-year-old Rory Addison, even though he had been virtually eliminated as a suspect.

The Seattle investigators called the woman who'd talked to the Bramhalls on the evening they died. Regretfully, she admitted that she had been mistaken about the time.

"I was going by which show was on television," she said, "but I was wrong; I talked to Burle and Olive at about eight fifteen—not at nine thirty."

That startling information meant Rory Addison's alibi had evaporated. According to his friend's and parents' timetable, he had been alone next door to the victims for almost an hour after their housekeeper left.

Detectives were determined to talk to him, but they were having trouble locating the tall suspect. One night when the night shift came on for third watch, Craig VandePutte, Gary Fowler, and Dick Reed went to Sarah Binford's apartment. She wasn't home.

Next they checked the Bramhalls' house again, this time with a search warrant in hand. They found the couple's wills. Not surprisingly, they had made generous donations to various charities. In their final documents, the childless couple stipulated that everything else they owned would go to their few relatives.

While opening doors, Dick Reed found a small ball-peen hammer in the kitchen's broom closet. That was odd.

If Burle Bramhall had loaned it out the night he died, what was it doing back in the closet?

Esme Svenson told Reed that she was absolutely sure that this was the hammer the "mister" had loaned to someone.

It had no blood on it at all.

The tips continued to flood the homicide unit's phones. A woman who lived nearby in exclusive Windermere reported that she had received a threatening phone call several months earlier.

"I don't have any idea who it was," she said. "But I could tell it was a young male. He told me I was evil. It truly frightened me—but he never called again. I finally figured it was some kind of prank."

She volunteered to listen to the tape of the 911 call to see if it might be the same voice, but she didn't recognize it.

A Seattle transit driver told Dick Reed he had driven a small, dark-complexioned man in "tacky" clothing to the Windermere area on the morning of August 3, and that the man had had a slip of paper with the Bramhall address on it. This was about 8:30. This information was, of course, about the workman from the Millionairs' Club whom detectives had already cleared.

Reed received a call from Cal Addison. "Rich Copley told me he picked Rory up and drove him to the Union Gospel Mission on the night of August third."

A quick check at the mission showed that Rory had been there the second night after the murders. The mission routinely booted out the sleepers early in the morning, and they spent their days on the street, hopefully looking for work.

Rory hadn't returned to the mission. He was keeping one step ahead of detectives.

The Union Gospel Mission employees assured Dick Reed that they would call the homicide unit if Addison checked back in.

Rory Addison's probation officer came into the homicide office, and he was both chagrined and frustrated. "I took Rory down to Western State Hospital on August second," he said. "We were both sure they would admit him, but they just told him he 'wasn't sick enough.'

"The shrink who talked to Rory said he only needed someone to talk to. And more medication. I saw Rory Thursday morning—the third—about eight A.M., and he seemed normal. I looked at him closely, but he seemed completely rational."

His probation officer filled the detectives in on Rory Addison's background. Despite his breakdown after his mother's suicide, Rory had managed to succeed in many areas, and his family had high hopes for him. Until he lost his mother, he looked and acted like a winner.

"He graduated as an honor student from Roosevelt High School," the probation officer said. "He was active in the debate team there. And he was very popular. He went to Claremont College in California, and then he was accepted at Oxford University in England for European Studies. You have to be really smart and accomplished to get into Oxford."

Rory's life was a string of successes, but that all

changed when his mother committed suicide in 1975. He was twenty then.

"When she died," the probation officer said, "Rory began to show signs of manic depression himself, along with paranoia.

"He went back to college in March 1976, and he was doing fairly well. But he hit a depressed cycle a year later. He cut his arm deeply in a suicide attempt. The records show that he had made kind of halfhearted suicide attempts before—but this time he would have died if he hadn't been discovered in time."

Rory had "flipped out" at the hospital and it had taken four men twenty minutes to subdue the six-foot, three-inch student. Terribly concerned, his family had admitted him to Fairfax Hospital, a private institution, and he'd been "very, very sick."

Rory Addison was on an emotional seesaw. It was clear that his family and his probation officer had tried their best to pull him off the emotional precipice where he stood.

"He got dramatically better by July and was able to go back to Claremont," his probation officer said. "But he cut his arm again in October and almost bled to death. He was in a hospital until Christmas and then he came back to Seattle."

Rory's father and stepmother had tried everything to help him. They arranged for him to receive therapy at the Sound Mental Health facility on Capitol Hill in Seattle. He lived in a halfway house. But he'd been violent there, too, kicking down doors.

Rory worked sporadically as a roofer, but he got into trouble for stealing pop and candy from a store. When he was confronted, he struck the manager and ended up in jail.

It was a tragic path for a boy who was in the genius category and had been expected to have a bright future as a lawyer. Rory Addison was put on probation and sent back to the halfway house, but he was picked up for shoplifting in the same store again in June. This time he went to jail for three weeks. Then he was released to another sheltered institution.

He broke probation again and was returned to jail until August 2. His probation officer had been sure Rory would be admitted to Western State that day on the judge's order. He needed help badly.

"Rory was clearly disturbed," his probation officer said flatly. "But they turned him away. I drove him back to Seattle and left him to catch a bus to his dad's house."

Rory had had many friends at Roosevelt High School but his obsession with the "demons in his head" and his constant depression had soon turned almost all of them off—except for the most loyal. Friends like Rich Copley and Sarah Binford kept hoping he would get better.

Even in the midst of his recent troubles with the law and mental illness, Rory talked of going on to graduate school. He'd wanted to go to the London School of Economics and the Institute of International Studies in Freiburg, Germany.

But where was he now? Wandering from flophouse to flophouse? A suicide himself? Detectives tried to locate him at the union hall where he sometimes obtained work as a roofer, but no one there had seen him.

At 6:45 P.M. on August 5, detective sergeant Don Cameron received a call from the Union Gospel Mission. Rory Addison had returned. Cameron and Don Strunk responded at once, and met Rory walking toward the elevator. Asked if he would return to headquarters for questioning, he said he wouldn't mind at all. The rage he'd demonstrated before seemed to be gone.

Advised of his Miranda rights, Rory talked of his activities on the day the Bramhalls were killed.

"I came back from Western State Hospital and took a bus to my house. It was about five P.M. when I got there. I had a sandwich, drank a Coke, and put my dirty clothes into the wash.

"About six, my brother came home," Rory continued. "I called my friend, Rich Copley, about 7:30 and asked him to pick me up. He didn't come until about 8:30 or 8:45 so I read *Newsweek* while I waited. When he got here, I'd just finished dumping the trash from the kitchen."

The rest of Rory's account of the deadly evening was exactly the same as Rich Copley had already given.

"How long since you've visited the Bramhalls?" sergeant Don Cameron asked.

"I haven't been in their house for over two years."

"Did you stop by Tuesday or Wednesday to borrow a hammer?"

"No, sir."

"Did you kill Olive and Burle Bramhall?" Cameron asked bluntly.

"No. And I'll take a polygraph any time you'd like."

Rory Addison was allowed to leave for the moment until an appointment for a lie detector examination could be set up.

Detective Gary Fowler spoke with Sarah Binford. She said he had called her about 12:30 A.M. on the morning of August 3.

"He sounded lonely. He said he was at the Savoy Hotel and wanted me to meet him to have coffee. I didn't want to go downtown, but I met him the next night. We talked about the murders in a general way, and Rory told me he hadn't been around when it happened because he'd been out with Rich."

As funeral services were held for the Bramhalls on August 7, there were whispers among those attending. Some mourners felt that the housekeeper—or *one* of their housekeepers—had something to do with their murders. Others weren't so sure. Some rumors were purely imaginative; others possibly had some basis in fact. Seattle homicide detectives attended the funeral, observing those who were there, listening for some clue, however small.

There was still the trouble with the Unification Church. Detective Gary Fowler received a call from the head of the "anti-Moonie" group, who had been out of town at the time of the murders.

"I received threatening phone calls about a year ago that I felt were from the cult members. They said they would blow me up."

And the Bramhalls had lived right next door to the Moonies.

The housekeeper involvement theory gained more credence when the wife of one of Seattle's richest and most influential civic leaders said that Olive Bramhall had confided in friends at the beauty parlor where she had her wigs coiffed that her housekeeper had run off with her keys.

This was not Esme Svenson, but the woman who had preceded her.

On August 8, Fowler received a call that ended all conjecture about who had killed the Bramhalls.

The caller was Rory Addison.

"Detective Fowler, I have some information on a homicide," Rory said. "Can you come and get me? I'm waiting by the monorail terminal."

Gary Fowler told Rory he would be down to pick him up in a few minutes, and to stay right where he was. Fowler and detective Wayne Dorman grabbed their car keys and ran to the police garage.

Rory Addison waited for them. The lanky young man had a large blue backpack, and a heavy load on his mind. Even before Fowler and Dorman could open the trunk to stow his backpack, he began to talk, his words burbling up under great pressure.

"What do you have for us, Rory?" Gary Fowler asked.

"I killed them—"

Before either detective could interrupt to read Rory his Miranda rights, he kept talking—and confessing.

"Have you looked at the wounds yet?" Rory asked. "When you do, you'll find Mr. Bramhall was hit once on the right side of the head with a hammer and Mrs. Bramhall three times. I used a sledgehammer, a poker, and a rock. He was lying with his head on a board. His false teeth were out. She was lying between the living room and the kitchen, wasn't she?"

Legally, what Addison was giving was a res gestae statement—a spontaneous utterance—which is admissible in a court of law. Still, Gary Fowler interrupted the suspect. "Wait until we get to the station. Then we can talk."

"Yeah. Okay, I understand."

Addison was ushered into an interview room and told that because of his voluntary admission of guilt, he was under arrest. He took this with equanimity, and listened quietly as his Miranda rights were read and explained to him. He signed the admonishment forms.

"Do you still want to discuss the Bramhall homicides?" Fowler asked.

"Yes. That's why I'm here."

Addison dictated two pages of his confession while Fowler wrote. Then he read the pages and signed them.

The bearded genius said he'd started hallucinating about a year and a half or two years after his mother's suicide. He said he'd heard voices telling him that Burle Bramhall knew about several tragic events in advance but did nothing to stop them. Although none of this was even remotely true, Rory Addison's mental disorder had convinced him that it was fact.

"Mr. Bramhall knew about a massacre in Brazil," Rory

said. This is a startling statement in light of the Guyana tragedy later in 1978 in which nine hundred followers of the Reverend Jim Jones had killed themselves with poisoned Flavor Aid.

Rory continued. "And he knew about a skiing accident, too, and a boating accident where six people died. I heard his voice one night when I was trying to sleep. He told me he'd been involved in several poisonings."

Rory Addison said he'd known that he had to do something to stop Bramhall from the evil things he was doing. But, first, he had tried to admit himself to Western State Hospital. Sadly—and tragically—they had turned him away with platitudes and told him to take more medication.

After he was turned down by the mental hospital, Rory said, he'd gone to his father's house and had something to eat.

"Then I sat down on the couch and decided to kill Burle Bramhall. I went over and asked to borrow a ball-peen hammer."

But Rory told Detective Fowler that the hammer he'd borrowed seemed too small to do the job, and he'd put it in the bushes between the houses. He then returned home and sat on the couch, he said.

But voices told him he must hurry to kill Mr. Bramhall before there was trouble.

"I went back and I saw the maid leave. I knocked on the door and told Mr. Bramhall that I needed a bigger hammer. He said he had one in the garage. We walked out there and he gave me a sledgehammer that was on the wall. I swung it at him when he turned away, but it hit the overhead door and he turned around, surprised. I swung the hammer again and he went down. I hit him again and his dentures fell out."

Next, Rory said, he went into the house where Olive Bramhall waited, unaware that her husband was dead. "I asked her for something to eat, and she turned to go to the kitchen. I hit her with the sledge. She fell and her wig came off."

Rory said he'd left the Bramhall house and returned home. Compulsively, he had begun to wonder if the victims were alive, and decided to go back. He was waiting for Rich to pick him up but he figured he had time.

"I grabbed a rock from a rockery in front of Burle's house, and a claw hammer from our basement.

"I thought that Mrs. Bramhall was still breathing so I hit her with the rock and the poker."

Whether either of the elderly victims was alive or not is moot; they were surely dead when Rory Addison left the second time.

"I rinsed off the weapons I used in the wading pool, and then I went to my house to put my clothes in the washer."

Then Rory said he called Rich again and sat down to wait. What bloody clothing was left he'd buried in the trash can—a task he had just finished when Rich Copley arrived.

It was an awful story, a combination of insane fantasy and cold-blooded planning.

Under the centuries-old M'Naghten Rule, a killer is considered sane in the eyes of the law if he can differentiate between right and wrong at the time his crime is committed. Most prosecutors stress that if a killer makes preparations to cover his tracks, he knew what he was doing was wrong.

Certainly, the voices that told Rory Addison that the Bramhalls were evil and dangerous were the whispers of a deranged mind; there was no gentler soul on earth than Burle Bramhall, and Olive had done her best to save Rory's mother when she was so desperately ill.

Yes, he covered his trail. He went out for an evening of drinking and dining even as his victims' blood was sluiced away in the washer at home. He gave detectives a solid alibi in his first meeting with them.

Even with his attempts to cover up his crimes, I believe that Rory Addison's motivation for murder was his paranoid psychosis. Medically and legally, Rory Addison was insane. Although I have written about scores of murder defendants who have claimed to have mental illness, Rory Addison's case stands out as one where I am convinced he did *not* know the difference between right and wrong at the time of his crime.

No one—not the detectives who arrested him, nor his parents, or friends, or probably even the public—could deny that the disintegration of Rory Addison's mind was a tragedy of major proportions. Two innocents died because of it, and a brilliant young scholar's life of potential service was ended.

Rory Addison was eventually found fit to stand trial,

and to participate in his own defense. But he didn't care about the outcome of the trial. Overwhelmed with remorse for what he had done, he pleaded guilty to two counts of murder in the first degree.

He asked judge Charles Dixon to sentence him to hang. He had tried to kill himself in jail by strangulation and with a broken lightbulb. But Judge Dixon could not sentence him to death; Rory had not been convicted of aggravated murder.

Instead, Rory Addison was sentenced to two consecutive life sentences. He would be fifty years old when he completed his two minimum sentences—if he lived that long.

The outlook for a deranged convict in Washington's penal system can be grim. There are not enough beds, not enough competent psychiatrists, and other prisoners detest the deranged prisoners they call "dings."

Where, if anywhere, the guilt lies is an open question. Why didn't the screening psychiatrist at Western State see that the bearded youth before him on August 2 was dangerous and violent, and desperately in need of confinement?

Under Washington State law, mental patients must be judged a threat to themselves or others before they can be admitted to a mental hospital. Apparently, the state's screening psychiatrist didn't think Rory Addison fit either category.

He was wrong.

Rory's father and stepmother, brokenhearted over his egregious crime, vowed to fight for a change in the mental health laws so that no other psychotic will be allowed to act out his sick fantasies. They had done all they possibly could for Rory. Sadly, it was not enough.

The ironic note is that Burle and Olive Bramhall, if they were here to speak, would probably forgive Rory. They fought for the underdog all their lives. All those 783 children Burle saved. The charities they contributed to, the poor they hired. If Rory had come to them, troubled, they would have tried to help, but he didn't come that way—he came to borrow a hammer.

The Seattle homicide unit did an admirable job of solving the murders of the Bramhalls, and they took a violent man off the street, but they took little pride in it. They, too, wished that time could be turned backward, that somehow Rory could have been stopped, treated, perhaps cured, before the awful events of August 2 ever happened.

I have tried to locate Rory Addison—thirty-four years now since the Bramhalls were murdered. He has disappeared into the mists of time. He may not be alive, and, perhaps improbably, he may be living a normal life. He would be close to fifty-five years old.

I have changed his name in this recall of the terrible night of August 2, 1978, because I don't think he had any control of his mind at that time.

And no one listened to him when he tried to get help.

"FIRE!"

Those who set fires deliberately are not necessarily killers. Some of them burn buildings because they are literally addicted to the sight of flames. Their addiction may be sexual in nature, or it may be they have a need to feel power by destroying something. Some need to gloat, knowing that *they* were the ones who caused sirens to scream in the night, that *they* were the reason firefighters rushed to respond.

The motivations behind arson are many: greed, revenge, sexual stimulation, profit through insurance. The motive, not infrequently, is a desire to be a "hero."

Arsonists often insinuate themselves into the crowds that gather to gasp at their conflagrations. That way, they can prolong the thrill they feel.

Some arsonists are merely pragmatic. They are professional fire-starters, highly skilled at what they do, often devising a delayed fire so that they are long gone before the flames actually blossom. They may be doing it for insurance purposes, or in reprisal.

And, of course, there are murderers who use fire to destroy the evidence of what they have done. When they use flames to destroy other human beings, they are extremely dangerous.

All too often, the fire-starter takes victims he doesn't know—nor does he care about that. He himself has no way of knowing how many he will kill. Once unleashed, fire takes its own path; it can grow to tremendous and deadly proportions, for fire is an unpredictable entity.

Still, arson investigators have something going for them. Even though the arsonist believes that flames will destroy evidence, fire is its own evidence. Trained investigators know how to look for their clues in the ashes left behind. What seems like useless rubble to the firebug may actually be a trail incriminating him as surely as if he'd painted bright red arrows to his front door.

Experts have found that most arsonists have limited imaginations. If a certain technique works once, it will be repeated.

Marshal 5, the Seattle Fire Department's arson investigation unit, had long been a shining example to other departments around the United States. They worked cases differently than police departments do, and I was curious to learn how clues could be left behind—even in an inferno—when I asked for permission to ride with Marshal 5.

The arson team was made up of former firefighters who had truly gone through a baptism of flames. They had all seen the tragedies caused by accelerants and the instruments used to torch them.

While I have to admit it was exciting to follow the

sirens and show the pass the fire chief gave me that allowed me into buildings that were "tapped," meaning fire controlled, but still with little licks of blue, yellow, and orange flame trying to creep back, I quickly found out why firefighters are called "smoke-eaters."

Marshal 5 was challenged by a series of fires that began in January 1975. They grew in intensity until they exploded in a veritable "towering inferno." The person who eventually emerged as a suspect appeared to laymen at least to be a most unusual choice. Before they zeroed in on one man, however, the investigators had to look at some of the strangest characters they had ever encountered.

The University Towers Hotel was located at Forty-fifth Street and Brooklyn Avenue in the University of Washington district. When it was constructed in 1931, it was viewed as very modern and soon became a landmark in Seattle. In 1933, the now long-defunct *Seattle Star* newspaper called it "One of the Seven Wonders of Seattle."

Initially called the Edmond Meany Hotel, it was built in the round, so that every room was a corner room. Revamped and remodeled into a plush hostelry, the "Towers" was much in demand by those who sought the finest in accommodations. It had a restaurant, cocktail lounge, ballrooms for conventions, meetings, and banquets, all heavily booked.

New Year's Eve 1974 was no exception. There was a large private party in the University Ballroom and the celebration was such a rousing success that the band was prevailed upon to keep playing until three o'clock in the morning. When the last celebrants left just after three, a hotel employee checked the banquet room thoroughly to be sure there were no smoldering cigarettes.

She was especially careful in checking the table where the last party had sat, but she found everything in order and locked the ballroom.

Half an hour later, Rodger Peck, who worked for a security agency and was on the night shift, entered the ballroom as part of his regular rounds. He found the huge room full of acrid smoke. Peck quickly located the source: flames flickered from a corner of the cloth at the table where the lingering guests had sat. Peck was able to extinguish the still small fire. Luckily, it hadn't had a chance to do any more damage than destroying the cloth itself and leaving a small scorched spot on the carpet. Peck felt the incident was so minor that he wrote "quiet night" for the overnight period on December 31–January 1 in the log that all security guards kept.

There could well have been a lighted cigarette that had fallen on the floor and gone unnoticed by the cleanup crew. A potentially dangerous situation, but Rodger Peck had found it soon enough. And that was especially fortunate because many of the hotel guests were a little tipsy after celebrating New Year's Eve. It might have been a daunting task to wake them all and clear the hotel if the flames had taken hold.

Slightly more than two months later, on March 6, 1975, a man passing the University Towers around 10:30 P.M. looked up and saw smoke billowing from an upper floor.

He immediately called the fire department and alerted the hotel staff.

Assistant manager Ralph Jefferson was in the restaurant when he heard that there was a fire on the sixth floor. He raced to the front desk, where a patrolman shouted, "It's on the eighth, ninth, and tenth floors!"

As the first wails of fire sirens approached, Jefferson joined Rodger Peck in the service elevator and the two rode up to the tenth floor. They split up there and Jefferson checked the eleventh floor. There was a faint odor of smoke there, but he saw no flames. He ran to the back stairway and grabbed a fire extinguisher before he headed toward the tenth floor.

Rodger Peck was already there. The men couldn't find any flames on that floor, either, and they moved down to the ninth floor. Now they could hear the pounding of running firefighters on the floor above them.

Peck ran ahead of Jefferson on the ninth floor and called, "Here it is!"

The manager relayed the information to firefighters, and then joined Peck outside the door of room 904. The security guard had obtained a fire extinguisher, too, and he had already kicked the door partially in; it was splintered in its frame but not quite open. Peck kicked the door again and ran into the smoke-filled room. Unerringly, he headed toward the right and sprayed the extinguisher over the bed. Firefighters, just behind him, had the flames out in minutes.

A tragedy of major proportions had been averted. Oddly, room 904 was unoccupied.

Rodger Peck told fire inspectors from Marshal 5 that he had been able to get into the room by crouching down to the floor.

"There was about three feet of good air," he said. "I was able to spray the flames with my fire extinguisher until your firemen got there."

"How did you know which room the fire was in?"

"I thought it was that room because I went along the hallway feeling the doors. The door to 904 was hot," he explained.

Rodger Peck said he didn't have a key to the room. "We never have room keys, but we do check doorknobs to see if unoccupied rooms are securely locked. I passed by 904 on my last sweep of the building, and I know it was closed and locked at that time," he emphasized. "But it must have been burning then. You know, there wasn't enough time for anyone to open that door unless they had a key and went in and set a fire."

Peck added that a guest who was staying in another room on the ninth floor had told him that he'd gone by 904 about 9:30. "He said he saw that the door was open then."

Investigators checked the registration book for the name of the last occupant of 904. A single man who listed his address as a town in New Jersey had stayed for two nights.

Ralph Jefferson ran his finger down the second column of the register. "He checked out shortly after noon today— he told me he had an early afternoon flight out of Sea-Tac Airport."

An arson fire in a densely populated hotel is disturbing enough; it was even more ominous when fire department investigators learned that a Seattle police emergency operator had received an anonymous call about an hour before the fire alarm call.

"It was a male," the dispatcher said. "No particular accent. He said, 'That hotel that has the law and order convention is going to burn up tonight—you mark my words.'"

Seattle police detectives began an immediate survey of every hotel in the Seattle area to determine which one—if any—was hosting a law enforcement convention. By the time they reached the University Towers, room 904 was already ablaze.

There were two law enforcement oriented groups in the hotel on March 6: the University of California Society for Crime and Justice, and the Northwest Indian Law Conference. It seemed unlikely that any attendee of those two groups would have set a fire. And no delegate from either convention had stayed in room 904.

Marshal 5 fire inspector K. D. Fowler surveyed the flame-involved room. With his trained eye, he determined that the fire had been deliberately set in three places—there were two scorched patches in the folds of the bedspread and another in the window drapes.

Fowler and Fire Department inspector Jim Reed compared notes, and they concurred that there were no combustible materials in the room that might have ignited accidentally. They agreed that someone had held a match or a cigarette lighter to the bedspread and the drapes.

If the arsonist intended to hurt law enforcement personnel, he had taken on a powerful adversary in the Seattle Fire Department.

There may be no other major city where fire investigators work so closely with the police department. Chief Frank R. Hanson organized his Seattle Metro Task Force on arson in June 1975. It included the Seattle Fire Department, the Seattle Police Department, the King County Sheriff's Office, the mayor's office, the Seattle City Council, the Seattle Chamber of Commerce, and representatives of the insurance industry.

All Seattle fire investigators are also commissioned police officers; they have the power to arrest suspects and the responsibility for preparing all arson cases for presentation to the prosecutor. At the time of the University Towers fires, two Seattle police detectives—Bill Berg and Hank Gruber—were assigned to work full-time with Marshal 5 at the fire department's Arson Investigation office.

The fire inspectors did the arson investigations and prevention analyses, while the Seattle police assisted in arson probes and offered the facilities of their crime laboratories and patrol surveillance.

The case before them began slowly, as slowly and silently as a tiny spark that smolders at length before it ignites. As it evolved, however, it would demand much of both departments.

*   *   *

At the University Towers, it would get worse before it got better—much worse. On Tuesday, March 11, only five nights after the fire in room 904, it was quiet and uneventful in the hotel.

And then Morris Babani, the night desk clerk at the Towers, heard banging and crackling noises coming from the mezzanine above the lobby. He asked Rodger Peck to check it out.

Moments later, Seattle police officers J. Hanna and F. Viegas walked into the lobby on their regular rounds. They were an hour into third watch and it was twelve minutes after midnight. Peck leaned over the mezzanine railing and yelled that there was a fire in the mezzanine.

Viegas used his police radio to call for help from the firefighters of Battalion 6, while Hanna bounded up the center stairway to the mezzanine. He grasped the knob of the metal door that led into the mezzanine interior. It didn't feel hot, but as he ran the flat of his hand up to the top panels of the door, he felt radiating heat.

The patrolman opened the door several inches. When no fire blasted out, he opened it a foot. Now he could see several small fires burning at floor level. They were individual fires with widely separated clear spots in between them. When smoke began to billow out from the room, Hanna realized there was nothing one lone man could do, and he slammed the door to keep the flames from igniting the rest of the mezzanine.

He hadn't seen Rodger Peck, and hoped Peck had managed to escape through another door. Hanna ran back to the lobby but he was unable to locate a fire extinguisher.

In the meantime, Officer Viegas took the elevator to the mezzanine. Several seconds had elapsed since Hanna had first seen the fire.

Officer Hanna was relieved to find Rodger Peck just outside the elevator. By the time Viegas opened the rear door to the mezzanine room, the entire place was in flames. He could see that the metal fire door had buckled from the intense heat.

It was 1:15 A.M. when Fire Inspector William Hoppe received the call for a full response to the University Towers.

Firefighters rate the dangerousness of fires by the diameter of the hoses needed to tap it. Initially, the flames on the hotel's mezzanine were referred to as a "one-and-one-half-inch" fire.

But it soon became more threatening. As Hoppe approached the location, driving across the Interstate 5 bridge, he could see a gray haze of smoke floating all around the top floors of the hotel. His radio now reported that a fire was burning on the eleventh floor!

A 2-11 alarm sounded. The head of Marshal 5, Captain Richard Hargett, responded from his home. More inspectors and firefighters were mobilized.

Hoppe looked at the horrific sight ahead of him. The University Towers resembled a scene from the hit movie *The Towering Inferno.* The hotel sign on the top of the Towers was completely obscured by smoke and terrified occupants of rooms in the upper stories were beginning to straddle windowsills. Hoppe saw the pitifully short ropes hastily fashioned from sheets that some hotel guests had flung over the sills.

Substantial billows of smoke poured from a window on the eleventh floor on the northwest corner of the building. He could also see that firefighters had made their way to the twelfth floor as they began to appear in the windows directly above the fire, hoping they could work best from that vantage point.

Bill Hoppe entered the lobby and found something close to chaos. One elevator was out of commission, and a plainclothes Seattle police detective was operating the remaining lift. The indicator on the stalled elevator showed that it was jammed at the seventh floor. Hoppe and Officer Viegas headed up the north stairs to the mezzanine level and from there they found they could follow another stairway to the seventh floor.

Fire had eaten away at the walls of the staircase for three floors, with the damage lessening as they climbed higher. At the seventh floor, they encountered heat and smoke, and they saw why the elevator was stopped there. Someone had deliberately locked the doors open, essentially rendering it useless. They put it into emergency service and Viegas rode it down to the lobby.

Guests, of course, were warned to stay in their rooms, and to place water-soaked towels over the crack at the bottom of the door. The elevator was too dangerous for anyone but professionals to use.

Bill Hoppe continued up the stairs from seven until he reached the eleventh floor. There was no question that someone had torched both the mezzanine and a room high above it. There were many undamaged floors between the fires.

The flames in 1109 had been tapped. Battalion chief Carl Peters had kicked the door down and two firefighters had followed him in with a hose. They were confronted with flames belching from under the bed. When the fire was hit with water, it went up the wall and across the ceiling with bright red flames.

In what was becoming a familiar pattern, it was clear that *two* fires were started in 1109—the fire beneath the bed and another below the desk.

This time, Bill Hoppe realized, they might find occupants with injuries—or worse.

On the seventh floor, two male guests had awakened to the smell of smoke. Almost immediately, they made all the wrong choices for surviving a fire. They'd gone into the hallway and found the passage obliterated by the thick pall of smoke. Attempting to find their way out, they rapidly became disoriented. They panicked. Stumbling, they felt along the walls and accidentally found themselves back in their room. They took deep breaths of the relatively fresh air before plunging back into the hallway.

They found one exit door and pushed against it ineffectively; in their fear, they had pushed it the wrong way. Had they pulled it, it would have opened.

Eventually they found a stairway and started down. The smoke lessened but the heat blasting up was like a furnace. One of the men held on to the banister until it burned away under his hand; he was burned severely on that hand, oblivious in his panic to the fact that the banister was burning. The pair came out on the fire floor—the mezzanine—and were led to safety by firefighters. Later, they would tell investigators that the door to the stairways on the seventh floor was open, allowing an easy path up for the fire and smoke below.

It sounded as if the arsonist wanted more than the excitement of fire: his (or her) technique was escalating. If they didn't find the firebug soon, someone was sure to die.

Inspectors Fowler and Hoppe went through the hotel to determine just how many doors in the building were open during the fire. They found that all the interior doors to the stairwells were closed during the fire *except* for the doors adjoining the center stairwells on the seventh, eleventh, and fourteenth floors. Someone had propped these doors open before the fire started! The Marshal 5 investigators found a small wooden wedge behind each door, and beneath it, an unburned portion of carpet. Each door closed only as far as the wedge. Moreover, burn and smoke patterns on the doors matched to show that someone had deliberately meant to leave these fire-blocking doors open.

They also discovered that all rear doors to the building had been locked from the inside and that someone had purposely opened rear windows and doors leading from the mezzanine level to the rear ground level.

The arsonist had obviously meant for flames from the mezzanine level to sweep up the stairwell and involve three upper floors—trapping the guests on those floors. If the firefighters from Battalion 6 hadn't arrived within

scant minutes of the first alarm, a tragedy of major proportions would surely have ensued.

On the chance that the arsonist was still in the hotel,
the fire department investigators ordered all exits closed
off. Seattle police officers and K-9 dogs helped Inspectors
Fowler and Hoppe in a room-by-room search.

They found no one who didn't belong in the hotel—
either as a member of the staff or as a registered guest.

As the search crews returned to the lobby, a man with a
deep voice phoned the hotel.

"Listen fast," he said. "There's a bomb someplace inside your hotel, and it's set to blow at one thirty A.M."

Since their just-completed search had been very thorough and turned up nothing that could be construed as a
bomb, the investigators tended to believe the caller was a
crank, someone who was making the worst of a bad situation. He was probably just trying to cause more trouble.

Of course, they couldn't be positive of that, and the rest
of the night passed with a sense of new danger.

Fortunately, nothing blew up, and guests, obeying directions to remain in their rooms and suites with the doors
locked, got a fitful night's sleep.

The Marshal 5 team and investigators from the Seattle
Police Department, however, worked through the night.

Three fires in one hotel in less than two and a half months
had to be more than coincidence. And there was a pattern
to the method the unknown arsonist was using. This fire of
March 10–11 had surely been meant to be a huge confla-

gration, and dozens of people might well have died. Despite the immediate response of firefighters, the damage had topped many thousands of dollars for the mezzanine and room 1109, plus the cost to replace three floors of the stairwell. Smoke damage was heavy.

Marshal 5 inspectors and the police detectives assigned to work with them began sorting through a weird assortment of suspects. Some would surely turn out to be red herrings, some the chronic confessors who haunt arson scenes, and, hopefully, one would be the arsonist.

Inspector Jack Hickam, like all of the Marshal 5 team, had once been a firefighter. He and Bill Hoppe fought flames back in the day where there were no protective masks to keep potentially deadly fumes from asbestos and other early building materials from entering their lungs.

I recall Bill Hoppe telling me that those fumes were nauseating, and that he often had to throw up over his shoulder, and keep on pulling smoldering insulation from walls and ceilings. Hickam was quite probably the biggest risk-taker in the arson unit, and he was certainly a genius at figuring out arson fires and how and where they began.

Now Jack Hickam surveyed the mezzanine area with a studied eye. The room was approximately forty by twenty feet, with three entrances through doors—one from a stairway leading down from the floor above. He found the point of origin located at the north wall, about thirty feet west of the north entrance door. There were two small chairs and a lamp, still plugged into a wall socket. The lamp showed no signs of having shorted out prior to the fire.

Two metal floor-standing ashtrays were next to the chairs. The chair nearest the west wall was completely destroyed by fire, and the other chair virtually incinerated.

Rodger Peck had said he was in the room at 11:30 P.M. and that everything had been normal at that time. Yet someone must have propped open the large door to the stairway, creating a strong draft that would take the flames up the well to the open doors on the upper floors.

The University Towers staff was naturally concerned about who might be prowling unseen through the huge hotel, and they were all cooperative. Peck said that he and Morris Babani, the desk clerk, had heard noises coming from the mezzanine just before the fire was discovered.

"We thought at first that the sounds were coming from our catering division, cleaning up after one of the banquets," Peck said.

But the noises had increased, and Rodger Peck said he had gone up the north stairs to the mezzanine—the same stairs that Seattle police officer Hanna had taken minutes later—and he had tried the door.

"I tried the door but I couldn't get it open."

Oddly, this was the same door that Hanna had opened with ease, although the door was very hot to the touch when he reached it.

"I went back to the lobby," the security guard continued. "I took the elevator back to the mezzanine, went through another door. As I walked out of the elevator, I could see black smoke seeping from the top of the fire door into the hall. It was then that I shouted to Morris that there was a fire.

"I ran back to the fire door, got the fire extinguisher, and tried to put out the flames. It's full of dry chemicals and they're supposed to work—but they didn't."

Peck recalled that he'd looked into the mezzanine room and had seen one large ball of fire.

"I had no choice then but to shut the door."

Jack Hickam wondered at the time lapse. He found it difficult to believe that there could have been such an involvement in flames within forty-two minutes—between 11:30 P.M. and 12:12 A.M., when the firefighters from Battalion 6 arrived to fight the fire in the mezzanine. The carpet in the mezzanine room had two pads—one hair and one rubber—which would account for the heavy, black smoke that clogged the stairwell. The type of accelerant used, if any, would be difficult to detect; the room was completely destroyed by fire.

Hotel lobbies are natural draws for what Washington State law enforcement personnel call a "220" or "219 and a half" and California police term "51-50s." These are the unfortunate individuals with mental aberrations that lead them to march to the proverbial tune of a different drummer. Some are homeless; some simply enjoy sitting in public libraries, parks, *and* the lobbies of posh hotels whiling away their time.

Security guards are always on the alert to spot mentally disturbed people who are an annoyance or a threat. Most of them aren't.

The University Towers was no exception with its roster of somewhat bizarre people to look out for.

Rodger Peck had run across many of them. He told

Jack Hickam a few of the more recent encounters. He wasn't sure of the exact date, but sometime between the second and third fires, he had found a little old lady sleeping at the top of a service stairway that led from the fifteenth floor up to the penthouse.

"Can you describe her?" Hickam asked.

"She was just a little old lady. She told me that she was about forty-five or forty-six, but she looked a lot older than that. She said she had no place to stay and that she had been sleeping here in the hotel for quite some time. But I never found her before."

Peck felt sorry for her because it was storming outside, but he told her she couldn't stay up there. The penthouse was very posh. An early owner of the Meany Hotel, Evro M. Becket, had lived up there for thirty years until his death in 1960. Now it was occupied by very wealthy guests who wouldn't be happy to find a bedraggled street person on their doorstep.

Rodger Peck explained that she would have to come down to the lobby, but she could sleep on a couch there until morning.

"Then I told the desk clerk on duty about this old woman and I said she was on her way down. But fifteen minutes passed, and we saw no sign of her," he continued. "When I went back to check on her, she was gone. I looked all over the hotel for her because I knew she didn't come down on the elevator. I finally saw her coming out of the Regent Room on the mezzanine. She told me she'd come down the back stairway—and that's where the fire was later.

"When I got off work in the morning, she was still sitting in the lobby."

The security guard said he had talked to her while she was in the lobby. "She didn't make much sense. I never saw her again."

Desk clerk Morris Babani told Bill Hoppe about another character who'd showed up at the Towers.

"On the night of March tenth," he said, "I was working at the desk at nine thirty when a man came in and asked me for some writing paper. He was about fifty, white guy, with a stocky build, gray hair, and he had a short, full white beard. He wore an army surplus green raincoat, and he had no socks on—only tennis shoes with the toes cut out. He was definitely not our usual Towers guest.

"He went over to the desk in the corner of the lobby that the guards use and started writing a letter."

Rodger Peck came on duty at 10 P.M. After he'd made his first round, he'd stood at the desk and talked with Babani because the stranger was using his desk.

"I saw the man mail some letters in the hotel mailbox," Babani said. "Then I lost sight of him for a while.

"Rodger made his rounds at eleven thirty and reported to me that he found the doors open in 1109 and 1110. He was surprised at that because he said he'd already checked the rooms out and found they were okay. He locked the doors and continued his rounds."

Around 11:30, the oddly attired man came in the front door again and began making calls on the pay phone that was about twenty feet from Babani's station. "I could hear him making calls to hotels and asking about room rates," the clerk said. "He came over at one point and asked me for change for the phone."

Morris Babani was growing nervous about the way the man was acting. "I looked over and saw that Rodger wasn't sitting at his desk in the lobby. This guy made some more calls, and then he asked for more change. I told him he would have to go downstairs to the bar. He did, and came right back up to the pay phone.

"Rodger came from the back of the lobby while this man was still using the phone. I asked him where he'd been, and he told me he had slipped around the corner so he could watch this guy without him knowing it."

"How long was Rodger gone?" Bill Hoppe asked.

"Oh, not long. He wasn't out of my sight for ten minutes at the most."

Babani was sure that Peck hadn't used the elevator, because he would have seen him.

"I told Rodger not to leave me alone in a situation like that one again. The way the guy with the beard was acting, I was afraid he was off his rocker, or maybe was planning to rob me. I was relieved to see him go, but I didn't notice which direction he went."

The desk clerk recalled that he and Peck had talked for a few minutes—and it was then that they heard noises from the mezzanine "like chairs being stacked. Rodger asked me if he should go and check and see what it was. I said, 'No,' that it was probably just Olaf that worked in catering."

But moments later, they heard more noise—this time like breaking glass and something "popping" from the mezzanine. Peck had seemed anxious to check out the noise, and as it grew in intensity, Babani said, "Go check it, Rodger."

Peck had headed toward the stairs and thirty seconds later called to Babani that there was a fire. Officers Hanna and Viegas had walked into the lobby at almost the same moment.

Babani also told Inspector Hoppe that Peck thought he recognized the man with the "open-toed" shoes as the same man who had "attacked him with an axe" a month before as he walked on a nearby street.

"Rodger asked if I thought I should call 911. I told him it was up to him—but he didn't call," Babani said.

Beyond the "little old lady" and the stranger with the white beard, the president of the corporation that owned the University Towers came up with yet another suspect.

"It was about a week before the last fire," the CEO said, "when I spoke with our employees in the Tally Ho Lounge downstairs. They told me they had been approached by a well-dressed man about thirty years old.

"He said he was a fire marshal and wanted to see our insurance papers. When they asked to see his ID, he said he didn't have to show them anything because he was an *Oregon* fire marshal.

"That made the bartender suspicious, and he refused to show any papers to the 'fire marshal.'

"The guy got huffy and said that maybe the police should be called in. That was just fine with our people and they said that was a good idea.

"They were leading this stranger to the office off the

lobby," the CEO said. "But, when they passed the desk, the 'Oregon fire marshal' kept walking—straight out the front door. He got into a 1970 or '71 bright red Chevrolet and he drove away so fast that his tires squealed."

"What did he look like?" Bill Hoppe asked. "Did they get a name?"

"Let me check—they wrote it down for me. "Six feet, one inch tall, clean-cut, wore a three-piece suit, tie, and a camel's hair overcoat with leather trim," the head executive said. "Oh—and they got a license number on the Chevy."

A check on the license number with the Department of Motor Vehicles showed that the car was registered to a man with an address in Seattle's north end. The car, which was financed through a Tigard, Oregon, company, matched the description of the red Chevrolet.

There was more. The registered owner's records had a red flag. Evidently he had a penchant for violent rages; he was known to erupt without any warning that he was about to attack.

The warning noted: "Carries hatchet under his left arm in a holster—also hunting knife in same place."

The fake fire marshal had a rap sheet listing arrests as far back as 1969 for narcotics possession, traffic violations, and DWI. Inspector Bill Hoppe scratched his head as he read about the stranger. He had resisted arrest in each case. His last arrest had involved a high-speed chase after he had single-handedly wrecked a Ballard area restaurant, and his car had finally hit a pole.

No one had seen this man in the Towers since the night

of the phony fire marshal incident. More important, he was able to prove his whereabouts on the night of March 10–11; he was miles away from the University Towers.

There was certainly no dearth of odd suspects. The University Towers Hotel was beginning to sound like it was Grand Central Terminal for weird characters.

Even so, the Marshal 5 investigators kept mulling over Rodger Peck's story. He always seemed to be Johnny-on-the-spot when the fires were discovered. They knew from long experience that the "hero" in a series of fires is often a prime suspect. And when they reviewed an assault complaint filed by a maid in the hotel three days before the first fire, it didn't add much to Peck's credibility.

The pretty young woman—Bernadette Casey*—told Inspector Fowler that she finished cleaning the rooms assigned to her on December 28 about 5 P.M. The weather was blustery and frigid, and she lived some distance from the University Towers.

"I had to be to work really early the next morning," she said. "They were nice enough to let me sleep in an empty room in the hotel."

"Did you know Rodger Peck?" Inspector Fowler asked. "Did you talk to him earlier in the day?"

She shook her head. "No. I didn't speak to him during the day or that evening—but one of the other girls told me that he was asking who I was. I just started working at the Towers."

At 2 A.M., Bernadette had retired to room 509. "I watched TV for a while and then I fell asleep," she said. "I'm a really sound sleeper. But I woke up around five A.M., and somebody was standing beside my bed. They were hitting me on the head with a hard object. I lifted my hand to protect my head, and somebody hit me again. I was really scared.

"Then I started screaming, and the person who was hitting me stopped and ran out of the room."

"Was it a man or a woman?" Fowler asked.

"A man. I saw him outlined in the doorway. He was about five foot eight or nine. I got out of bed and followed him. I don't know what I thought I could do. I watched him as he ran down the hallway toward the center stairway."

Bernadette said she had seen her assailant in profile for a second as he turned toward the doorway. It was light in the hallway.

"He was African-American—or maybe Hispanic," she said as she closed her eyes to bring back what she saw that night. "He had short hair, and he wore a light blue shirt and navy blue or black trousers. He wasn't wearing a coat."

"Did you recognize him as someone you had seen before?"

"I think he looked like one of our security guards," she said quietly. "The one named Rodger."

With the first shock over, Bernadette had still been very afraid. She called down to the desk and in less than five minutes, two other maids and Rodger Peck came to her room.

"He seemed awfully nervous—he was kind of trembling," the maid said. "His voice was really high-pitched. Maybe it's always like that. I don't know."

Bernadette Casey said Peck had actually told her that he knew she suspected him, even though she hadn't said anything like that. He hastened to explain to her that he had been down in the lobby.

She couldn't be sure that Rodger was the person who attacked her, and Bernadette didn't want to accuse the wrong man. She chose not to file charges.

Peck's association with the University Towers hadn't been entirely smooth. He had been reprimanded on occasion for sleeping on the job. On the night of the March 6 fire in room 904, a memo to Peck was waiting for him in an envelope on the night manager's desk. Ralph Jefferson had intended to give it to Rodger, but he forgot about it when the security guard first came on duty. After the excitement of the fire, he remembered it, but when he looked for it, it was gone.

The memo had been a warning for Rodger. It said that if he didn't "shape up," he would be fired.

Was it possible that Peck had found the note, and become angered enough at the hotel management to torch a room?

None of the other employees who had access to the night manager's desk was aware that memo existed. The arson inspectors felt that if anyone other than Peck had taken it, the hotel grapevine would have rapidly circulated gossip that Peck was in trouble.

But no one mentioned it.

When Rodger Peck applied for a job at the University Towers, he had given a job reference from St. Joseph's Hospital in Tacoma that indicated he was a paramedic. In truth, he had been only an orderly.

Marshal 5's arson investigators tried to follow the trail back to Rodger Peck's life before he hired on at the Towers. He had left his St. Joseph Hospital job for unknown reasons. He wasn't fired; he had simply walked away from that job after only three months.

Before his last job in Tacoma, Peck had worked as an orderly in a hospital in Fresno, California. Fresno police had no record on the guard beyond a current traffic warrant.

And suddenly it was as if he hadn't lived at all before that. They wondered if he had used different aliases.

All of the fires in the University Towers had been set in the same fashion; they weren't sophisticated. The arsonist had held flames—matches, probably—to combustibles that were easy to burn. Rodger Peck had discovered them all. In the room fire on March 6, he had seemingly known exactly where to find the fire. He claimed that smoke had come from beneath the door of room 904, and that the door was hot, yet the manager with him said there was no smoke, and the door wasn't even warm.

The investigators found there couldn't have been enough flame involvement at the time of discovery to send smoke through the door cracks. Still, Peck had turned immediately toward the slight flickering of flames as he entered the room.

How had he known so much?

In the major fire of March 11, there were several factors that didn't fit. Peck claimed to have been in the lobby at 11:30, but Babani *knew* he wasn't there. Babani had looked around the lobby for Peck in vain because he was very nervous about the strange man in the cutout shoes. The bearded man could not have set the fire. Babani had had him in sight during the crucial time, except for the few minutes when he went down to the cocktail lounge for change. The fire had been started by someone above the lobby, in the mezzanine.

Peck's excuse for his absence was, of course, that he was hiding "around the corner" to observe the peculiar visitor.

When Peck went to check out the strange noises in the mezzanine, he claimed he couldn't open the door above the center staircase. He said it was locked. It was not locked. Seattle police officer Hanna was able to turn the knob easily a few moments later.

Peck said he'd taken the elevator to the mezzanine. He hadn't—or Babani would have seen him.

Rodger Peck told Officer Viegas that there was a "ball of fire" in the mezzanine. But when Hanna opened the "locked door" he had seen widely separated areas of flames, as if the fire had been started in several spots.

There were approximately twenty minutes when Rodger Peck could not be accounted for. He claimed to have checked the mezzanine at 11:30 and found it normal. The fire had to have started before then to reach the intensity it had when Peck "discovered" it shortly after midnight. His own log put him in the vicinity of the fire in room 1109 when it started.

Rodger Peck lost his job with the security guard agency, but he was a man full of pride. He pretended to the arson investigators that he was merely waiting reassignment. He also became aware that a stakeout had been placed on his apartment, but he gave no evidence that he was concerned. He called Inspector Fowler on March 24 to ask if there had been any progress on the investigation. When Fowler suggested that Peck take a polygraph, he changed the subject as if he hadn't heard.

After more conversations with the arson investigators, Peck finally agreed to come into the Marshal 5 offices and talk to Inspector Jack Hickam. He didn't object to having the interview taped, and actually seemed at ease during the long discussion. The former security guard had easy explanations for everything. He went into great detail about the attack on Bernadette Casey by the unknown man in the blue uniform, pointing out frequently that it could not have been him.

Peck explained how he made his rounds, sometimes taking the stairways, sometimes the elevators. He didn't think it was unusual that all the arson and assault incidents had taken place on the nights he was on duty.

Jack Hickam was a master at interrogation. He had a friendly face and a big grin, and by the time suspects realized that he'd led them down the garden path, trapping them in their own lies, it was too late.

But Rodger Peck wasn't fazed by Hickam's approach. Even as Hickam pointed out all the discrepancies in Peck's version of his actions on the nights in question, Peck continued to insist that he had just seemed to know where the fires were.

"Is there someone mad at you?" Inspector Hickam asked easily.

"I hope not. I hope I don't have an enemy within three thousand miles of here."

"Well," Hickam continued, "I mean it looks like maybe you are finding an awful lot of stuff happening when you are there. Or is there someone mad at you who is trying to make you look bad?"

"Not that I know of. I figured the only reason I find it is because I am there more than the rest of them, but everything has happened when I am there, except that they received one bomb threat when I wasn't there. That should be in the report."

Peck fell easily into the role of an innocent man. He added more and more details that no one but the arsonist should have known. He professed willingness, at first, to take a lie detector test, but then seemed concerned that secrets of his personal life would be revealed.

Hickam assured him that only questions about the fires would be asked. They didn't care at all about the rest of his life. Even so, the ex–security guard began to perspire.

Everything fit. Yet, as with other detectives who face frustration after frustration in bringing a circumstantial case to court, the arson unit investigators were told that, unless they could come up with physical evidence, charges against Peck would not be filed. It was a crushing blow after weeks of work. More than that, they feared a recurrence. The thought of Rodger Peck was uppermost in their minds.

But their hands were tied.

It was almost a year later, on January 29, 1976, when arson inspectors' fears were realized.

After being fired by the security company, Rodger Peck had returned to hospital work. He was currently employed as an orderly in the Coronary Care Unit of Providence Hospital on "Pill Hill," in downtown Seattle.

The charge nurse on duty on the evening of January 29 took a break in the lounge of 5 West. She asked Peck to answer a call light in room 506. Peck nodded obligingly and walked down the hall toward that room.

Minutes later, another attendant smelled smoke. This was, of course, an ominous situation in a ward where oxygen tanks abound. The orderly walked down the hall, sniffing the air so he could locate any fire. When he traced the smell to room 509, he was horrified to find the bed there enveloped in flames. Fortunately, there were no patients in the room at the time.

And there was a hero who rushed in to fight the fire. That hero was none other than Rodger Peck. Peck took over efficiently, extinguishing the fire on the bed before it could reach nearby oxygen tanks, and closing other patients' doors.

Bill Hoppe was working the night shift for Marshal

5 that night, and he left the unit's station near Pioneer Square and was up the hill at Providence in no time.

He quickly deemed the hospital bed fire as arson. He did a test burn on a similar bed linen drape and found that a handheld flame would ignite the spread in one minute and forty seconds. In talking to the nurses and orderlies on 5 West, Hoppe learned that was exactly the period when no one saw Rodger Peck before the fire bloomed in room 509.

There were no injuries, and the damage to the bed-spread and mattress was no more than a hundred dollars. But it could have been a holocaust, in the worst possible location. Helpless patients, many too ill to be moved, dozens of oxygen tanks—and fire.

But again, this was a circumstantial case. No one had seen Rodger Peck in room 509 before the fire.

Although the arson team was sure that Peck was responsible for the bed fire, he was viewed as a hero around Providence Hospital's 5 West.

On March 10, 1976, Rodger Peck was at work on 2 West. In room 230, a patient recovering from abdominal surgery waited for a doctor and nurse to remove stitches from the wound.

As the nurse headed for 230, she didn't know that the patient had unexpectedly gone to have X-rays done.

She opened the door—and was shocked to see that the patient's bed was entirely engulfed in flames. The nurse rushed to the bed, unaware that the patient was no longer in the room. She fought through the flames trying to find the patient and yelling "Fire!" When she finally realized that the bed was empty and the patient was nowhere in the room, she left and closed the door behind her.

The fire alarm box was in room 234 and she pulled the alarm. Then she returned to the room where the fire was.

It was no longer empty, and the fire was only flickering along charred edges of sheets and pillows.

Once again, Rodger Peck had "sensed" just where the fire was when he heard the nurse scream. That was remarkable, of course, because there had been neither flames nor smoke outside the room.

Once again, it was the hero: Rodger Peck. He had somehow reached room 230 and managed to spray the fire extinguisher over the bed until the fire was almost out.

There were many, many rooms on 2 West, but Peck had gone unerringly to room 230. He had finally run himself out of luck. This time there would be no pats on the back, no compliments on his quick thinking.

The arson investigators determined that the cause of the fire was arson. Someone had lit paper from a crossword puzzle book with a match and then held that paper to the drapes around the bed. With the fire burning fiercely, that "someone" had left the door ajar enough so that the flames could gather momentum.

No one on the floor could remember where Rodger Peck was just before the fire started. He was running true to form—he'd been the invisible man before the fire, and then the indispensable hero.

Damage was limited to the mattress, bedding, and the nurse's call indicator. Rodger Peck was like a sniper firing wildly into a crowd, neither knowing nor caring how many might die.

This time, he had pushed his luck too far. On March 11—exactly one year to the day since the last fire at the University Towers Hotel—Inspector Fowler and Seattle police detective Bill Berg arrested Rodger Peck and booked him on five counts of arson. His bail was set at ten thousand dollars.

He went on trial May 25. It is a difficult task to convict someone on arson charges. Peck's first trial resulted in a hung jury. He remained in custody until his second trial on September 3.

By now, Rodger Peck had grown cocky and he seemed to enjoy his time on the witness stand. He was the center of attention, something he had long aspired to. Perhaps he simply could not resist talking about fire. As his defense attorney turned pale and the jury members exchanged glances, Peck regaled the jurors with accounts of the many fires he had witnessed. As he warmed to the subject, he seemed at ease in the witness chair; he apparently saw himself as the definitive expert on fire.

He was so caught up with the sound of his own voice that he convicted himself. After only two hours of deliberation, the jury found Peck guilty on four of the arson counts. On September 27, Rodger Leon Peck, twenty-nine, alias Rodger Bridges alias Rodger Williams alias Leon Rodgers, was sentenced to four life sentences—to run concurrently.

With that sentencing, the Seattle Fire Department's

Marshal 5 team heaved a sigh of relief. Peck had backed himself into a corner. They were always sure that this serial arsonist would be arrested and convicted one day.

But they feared that many innocents might die before that happened.

Rodger Peck was elusive, but he was not particularly clever. His case is an example of how difficult it is for detectives and prosecutors to bring an arsonist to trial. There are many inequities in the system. But with the advent of computers, Internet communication, and security cameras, fire-starters are being tracked and identified much more effectively than ever before.

Rodger Peck has served his sentence and hasn't come to the attention of the Seattle Fire Department's arson unit since he was paroled. But any potential arsonist in the city of Seattle should be forewarned that he is facing one of the most sophisticated and efficient fire departments in the world. Inevitably, all arsonists leave patterns, with the same MOs used again and again.

They also leave behind ashes that are full of evidence to an experienced arson investigator.

AN OBSESSION
WITH BLONDES

The Candy Store was a neighborhood tavern, and the two young Portland, Oregon, women had been there often; in 1975 it seemed as safe as going to a local drugstore for a Coke. The pretty blondes had a beer or two, talked with friends, and played the pinball machine. They watched and kibitzed with the pool players.

There were a few strangers in the place—one a tall, good-looking man in jeans and a plaid shirt. He seemed to be attracted to twenty-three-year-old Marci Brunswick* and made small talk with her while she played pinball. He offered to buy her a beer, but she refused because she had to get home and she didn't really know him. She assumed, however, that others in the tavern knew him because she'd seen him playing pool with some of the regulars.

Shortly after 1 A.M., Marci left alone and walked to her car, which was parked in the lot behind the Candy Store. She'd had a bad cold for a week and she was tired. As she backed her car from its parking space, she heard someone call to her from the rear door of the tavern.

It was the man she'd talked to earlier. She rolled down

the driver's window and waited to hear what he wanted, and then her car stalled. She tried to get it started again as he walked toward her, but the starter gave only a few half-hearted grunts and then died.

"You've probably just flooded it," the man said easily. "Slide over and let me try."

He seemed okay and she was in a jam. Marci slid over. He turned the key and floored the accelerator pedal but the starter barely beeped.

"Looks like you're stuck," the stranger said. "Tell you what, I'll push it back into the parking space and I'll give you a ride home."

She studied his face. He looked harmless enough, and he didn't seem at all intoxicated. It was either accept his offer of a ride home, or go through the hassle of trying to get her car started and probably ending up having to take a cab.

Marci accepted his offer and waited while he pushed her car backward into a space against a nearby building. Then she followed him to the red El Camino pickup truck he pointed to.

She was barely seated before she had reason to regret her decision. The man hadn't seemed drunk at all, but now he was pulling his vehicle out onto a one-way street—and going the wrong way. For three blocks, he raced down the street as she pleaded with him to turn off. She was certain they were due for a head-on collision.

Finally, he turned a corner, and soon they were on the street where she lived. She pointed out her apartment house.

"There—that driveway," Marci said. "You can just let me out there at that driveway."

But the man behind the wheel didn't slow down at all. He kept going until she insisted that he stop his car. At length, he pulled into a gas station, turned around, and headed back to her apartment. She pointed out the driveway again, but the driver not only didn't stop, he stomped down harder on the gas pedal.

At first she'd been exasperated. But now a buzz of fear rippled along her nerves and started her adrenaline going. This guy was obviously a "cowboy," playing childish games with an automobile. He seemed determined to keep her in the car with him. At this point, Marci wasn't worried about being molested or hurt—except in a car accident.

But she knew she wanted out.

She grabbed the door handle on her side and opened the car door partway, preparing to jump. She vacillated a few moments too long, though, and she saw they were going over fifty miles an hour.

The man in the plaid shirt reached out and grabbed her arm, pinning her inside. He read her mind and said quietly, "That would be suicide, you know."

Marci looked down at the ground rushing by in a blur and agreed with him on that one point. If she tried to jump, she could very well die.

Now she had no choice but to pretend to go along with his perilous games. She just figured he would drive her around for a while to prove that he had her under his control. Then she believed he would let her go.

But the tall stranger had other things in mind. He drove north to the corner of NE 162nd and Glisan and pulled into a darkened gas station. This time he didn't turn around. He parked on the south side of the station, where they wouldn't be visible from the street.

He turned to her and said bluntly: "Take off your clothes."

Her first reaction was disbelief. She had a crazy random thought. She had a bad cold and it was a frigid early November night. She would freeze if she had to take off her clothes.

Only then did she face the reality of what he meant to do to her.

"I won't!" she said firmly.

His response was to grab her around the neck. She still had her car keys clutched in her hand, and she thought of scratching him in his eyes with them. But she quickly dismissed that idea, afraid he'd hurt her more if she tried to resist. There were no lights on in the area around them and she realized that probably no one would hear her if she cried out for help.

But she did scream, an ineffective croak because of her laryngitis.

Her captor's face twisted as his expression showed his rage. "I will hurt you if you scream again or try to fight me."

Brutally, he pushed her down on the seat of his pickup and pulled her bra and blouse up. He began kissing her breasts, then he yanked off her jeans and fondled her crotch.

Marci Brunswick prayed out loud; there seemed to be

no way to get away from him, short of divine intervention. Her prayers irritated the rapist.

"Why do you keep yelling for God?" he asked harshly.

"I hoped maybe there was one," she whimpered.

"Well, there isn't. And even if there is one, He's not going to help you now."

He continued to kiss her naked body. Perversely, he told her he loved her.

That was too much. Marci hissed, "No, you don't!"

"How do you know I don't?" he demanded.

"Because if you did, you wouldn't be doing this to me."

The rapist seemed insatiable, and now he demanded that she fellate him, but she protested that she couldn't, that she'd get sick if he put his penis in her mouth. She was seized by a violent coughing fit, and the man relented on that particular sex act.

Marci Brunswick was a slender five foot six and 118 pounds. She estimated that her attacker was over six feet tall and probably weighed two hundred pounds. If she fought, she believed he would kill her. Of the two evils, she decided she would rather be raped than murdered. So she submitted.

He was offended because she lay passively with gritted teeth while he forced himself on her. He complained that she wasn't responding to him like he wanted her to. But she couldn't; it was all she could do to keep from vomiting.

When he ejaculated, his attitude changed radically. He suddenly became apologetic. He tried to explain away his brutality.

"Being nice to girls doesn't work."

He told Marci that he'd been married for five years and learned that women didn't appreciate kindness in a man, so he had decided to be mean.

"But that doesn't work, either, does it?" she asked.

"No," he admitted.

Marci lied to her rapist and said she wouldn't go to the police. She just wanted to go home and forget about what had happened.

Reassured now, he allowed her to get dressed. She couldn't find one of her shoes, and he even lit matches to help her look for it inside the pickup. She'd noticed earlier that the ceiling light in the vehicle wasn't working. She had been able to see him only as they passed under streetlights.

Her shoe mattered little to her; getting away from him was the important thing. As he was busy looking for the shoe, she quietly edged farther and farther away from the El Camino. She wanted to run, but she thought he would chase her if she did, so she forced herself to walk slowly. His moods were so mercurial that he might change his mind about releasing her.

She heard the pickup's engine start up and was tremendously relieved to see its taillights disappearing down the street.

It was after 1:30 A.M. and she had several blocks to walk to her apartment. She cut through yards and walked in the shadows as much as she could in case he came back looking for her. Only when Marci finally got back to her apartment did she allow herself to break down and cry. And then she called her girlfriend who'd gone to the tavern with her. She told her what had happened, and her friend immediately called the Candy Store and asked them who the man was.

No one knew.

Candy Store bartenders and waitresses hadn't seen him before, but some of them felt they might be able to identify him in a police lineup. *If* he could be found.

Marci Brunswick called the Multnomah County Department of Public Safety, and deputy O. R. Pollard responded. He took her at once to the Holladay Park Hospital, where the frightened woman was examined and treated. The ER doctors found motile semen in her vagina, and she had dark bruises on her inner thighs indicating that she had been raped.

Marci was met at the hospital by a member of Portland's Rape Victims Advocates—volunteers who stand by the victims of sexual assaults from the moment a complaint is made throughout the entire investigative and court procedures, giving them emotional support and explaining what they can expect.

Fortunately, there are many such programs in the country, and Portland's is one of the very best.

The preliminary investigation began at once. Multnomah County utilized the team-policing system. Deputy Pollard questioned Marci initially, then passed on all information he gleaned to detective Robert Walliker. Walliker was in charge of following up on all sex offenses. All of Marci Brunswick's underclothing was preserved for lab testing, along with slides from the hospital that might allow the semen stains to be correlated with the yet-unknown rapist's blood type.

In 1975, DNA matching was only a brave new world of forensic science, as yet unknown to criminalists.

But Marci was a good witness. She described her assailant as a white male, five feet, ten inches to six feet tall, weighing between 175 and 200 pounds. He'd had no facial hair and fairly short dark hair, and his plaid shirt was blue and gray, his jeans faded. His El Camino pickup was red to maroon in color, and she picked the 1965 to 1970 models out of a car identification display. She had seen a tape deck in the glove compartment, along with several music tapes.

The shoe that she abandoned in her flight was a well-worn lace-up type, known as a "Get There" shoe. And Marci recalled losing something else—a distinctive hammered brass earring, square-shaped and very large. She recalled the rapist's facial characteristics for a police artist, who put together a composite picture. This was immediately dispatched to all county patrolmen so they could be on the lookout for anyone resembling it.

Marci Brunswick had no idea what the rapist's name was, what he did for a living, where he lived—or any details about him. He had been careful to be only a shadow person.

Detective Walliker's files on recent attacks didn't turn up another suspect with a similar MO or description. Either this was the assailant's first reported rape or he was new to the county.

Unfortunately, the Multnomah investigator didn't have

long to wait before he heard reports of similar sexual attacks in Portland.

It was very early on the morning of November 8, just after 1 A.M., when someone knocked on the door of an apartment house not far from the site of the attack on Marci Brunswick. Eleven-year-old Hank Jenner,* his thirteen-year-old sister, Nadine,* and four-year-old sister, Reecie,* were home alone. Hank woke first and went to the door. He'd been warned not to open the door to strangers, but he was half-asleep and too short to peer through the peephole high up on the door. His mother was out for the evening and he just assumed she had forgotten her key.

As the door swung open, he saw a man standing there, a man he didn't know. The stranger seemed to be in a hurry as he asked if Hank's parents were home.

"No," the drowsy youngster answered.

"Is there anyone else here? Anyone older?"

"My sisters are here."

The man explained that it was very important that he talk with the older sister and the little boy let him in. He strode past Hank into a bedroom where Nadine lay sleeping. Reecie was sound asleep beside her.

Nadine woke to find the stranger hovering over her bed.

"Your parents have been in an accident," he said bluntly. "Your father is in very bad shape, but your mother's only slightly hurt. I've been sent to take you to the hospital. Your mother needs you there."

It is one of the oldest—and cruelest—ruses used to lure children into the hands of attackers. This is also one of the examples used most often by teachers and parents to warn children.

But Nadine Jenner had been awakened from a sound sleep and the man's words filled her with anxiety. If her mother needed her, she would go.

"I'll get dressed," she told the strange man. And he left her room as she threw on her clothes. As she stood half-naked, preparing to put on her bra and blouse, the man walked back in. She was peripherally aware that he was watching her, but her concern for her parents overrode any feeling of uneasiness she had. She knew her mother had gone with a date to a business dinner, and not out with her father. The Jenners were divorced. Nadine figured that the hospital probably thought both the injured people were her parents.

She fumbled for her shoes and the man said, "Never mind your shoes. Your mom wants you down there *now*!" Stocking-footed, she followed him to a red El Camino pickup parked at the curb in front of her apartment house.

Nadine looked older than an eighth grader. Even though she was only five feet tall and weighed just 103 pounds, her body was quite well developed. As the El Camino hurtled through the dark streets, she tried to question the man at the wheel about the accident.

"Your dad's all torn up," he responded, "and your mom told me to get you because I can get you there quicker than the police."

"Who *are* you?" she asked, more awake now from the cold night air coming in her window.

"I was at a party with your mom."

Nadine was puzzled. His clothing certainly wasn't what people wore to parties. Her mother had been all dressed up when she left. This man wore dark blue pants and jacket and a light blue shirt. His outfit was like a gas station attendant would wear. There was a patch over his right breast pocket that said HUSKY.

He was staring at Nadine now, especially as they passed under streetlights. "Your mother talked about her beautiful daughter."

Nadine didn't say anything. The man made her nervous.

They drove south first, and then eastbound for several miles. She looked for a hospital, but she didn't see any, or, for that matter, any signs that had a hospital image on them.

Suddenly the pickup pulled into the parking lot of a veterinary hospital. Once the man had parked, he dropped all semblance of being a messenger sent to take Nadine to the hospital. He stared at the pretty blond teenager who was cowering against the passenger door.

And then he told her in gutter terms what he was going to do to her.

He reached for her breasts and touched them roughly, telling her he'd heard she was very well endowed. She screamed as loud she could, but the stranger quickly clamped one hand over her mouth, and slapped her with the other.

"I will kill you," he growled, "if you don't stop screaming."

Nadine was virtually immobile from fear, and she didn't fight back any longer. The man took off all of her clothes and attempted to have intercourse with her. Not surprisingly, the girl barely in her teens was a virgin, and his efforts to penetrate her failed. Disgusted, he ordered her out of the vehicle.

"Lie down there," he ordered.

She looked at the spot he indicated and saw a pile of rough boards, studded with nails and filthy.

"There're too many boards," Nadine protested.

"Well, move them!" he said.

"I can't move them," she sobbed. "There's too many."

"Well, then suffer."

And suffer she did, subjected to various deviant sex acts that probably have given her nightmares ever since. Now her terror was mixed with pain and her mind mercifully blanked out many of the details of the attack. ER doctors who examined her later would detect signs of gross perversions inflicted on the helpless thirteen-year-old.

Nadine was sure the man would kill her when he was finished with her, so she was surprised to find that he was going to allow her to get dressed again. He ordered her into the pickup. Huddled in her corner of the front seat, she wondered where he was taking her next.

The man's voice was gentler now. He seemed almost solicitous for her well-being. He asked her if she was going to tell her parents. That was the first hint that she might see her parents again. She knew that a "yes" answer might mean her death, so she lied and said, "No."

Her answer elated the man in the blue shirt. He told her she was "simply outrageous!" a then-current compliment.

"You're really sharp," the man continued. "Will you forgive me?"

"Maybe," she hedged, knowing she'd never forgive him but afraid to say so.

Encouraged, the rapist said, "I'll be your man if you want to be my girl."

The very thought of any continued relationship with this man unnerved Nadine. She burst into tears. He didn't press the matter but apparently he believed her when she said she wouldn't tell anyone because he drove her to the front of her apartment building. When he let her out, he asked again if he could call her up sometime.

She said something under her breath and ran as fast as she could for the front door.

It was 3 A.M. Nadine's mother had been home for only a few minutes. She was beside herself after hearing Hank's chilling description about how Nadine had left with a man to go to the hospital because of an "accident." Horror-struck, Jesse Jenner* had been debating what to do when Nadine, sobbing and hysterical, burst in.

Her mother called the sheriff and then drove Nadine to Holladay Park Hospital. Deputy Tim DeBauw met them there. The ER crew at Holladay told Debauw that Nadine hadn't been damaged physically except for the cuts on her back from the scrap, nail-studded lumber on the ground where her abductor initially attempted to force inter-course, and a number of purpling bruises.

They were more concerned about Nadine Jenner's emotional state. They were having difficulty quieting her hysteria. She was in no condition to be questioned at the moment. Jesse Jenner comforted her daughter.

And then Nadine seemed to pull herself together through force of will. She wanted to help the investigators find the man who had lied to her and then attacked her.

She described the man right down to the HUSKY emblem on his shirt. She knew that his pickup truck was either an El Camino or Ranchero, red with a dark interior. It had a bench seat in front and a "crummy" tape deck mounted in the glove compartment.

"The same tape played the whole time," she said. "It was kind of a country-western and rock-and-roll combination."

Nadine was sure there had been no canopy on the pickup's bed, but she thought she'd seen a tire in the back.

"It wasn't too dirty inside—but it didn't smell new," she said. "You know, like a new car smells."

Detective L. Pike worked on a composite picture from Nadine Jenner's later description. She was able to take Deputy DeBauw and Detective Pike to the exact location behind the veterinary hospital where the attack had taken place.

"Right there," she said, pointing. "That's where he hurt me."

They saw the boards she was forced to lie on, and marveled that Nadine hadn't been cut more than she was.

There were tire marks in a grassy area nearby that confirmed that a vehicle had been parked there recently, but grass isn't conducive to clear, identifying photographs or moulages.

They found a damp cigarette butt next to the tracks. The investigators bagged and labeled it, but, again, this was long before DNA could be extracted from any body fluids left behind by a criminal.

Although she felt safe when the detectives were with her, Nadine was desperately afraid the rapist would come back. She said he seemed to know everything about her family.

"While he was hurting me," she said, "he even threatened me that if I didn't cooperate, my little sister, Reecie—she's only four—would be next."

Detective Walliker and his team were gearing up to canvass all the Husky gas stations within a ten-mile radius when another report came in at 8:30 A.M. This was only five hours after Nadine's report. Deputy Frank Hannah had taken this latest complaint, and the modus operandi, the attacker's description, *everything,* matched what Nadine Jenner had told the sheriff's men.

The newest victim was nineteen-year-old Sonia Lindell.* The strawberry blonde reported that a man had followed her car as she drove home from a babysitting job at 5:15 that morning. He had pulled his red pickup into her driveway and parked behind her.

"The driver got out," Sonia said, "and he followed me to my front door. I wasn't aware how close behind me he was—not until we were just inside my own doorway. He asked me if my husband was home. I was startled and I answered too quickly. I told him that I didn't have a husband. That was the wrong thing to say."

Evidently, that was all the man needed to know. "He put his hand over my mouth when I started to scream and grabbed me in a headlock. I think that's what it's called.

And then he said he would break my neck if I didn't do what he said."

The man ordered her to remove her clothing, but she stalled, saying an elderly relative lived with her and might come downstairs any minute.

Her ruse didn't work. Instead of leaving her alone, the stranger grabbed Sonia and forced her to go with him.

"I only weigh ninety-two pounds, and I had no choice but to do what he told me," she said. "He led me out to his El Camino pickup, and told me to crouch down on the floorboards."

Sonia Lindell was a victim of odds; lightning isn't supposed to strike twice in the same place, but Sonia Lindell had been raped once before. And now it looked as if it was going to happen again. For her, a sexual attack could be fatal. Her health was not good. She had painful rheumatoid arthritis *and* a skin condition that resulted in hemorrhaging if even slightly more than normal pressure was exerted on her skin's surface. Doctors had told her that she had to avoid any trauma or else they couldn't promise her survival. If somehow, some way, she couldn't talk this huge man out of hurting her, she was as good as dead or disabled.

As they drove along, the man looked sideways at her and said, "Do you know what I'm going to do to you?"

"No," she lied.

"Are you sure you don't know?" He was having fun playing with her like a cat with a mouse.

"No, I don't."

"I'm just going to rape you," he promised, as if such a statement would ease her mind.

TWO STRANGE DEATHS IN CORONADO

Becky Zahau was a beautiful Burmese woman, the girlfriend of an industry giant. She died far too young.

Jonah Shacknai's innovative sense and business acumen made him a billionaire at a comparatively young age. He also suffered unbelievable tragedies.

Maxfield Shacknai was bright and loving, a little boy who was entranced with soccer. He suffered a mysterious accident in his father's mansion in July 2011.

Although Dina Romano and Jonah Shacknai divorced, they shared a deep love for their son, Max.

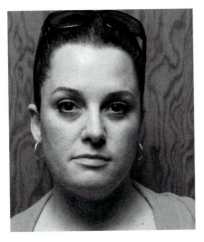

Nina Romano was Dina's twin sister, although they were not identical. One of them was outside the Spreckels Mansion the night Becky died.

Rebecca Zahau was born in Burma, but her family fled to Germany after her father was harassed for his religious beliefs. She came to America to be married, but it proved to be a sad mismatch. (*Zahau family*)

Mary Loehner and her sister Rebecca Zahau at the beach. Mary and her family are trying their best to find some kind of justice for "Becky." They don't believe she committed suicide. (*Zahau family*)

Becky Zahau and Jonah Shacknai had vastly different backgrounds but they seemed very happy together. She loved him—and *not* his money.

Adam Shacknai, Jonah's younger brother, was a tugboat captain in Memphis, Tennessee. He rushed to his brother's mansion as soon as their father called to tell him that Max had been critically injured. He was in the guesthouse of the mansion and Becky was in the main house on the night she perished. Adam called 911 and asked for help for her.

The front entrance to the Spreckels Mansion with police crime scene tape.

An aerial view of the Spreckels Mansion in Coronado, California, marking the main house and the smaller structures.

San Diego County sheriff's investigators and Coronado police detectives walk along a driveway on the murder site's grounds. Detective sergeant Angela Tsuida, in the center wearing tan slacks, was appointed to head the probe for the sheriff.

The lavish Spreckels Mansion was a Coronado showplace that once hosted the future Duke and Duchess of Windsor, Edward VIII and Wallis Simpson.

Broken chain where the chandelier hanging over the foyer—two floors down—snapped or was cut and Max fell.

Landing where Max fell. Looking down to the foyer. Max may have been going too fast on his scooter. It was found beside him two floors below.

Max and Jonah, father and son, posing together.

Becky Zahau's driver's license from Arizona, where she worked as an ophthalmologist's surgical assistant.

ARIZONA
Driver License

Number   D06141419
Expires   03/15/2044
Date of Birth 03/15/1979
Issued   08/01/2008

REBECCA M
6901 E CHAUNCEY LN APT 3149
PHOENIX AZ 85054-5145

Class D   Sex   F
Eyes BRO   Height 5-04
Hair BK   Weight 105

Table with broken leg. Adam said he pushed it over beneath where Becky was hanging and managed to cut her down.

A cryptic message painted on the outside of the door to Becky Zahau's office/spare room. SHE SAVED HIM CAN YOU SAVE HER. No one ever discovered who wrote it or what it meant.

A reddish-orange towrope for waterskiing tied to the white iron frame of the bed in Becky's office. Note paintbrush and criminalist's marker.

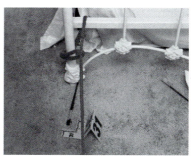

The towrope stretched from the white iron bed leg, across the floor, over the railing, knocking down a chair on the way. Did Becky Zahau tie herself up with it and deliberately plunge over the high wrought iron railing? Was she even up there in her last moments of life?

DOUBLE DEATH FOR THE KIND PHILANTHROPISTS

Probers learned that Mrs. Olive Bramhall met death as she approached her kitchen to prepare food for the maniacal killer

Olive Bramhall was struck from behind as she walked toward her kitchen to prepare a snack for someone she trusted. She and her husband, Burle Bramhall, were a happy, elderly couple who still enjoyed their lives when they were murdered. (*Police file*)

Burle Bramhall kept a full supply of tools. He liked to fix things around the estate where he and Olive lived. Unwittingly, he loaned the death weapon to his killer. Detectives found the bare spot on his wall of tools with an outline traced in the pattern of a sledgehammer. (*Police file*)

The lifelong philanthropist didn't have a chance against his much younger attacker. His body lay in his garage, next to his Mercedes. (*Police file*)

Wealthy industrialist Burle Bramhall was bludgeoned to death in his own garage. One of the family's two cars was missing

Photo of Dick Reed, Seattle homicide detective, who was called out from home to investigate the Bramhalls' murders.

An aerial shot from a police helicopter of the Bramhalls' mansion and grounds. They lived there for many happy years, unaware of how close danger was to them. (*Police file*)

The fireplace and indoor garden in the Bramhall home. The killer used the fireplace poker to murder Olive, and a five-pound sledgehammer to murder Burle. (*Police file*)

FIRE!

The University Towers Hotel's fire belches smoke and flames as Seattle firefighters scale ladders on two sides of the building, trying to reach anxious guests who stand in their windows. Arson investigators soon found that this was not an accidental fire, and they questioned a number of possible suspects.

Marshal 5 investigator Bill Hoppe of the Seattle Fire Department. Hoppe was the first on the scene to probe the rapidly burning fire at the University Towers Hotel. (*Ann Rule*)

AN OBSESSION WITH BLONDES

Retired Multnomah County, Oregon, sheriff's detective Bob Walliker and his dog Cody. Walliker headed the sex crimes unit for many years and tracked and arrested the suspect who stalked pretty blond victims. (*Bob Walliker*)

THE LAST VALENTINE'S DAY

Dina Peterson walked to a pizza parlor with a girlfriend, went in her front door, and exited out the back. Relatives heard a "scuffle" in the backyard but believed it was Dina with a friend. They never saw her alive again. It would take more than three decades to find Dina's killer. (*Police file*)

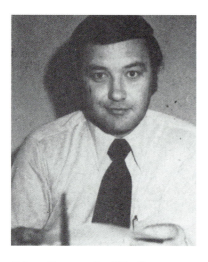

King County sheriff's lieutenant Richard Kraske, who directed the investigation into Dina Peterson's murder. (*Ann Rule*)

King County sheriff's detective Randy Hergesheimer worked tirelessly to find Dina's killer. Sadly, he did not live to see the murderer arrested and convicted. (*Ann Rule*)

Dina's body was found in her own backyard—only a few feet from her home. Her little dog had stayed with her all through the chilly night. (*Police file*)

This man had a huge crush on Dina Peterson when they were both teenagers. For years, investigators focused on Dina's boyfriend—not this man. But the convicted murderer wanted her so badly that he stabbed her to death. With someone else's knife. (*The Seattle Times*)

THE MAN WHO LOVED TOO MUCH

Sue Ann Baker was a popular bartender in a Seattle cocktail lounge. The staff there grew worried when she didn't show up for work on Halloween. Nor did she come to the Halloween party that she had organized and promised to supervise that evening. (*Police file*)

Seattle police homicide detective Dick Sanford worked with fellow detective Gary Fowler to find the suspect who had killed Sue Ann and then laid her out like a dead princess under a coverlet of roses in her bed. (*Ann Rule*)

Ted Fonis was one of the team of Seattle Police Department detectives who investigated the murder of Sue Ann Baker. (*Ann Rule*)

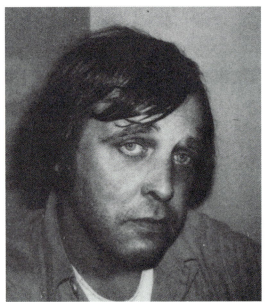

The man who claimed to love Sue Ann, but lived to regret mightily what he had done to her. (*Police file*)

TERROR ON A MOUNTAIN TRAIL

Mark Leslie Rivenburgh, twenty-nine, an army Ranger whose commanders found him exceptionally proficient and dedicated. This is a booking photo after he was arrested for sexually attacking two young female hikers on Washington State's Mount Rainier. (*Police file*)

Mark Leslie Rivenburgh at sixty. After his release from prison on sexual offense charges, he reoffended, this time committing murder. (*Prison file*)

All the entrances to Mount Rainier National Park were blocked in an attempt to trap a wanted sex offender inside the park. (*Police file*)

NO ONE KNOWS WHERE WENDY IS

Wendy Ann Smith seemed to vanish instantly in the dusk of a summer day. She was only nine years old, and she still trusted almost everyone. (*Police file*)

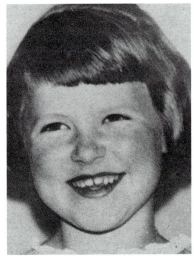

Anne Marie Burr vanished from her home in Tacoma, Washington, in 1963. Investigators who were searching for Wendy remembered her. She has never been found, and the circumstances of her disappearance were very similar to Wendy Ann's. Tacoma is close to the U.S. Army's Fort Lewis. (*Police file*)

This young man was one of the most helpful in Wendy Ann's family's neighborhood when search parties were formed to look for her. He was so eager to assist that he sometimes got in the way, being always underfoot. (*Police file*)

The man pulled over to the side of the street a few blocks from her home and parked, and, true to his pattern, he told her to remove clothes.

Sonia decided to try the truth on him; she had nothing to lose. She told him she'd been raped before, and that she had a medical condition that would be serious if she even tried to resist him.

Suddenly his attitude changed. He seemed to believe her and questioned her closely about her condition, which she explained to him. He appeared to be concerned.

"The only reason I have to rape you," he said, "is because I've never raped anyone before. I guess I was curious."

Sensing the change in his attitude, Sonia pressed her advantage, asking him about his problems. He responded to her concern and asked her if she would mind going to a restaurant to have coffee and talk. He smelled slightly of alcohol but didn't seem to be intoxicated. And Sonia Lindell had little choice. At least they would be around other people in a café.

She quickly agreed and they drove to a Fancy Dan's restaurant, where they talked about her abductor's marital problems. Bizarrely, the stranger seemed to Sonia to be a completely different person now. He talked on and on about his ex-wife, and his disappointment that his marriage had broken up.

He apologized for threatening to rape her and she accepted his apology, wondering what was going to happen next.

"He told me first that his name was Tom," Sonia told the

investigators. "But then he told me his name was Ernest. He said he worked at a Husky truck stop near Troutdale. And then he actually asked me for a date tomorrow night!"

Strange as it seems, it isn't that unusual for a rapist to convince himself that his victim will want to see him again. It may be a manifestation of ego, or only a reflection of what detective Bob Walliker called "the male chauvinist rapist."

"These guys seem to believe that women are 'just asking for it' and will naturally be more than glad to see the attacker again."

"Tom/Ernest" had seemingly forgotten how he had "met" Sonia and had become quite charming.

It was daylight now. Sonia debated running to the ladies' room and hiding, but there were only a few women working in the café. He could easily overpower any of them.

She didn't recognize it, but Sonia Lindell was suffering from shock and her thinking was skewed. In that blurred shock state, she contemplated how normal her captor now acted, even convincing herself that he hadn't *really* intended to rape her.

Incredibly, she took a chance and let him drive her home. He made no attempt to harm her and went directly to her apartment, even opening the car door politely.

Once she was safely inside with a locked door between them, Sonia realized what a stupid choice she had made; she felt lucky that Tom/Ernest hadn't driven her out into the country, raped her, and possibly even killed her. She waited until she stopped shaking before she called to report her strange and terrifying night. Deputy Hannah responded at once.

Hannah, aware of the first report that DeBauw had handled, now contacted his fellow officer and told him that a very similar suspect had told one victim that he worked at a truck stop in Troutdale.

The "team policing" approach gives field officers more responsibility in investigative work. The deputies follow up on complaints in many instances instead of referring all investigative work to detectives in the Investigation Unit. DeBauw and Hannah contacted the truck stop manager and learned he did have an employee named "Ernie" who drove a red El Camino.

"Ernie called in sick this morning," his boss said.

The suspect's employer told the detectives that "Tom" was actually Ernest Leroy Donatelli Jr.,* twenty-four. The investigators obtained his address from the station manager, drove there immediately, and located Ernest Donatelli Jr. He matched the descriptions given by the three victims they knew about. Advised of his rights under the Miranda rule, he agreed to be transported to precinct headquarters for questioning.

Donatelli seemed completely baffled that Sonia Lindell had reported him. "I followed her home early this morning, and I asked her out for coffee," he said easily. "I can't understand why she would say I raped her or anything like that. I wasn't rough with her at all."

Bob Walliker arrived to continue the interview and Donatelli agreed to have it taped. Walliker began by questioning the suspect about the most recent complaint, the one filed by Sonia Lindell.

Donatelli continued to appear shocked that Sonia had reported him.

"I just saw her driving and she waved and smiled at me. She seemed so friendly that I followed her all the way home. I wasn't looking for sex, and all we did was have a conversation. When I went to her front door, I asked her if she was hungry and invited her out for a bite to eat."

As Walliker's questions grew more intense, however, Donatelli grudgingly admitted that perhaps the woman had been frightened, and that the thought of sex with her might have crossed his mind.

"But I didn't want to force her, you know," the suspect said. "I do kind of recall her saying, 'If you're going to rape me, go ahead. I'm not going to resist you.'

"But I *wasn't* going to rape her. I don't even know why she said that."

Again, he disclaimed any use of force.

"I don't know why she just happened to take her clothes off."

He finally admitted that he had intended to rape Sonia and said he felt "sorry" about that.

When Bob Walliker asked about the incident following an evening at the Candy Store Tavern, Ernie Donatelli admitted that the attack on Marci Brunswick had taken place the way she'd described it. However, his phraseology on all of the sexual attacks was decidedly euphemistic: he had not "raped" his victims; he only "had sex" with them.

He said he had watched Nadine Jenner walk in and out of her apartment house and found her very attractive.

"I thought she was much older," Donatelli said. "I didn't know she was only thirteen."

The tall, good-looking suspect said he had separated recently from his wife of five years and had suffered from sexual deprivation since. His method for relieving this had obviously not proved either socially or legally acceptable.

Donatelli's clothing at the time of his arrest showed mud on the knees of his blue work pants and on the lower right leg. Lab tests on his clothing showed a positive reaction for semen on the shirt and underwear along with blood smears of type A blood. That was Nadine Jenner's type, although it is a very common classification.

Walliker and Oregon State crime lab criminalist Bonnie Garthus processed the red El Camino. It proved to be a virtual treasure trove of physical evidence. Although Marci Brunswick's shoe had disappeared completely, her square hammered brass earring still lay, apparently undetected by Donatelli, just behind the seat. Acid phosphotase tests on the car's seat turned the characteristic bright reddish-purple that indicates a positive reaction for semen. The investigators found head and pubic hairs. The tape deck still had the tape engaged that Nadine had described. There was a tire in the truck bed.

And the vehicle's overhead light had been deliberately removed so that it would have been difficult for an unwilling passenger to observe the suspect's face.

Donatelli's three fair-haired victims picked his mug shot from a lay-down of photos that Bob Walliker showed to them. Walliker had built a tight case against the sexual predator and there was no way he could deny the attacks. Instead, Donatelli chose to go the "insanity" route in his defense. He was examined by psychiatrists who said he did indeed regret the attacks but that his regret seemed to be normal. "It's the regret that any man would feel at getting caught for his crimes," one psychiatrist said succinctly.

Perhaps to beef up his insanity claims, Donatelli attempted suicide in the Rocky Butte Jail. He succeeded only in breaking his leg and was forced to appear in court in a cast and on crutches.

The man who had demonstrated his anger and hostility toward his estranged wife by terrorizing three female strangers pleaded no contest to two counts of first-degree rape (in the cases of Marci Brunswick and Nadine Jenner) before Circuit Judge Roth on February 6, 1976. On March 16, Judge Roth sentenced Ernie Donatelli Jr. to twenty years in prison, to run concurrently with another twenty-year sentence.

He also had to pay reparations to his victims. In more cases than not, Oregon courts awarded rape victims restitution in amounts ranging from five hundred to three thousand dollars, one more deterrent, hopefully, for the men who considered any attractive woman alone and vulnerable as fair game.

Ernie Donatelli Jr. served his sentence and was released decades ago. As I attempted to find his whereabouts today, the Internet did not list his address or even the state where he lives. I am troubled, however, to discover in a national gun control register that Donatelli recently applied for a gun permit. And it was granted.

Somewhere in America, Ernie Donatelli Jr., who would be in his sixties now, is carrying a deadly weapon. One would hope that he no longer feels a sense of entitlement that spurs him to fixate on helpless women and act on his obsession.

THE LAST
VALENTINE'S DAY

It was Valentine's Day 1975 when an inexplicable homicide occurred in one of Seattle's northern suburbs. The vast majority of murders have some kind of motive—even though it may not be obvious in the beginning—but there seemed to be a total lack of rhyme, reason, or motivation in the brutal death of sixteen-year-old Diana "Dina" Peterson. Stymied, King County sheriff's detectives worried that Dina's death might well end up in the "Losers File"—an outcome they all detested. Their efforts to solve one of the decade's most baffling murders kept circling in frustrating spirals, and they seemed to be no closer to solving it than they were in the beginning.

This homicide did land in the sheriff's cold-case file. I originally wrote the story for a magazine way back in 1975, even though it had no ending, hoping that maybe someone would read about what happened and come forward with information that could help.

But no one did. Not then.

*   *   *

377

George and Leanne Peterson had a large and happy brood. They had nine children, including a foster daughter, ranging in age from eight and a half to twenty. They had lived in the yellow split-level house on NW 192nd Street in Richmond Beach for almost two years. Their home was welcoming and friendly, and their kids and their friends came and went constantly.

George Peterson worked hard at the service station he owned, and he spent a good part of his "free" time transporting one child or another to basketball practice, school functions, or on errands. He was a strict father, and Leanne backed him up. They knew where each of their youngsters was most of the time—but it was complicated and difficult keeping tabs on nine children who were all involved in their own activities. Their older offspring had more freedom as they matured.

On the morning of February 15, 1975, George Peterson arose at six. It was a Saturday, but he wanted to get to the station early and work on his books before the rush for gas began. He'd had a restless night, waking each time one of the older girls returned. Now, he peered into sixteen-year-old Dina's room, and saw her bed was undisturbed; perhaps she'd slept with one of her sisters, or had decided to spend the night with a girlfriend.

No. That couldn't be. Dina was grounded and wasn't supposed to go anywhere except to school and her own yard. Her mother had given her some leeway the night before, allowing her to walk to a nearby pizza parlor with a girlfriend. But when George fell asleep, she wasn't home yet—and Leanne Peterson was half-angry, half-concerned.

As Peterson walked toward his car in the carport, he heard Dina's little black dog, Oscar, barking frantically. The dog wasn't known for his silence, but there was something in the frenzied yapping that disturbed Peterson. He moved into the backyard and saw Oscar running along the top of the rockery there. Oscar shivered in the cold; he had been outside all night.

As he approached, Oscar suddenly growled at him, something he never did, and then leapt off the rockery and ran out of sight. Curious and somewhat alarmed, Peterson peered over the stone barrier.

And he drew in a deep gulp of frigid air, so shocked that it seemed his heart had stopped beating. His daughter Dina lay on the cold ground on her back, her eyes slightly open.

Her father scrambled down to where she lay, and knelt beside her. He touched her face gently. Her skin was as cold as ice and he knew that she was dead—improbably, uncomprehendingly, lying dead in her own backyard.

Peterson stumbled back to the house and called their family's priest first, and then dialed the King County police. Knowing in his heart it would do no good, he grabbed two blankets and covered Dina.

Then he woke his wife and told her that Dina was dead. There was no easy way to say it. They waited hopelessly for the deputies. Their other eight children slept on; they would have to know the truth soon enough.

King County police patrolman Eric W. Anderson was dispatched at 6:22 on that freezing morning. George Peterson's disjointed call had resulted in the dispatch of a fire department aid car, with the indication that a "possible assault" had taken place.

Anderson pulled up behind a King County Fire Department District #4 emergency vehicle that had reached the scene only a moment before. Anderson followed George Peterson's directions to the backyard and caught the "thumbs down" signal of EMT Lieutenant Leroy McVay, who had just checked Dina Peterson.

It might have been an assault call to begin with, but the girl on the ground was dead.

Patrol sergeants Larry Danielson and Harold Hansen arrived to supervise patrol units racing to the scene. Lieutenant Richard Kraske of the Major Crimes Unit was notified that an apparent murder victim had just been found. Kraske called homicide detectives Roger Dunn and Rolf Grunden at home and directed them to the scene. They were joined by their sergeant, Len Randall.

Officer Steven Brown secured the crime scene from neighbors who were sure to come out of their homes when they saw the lights and heard sirens. He cordoned off the house and yard with yellow crime scene tape. The homicide men would be the only personnel allowed beyond that barrier. They didn't want possible evidence touched or trampled.

Initially, it looked as if Dina Peterson had been beaten to death. There was blood on her face. But the investigators wondered how a healthy teenager could be attacked and beaten in her own backyard without someone hearing her cry out.

The houses along 192nd were barely fifteen feet apart,

and Dina's body was only sixteen feet from the patio of her own house. Surely there would have been some unusual noise or sounds of struggle—something that would have been heard by neighbors or her own family.

Investigators planned to canvass the neighborhood for any possible witnesses, but first they had to work the crime scene and preserve as much physical evidence as possible.

The pretty brown-haired teenager was fully clothed in jeans, sweater, and a long coat—all buttoned tightly. Her shoes were still on her feet. If a sexual motivation had been present in the mind of her killer, an overt attack had not been carried out. Maybe she had fought hard enough to scare him—or her—away. But it didn't look as if she had fought; it was more likely that someone had crept up out of the dark before she had time to respond.

It was still half daylight, with some ground fog not yet dispersed. The detectives held their flashlights at an oblique angle, hoping it would enable them to see any blood in the area near Dina's body.

They could see dark splashes on some wooden slats near the younger children's sandbox, and several loose boards nearby also bore bloodstains, as if they had been used to strike her. There was more blood on the stones in the rockery.

Detectives found footprints leading away from the girl's body—deep, widely spaced prints, which indicated the person who made them was running. Unfortunately, the frozen ground wasn't conducive to showing deep prints, and they stopped only a few houses away. Rolf Grunden cast these footprints with a plaster-of-paris moulage. The moulage showed only a partial design pattern of the sole of the wearer's shoes.

The sandbox above the body contained sand that was disturbed, as if the initial struggle had taken place there, but criminalist Kay Sweeney was unable to find any usable footprints or physical evidence there.

Dina Peterson had been dead for hours. Rigor mortis was already well developed in her jaw, where it usually begins as muscles grow taut after death. This eliminated the possibility that she had risen very early to walk her dog. She had probably been lying dead in her backyard for the entire night.

The sheriff's investigators were still able to open one of her tightly clenched hands, and they found dirt and grass inside. Dina might have tried to hold on to the rockery or the weeds as her assailant dragged her.

Dunn, Grunden, and Sweeney took photographs of the teenager's body and the surroundings, and measurements for triangulating the area. King County detectives made it a point of triangulating all homicide scenes so they would be able to know *exactly* where the victims were originally found.

The detectives finished their measurements and pictures in the backyard of the Petersons' home and were finally ready to turn Dina's body over. But as they did so, they received a startling surprise.

Dina Peterson hadn't been beaten to death. A bone-handled hunting knife had been plunged into the center of her back! There were no other possibly fatal wounds at all—just the single deadly knife thrust from behind.

Media reporters had already been told that the girl had apparently died of a beating, and their early morning newscasts used that. The sheriff's detectives agreed they would keep this new information secret. It was quite possible that only Dina's killer knew how she died. Quickly, the investigators moved in close and surrounded her body so no onlooker would be able to see the knife as Dina's body was lifted from the ground and placed in a body bag before the King County medical examiner's deputies loaded it into their van.

An autopsy would, hopefully, give them more information.

In deep shock, George and Leanne Peterson nonetheless tried to reconstruct for detectives what had happened the night before.

George Peterson told Roger Dunn that he had not seen Dina since the family had dinner together from about 6 to 6:30 the night before. He explained to Dunn that he had left the house after that to take some of his younger sons to basketball practice and do some other errands.

"I got home around 8:30 and went to watch TV about 8:45—but I was reading the paper, too, and I fell asleep. I woke up at 11:30 because the TV was blaring and I turned it off," he recalled. "Then I woke up at 1:30 in the morning when one of our girls came home from a date. She knocked on the front door to get in. I checked the patio door leading off the recreation room and found it was locked. I looked in Dina's room, and she wasn't there. I was worried and a little angry that she was still out."

George Peterson explained that if Dina had any faults, it was her tendency to stay out longer than she was supposed to. In fact, that was why she was grounded on Valentine's Day. She'd stayed out too late the previous night, visiting her boyfriend, Tim Diener, who lived next door. It was too easy for Dina to sneak over to Tim's house; all she had to do was open the Petersons' sliding glass door in the basement and skip over to the sliding door that went into Tim's room.

Her dad had caught her on February 13 and grabbed her by the arm. "I was angry," he said. "I told Dina, 'You don't go there anymore!' "

When Peterson glanced into Dina's bedroom at 1:30 A.M. on February 15, her bed was neatly made, the bolster pillows in place. But she wasn't there. He thought she was deliberately defying him.

Her room had looked the same way in the morning just before he found her body.

In any household with teenagers, parents never really sleep well when one of them is out, and Peterson couldn't get back to sleep by 2:15. He said he'd taken three aspirin and went back to bed, and finally to sleep. At 3:30, Leanne Peterson had gotten up to let their oldest daughter in. Finally, all had been quiet until George got up at 6.

Peterson said he had heard nothing unusual during the night, certainly no cries for help or screams.

Dina's mother tried to recall for the detectives what

had happened the night before. Dina had been grounded for Valentine's night because she'd stayed out past curfew. She hadn't done anything shocking; Tim's parents were home and Dina just forgot about the time.

But her parents wanted to make a point so she wouldn't do it again.

On Valentine's night, Dina tried to get her mother to change her mind about the grounding. First, she asked to go to a friend's birthday party, and Leanne refused—but Dina didn't seem very disappointed.

Dina tried again. She pleaded to be allowed to go to a basketball game at school and the Valentine's Day dance that was to follow. Her foster sister was going, she argued, but her mother explained that Dina was the one who was grounded.

She pouted a bit but eventually settled down in the Petersons' recreation room to watch TV with a girlfriend, and a neighbor boy, Jim Groth, also sixteen, whom she considered a platonic friend. Her sister Marilyn said later that Jim was kind of an old shoe.

"Jim would just show up—and it was hard to get rid of him," she said. "Dina had no interest in him, but she didn't want to hurt his feelings."

Shortly after 9 P.M., Dina and her girlfriend had begged to be allowed to walk to a nearby restaurant to buy a pizza. They would eat it there, and they promised fervently that they would be back by 10:30.

Dina's mother finally relented and the two girls joined one other teenager to walk the few blocks to Michael's Restaurant on NW 195th.

Jim Groth had elected to stay in the basement to watch the end of a TV movie and wait for the girls to return.

Leanne Peterson heard Dina come in the front door about 10:30, relieved that she was home on time, just as she'd promised.

Dina's sister Marilyn had come home from a birthday party shortly before and she was sitting on her mother's bed, chatting about the festivities.

Within a few minutes, Leanne and Marilyn heard a little "scuffle" in the backyard of their home and two "playful" screams. It didn't sound out of the ordinary. There was horseplay in their house and yard often. The motion light in the backyard came on, too.

"We heard something like 'Don't!' and 'Stop it!'" Marilyn said.

Leanne thought it was Dina and one of her friends and the sounds did not indicate at all that Dina was distressed. But her mother was afraid the noise might annoy the neighbors so she'd gotten out of bed, put on a robe, and gone downstairs to the recreation room.

Outside in the dark yard, she'd seen two people in what looked like a playful wrestling match near the rockery. She even opened the sliding glass door in the recreation room and called Dina's name several times, telling her to be quiet.

There was no answer, but she wasn't concerned. She let Dina's little dog out, knowing Dina would bring him in with her. Leanne Peterson locked the door so Dina would have to knock to get in, and then Leanne returned to bed.

When Len Randall asked Leanne Peterson about Jim

Groth—who had been waiting for Dina and her friend to return—her mother nodded.

"I found him still down in our basement rec room, watching TV all by himself," she said. "I asked him what he was doing there, and he said he was waiting for the girls to come back with the pizza. I told him they were going to eat their pizza in the shop, and I sent him home. That would have been about ten P.M."

As the homicide crew worked at the scene in Richmond Beach, the temperature dropped dramatically and now snow sifted over the scene. They hurried as much as they could before the white drifts covered any physical evidence they might yet find.

Dina's anguished parents tried to think of who might conceivably have wanted to hurt their ebullient daughter. She wasn't a girl who confided all her secrets to her parents, but then that is standard teenage behavior.

Usually, high school students' peers often know more about them than their own mothers and fathers do. The detectives hoped to find Dina's friends, who might know if she had reason to be afraid of anyone, or if she was secretly worried about anything.

Overwhelmingly, the friends who were Dina's age said she was a good girl, an obedient teenager for the most part, and upset when she broke her curfew. She was very close to her family. Her boyfriend, Tim Diener, was nineteen, out of high school and worked at The Boeing Airplane Company.

"She trusted just about everyone," one girl said.

Dina Peterson was a "helping" kind of teenager who reached out to people with problems.

"We used to always tell the kids to feel free to bring home their friends anytime. But Dina usually didn't. We didn't really know how many friends she had. She kind of collected people with problems. Maybe she had empathy for them. I don't know," Leanne Peterson recalled sadly. "Whenever I objected if she brought someone home who seemed like they had too many problems, she would tell me they were beautiful human beings but that nobody understood them."

The night before she was killed, Dina had baked two pies. In the crusts, she'd pricked out patterns with a fork. One spelled out "Welcome All Strangers" and the other said "Smile—God Loves You."

Had Dina met a stranger who was not a beautiful person?

But when? She'd been gone to the pizza parlor for only an hour. Had someone deadly followed her home?

Detective Randy Hergesheimer joined the investigative team; he would take over responsibility for the case.

The first thing for the team to do was trace Dina's movements *after* she left her home at 9:30 on Valentine's night. The detectives talked to the two sisters who had accompanied her to the pizza parlor. They verified that the trio had called the restaurant, ordered a pepperoni pizza, and then walked there to eat it. They'd started walking home shortly before 10:30 because Dina was anxious to keep her promise to her mom. Halfway home, Kathy

Strunk and several friends from school stopped and offered them a ride. It was cold out, and even though they were close to home, Dina and the sisters had climbed into the back of the pickup truck.

When they got to the Petersons' house, Kathy Strunk said that Dina had gone inside immediately, through the front door. The other teenagers had stayed on the sidewalk in front of her house talking to two of the girls in the truck. They gave the detectives the names of the other two girls.

One of the other girls told detectives that Dina had been so concerned about getting home on the stroke of 10:30 that she'd barely waved goodbye as she ran to the front door.

"We four stood there talking," Kathy said. "Sometime—maybe about ten fifty—I heard a sound from the backyard of Dina's house."

"What kind of sound? A scream, or something like that?" Hergesheimer asked.

"No," she said. "Not like that. It was like a person hitting the ground after jumping off of somewhere, and then I heard just running steps."

The owner of Michael's Restaurant recalled that the three girls had been in his pizza place around 10 P.M. "They called in to order a pepperoni pizza," he said. "They split it three ways and ate it here. It would have cost $2.84. I remember them especially because they all dug in their jeans to come up with enough nickels and pennies to pay for it." He identified a picture of Dina Peterson as having been one of the girls.

Detectives still had dozens of teenagers and neighbors

to talk to. But first, they attended the postmortem exam of the sixteen-year-old victim.

Dina had been completely clothed when her father found her, wearing the same clothes she wore to the pizza parlor: blue jeans, all of the buttons—even on the inner waistband—buttoned, an emerald-green long-sleeved sweater, a blue full-length coat, white bra, pink panties, red socks, and brown suede shoes.

There was a single rip in the back of the coat and a corresponding tear in the sweater—both caused by the knife in her murderer's hand.

Dr. Patrick Besant-Matthews, the King County medical examiner, performed the autopsy. The forensic pathologist took blood samples, vaginal smears, hair samples, fingernail clippings, and a few soil samples. Even a couple of stray hairs that still clung to her clothing were preserved. They were probably from her own head, but no one could be sure of that.

It was 1975, and no one had heard of DNA matching at the time. However, if the hairs still had "tags" at the scalp end, they might be able to ascertain blood type.

Dina Peterson was petite at five feet, two inches and she weighed only 117 pounds fully clothed. Besant-Matthews found one puzzling factor as he surveyed her body. The lividity pattern on her corpse was not in keeping with the supine position of her body when Dina was found.

When the heart stops beating and pumping blood, the life fluid drops to the lowest part of the body. If the victim is moved before this pattern—called lividity—is set, there will be a second staining on the new bottom body portion. Only it will be much lighter: pink instead of purple.

Dina Peterson had *two* patterns of lividity. Besant-Matthews and the detectives attending her autopsy could see that she had lain on her face for some time after she died. But someone had turned her body over during the night. The striations of bright purple livor mortis were on the front of her body; lighter pink areas marked her back.

Few laymen understand livor mortis, or, for that matter, rigor mortis. Nor do they understand how accurately these postmortem changes can tell time and manner of death, and if the victim has been moved after death.

The King County detectives had questioned everyone on the scene carefully. Her father had not turned Dina over; he had only touched her face and then covered her with blankets. Even so, they asked him if he owned any knives. Chagrined at what they seemed to imply, he led them to his workshop. All of his tools, including knives, hung from their labeled spots.

Homicide detectives *do* often have to ask difficult questions, and they explained that to Dina's father.

Patrol officers recalled that the priest who'd administered last rites had not touched her at all. The EMTs had merely looked for a pulse and noted the rigor in her jaws.

Who, then, had turned Dina over?

The autopsy continued. There was blood in Dina's right ear, nose, and mouth. Her legs were skinned and bruised. She had some facial bruises and scratches, which might have been sustained as she fell, or they could have resulted from being hit in the face.

It seemed probable that she had struggled for her life—if even for a short time—but she was tiny and would have been very easily subdued by a larger attacker.

Dina's cause of death was, however, the single knife wound nine inches above her waist. The bone-handled knife was only one and five-eighths inches to the left of the midline of her back. It had pierced her back almost five inches deep and penetrated her left lung, causing rapid death from hemothorax—blood hemorrhaging into her lungs. The thrust of the knife was downward, suggesting her attacker was taller than she was. She could not have lived very long before she drowned in her own blood.

There were no defense wounds at all on Dina's hands. That was interesting. She must have been taken by surprise, perhaps by someone she completely trusted.

A homicide where there is only a single knife thrust is very unusual. Pathologists and detectives are far more likely to find victims who have been stabbed again and again in a frenzy of anger or passion.

What did just one wound mean? A killing done on impulse? A cold-blooded murderous erasure of someone the killer wanted to get rid of?

An accident? No, not an accident—not when a knife had plunged so deep.

Dina's stomach still contained barely digested bits of pizza. Dr. Besant-Matthews estimated that the time of death would have been between 10:30 and 11:30 P.M.

It was tragically apparent that the "friendly scuffle" her mother had observed had been Dina's death struggle. And that knowledge was devastating to Leanne Peterson, even though she had no way of knowing the truth at the time.

Detective Randy Hergesheimer questioned Jim Groth, the sixteen-year-old boy who'd spent the early part of Valentine's night watching television with Dina in her recreation room. Groth was nervous—but that was to be expected. He told Hergesheimer that he had remained in the Petersons' basement after the girls left.

He sat on the couch there until about 10 P.M. He was watching a movie, titled, ironically, *Murderers' Row.*

"I left by the back—the patio—door, after Mrs. Peterson told me to go home," Groth said. "I couldn't figure out how to lock the door from the outside, though, so I left it unlocked."

Jim Groth recalled that he had then walked to a bowling alley, where he stayed from 10:45 until shortly after 12:30.

"Then I walked home and my mother let me in."

Groth added that he had stopped on his way home to visit a friend, Tim Diener, who was, of course, Dina's boyfriend.

"Tim was sound asleep," Groth said. "In his bedroom—it's in the basement. So I just went on home."

Jim insisted that he and Dina had been only friends, and if Dina felt romantic about anyone, it was Tim Diener.

Dina's friends had already confirmed this, but they also suspected that Jim Groth had a crush on Dina.

Dina's sister Marilyn believed that. "He was always hanging around, and he would wrestle with Dina. It was the only way he could touch her."

Jim Groth had some scratches on his arms, but he explained those away—saying they came from bushes with brambles that he ran into in the dark as he took a shortcut through the backyards to his house, which was two doors down from the Petersons.

The investigators also talked with Tim Diener, whose basement bedroom was only about twenty-one feet from the Petersons' house. *He* was the one most closely connected to Dina—both geographically and emotionally. He seemed shaken and his eyes were red as he told them that he and Dina had been dating since August, and that he was very fond of her.

"Her real name is—*was*—Diana, but we always called her Dina or Dynamo."

"You two ever argue—fight?"

Tim shook his head. "We never had any serious fights."

"When was the last time you saw her?"

"We spent most of the afternoon together on Valentine's Day. She came over to my house and we visited with some of our friends. I asked her to make some brownies for my family's dinner, and she did. My folks came home while Dina was still there."

"When did she leave?"

"It was about a quarter to six. Dina said she had to get back to her own house for dinner."

Diener said he hadn't seen her after that. She was

grounded at night, so he'd gone to Snohomish County and spent the evening with friends there.

"I got home just before eleven and I went to sleep with the TV on in my room. The TV was off the air and humming when it woke me up at six."

Diener said he'd heard the commotion outside and seen the police and fire department aid cars outside Dina's house.

"That was when I found out what happened."

Randy Hergesheimer and his crew verified that Diener had been with friends during the evening, and they talked with the youth who had driven him home at five minutes to eleven.

One of Diener's relatives, who lived in a nearby house, said he had seen Tim come home at approximately 10:45 in his friend's pickup truck. "He went right into his house."

Tim Diener seemed to have a good alibi with witnesses to back him up. But he failed a lie detector test.

Sheriff's detectives served a search warrant on Diener's home, and they found a pair of trousers with blood on them. There was not enough, however, to determine the blood type.

Jim Groth also agreed to take a polygraph test to validate his truthfulness. The results, however, were surprising. The polygrapher viewed the charts and felt that Groth was also being deceptive in some areas.

Now the sheriff's men had *two* possible killers. Even so, they suspected that Tim Diener was the more likely suspect.

The probe bounced back and forth as they looked at all possible suspicious people.

And then, a few days later, on February 18, Jim Groth admitted to Randy Hergesheimer that he hadn't told the complete truth in his first statement. He had lied—but only because he was frightened. He had a juvenile record for underage drinking and drug use, and he was afraid he might be tied to Dina's death.

This time, Jim Groth said that it was true he had gone to the bowling alley after he left the Peterson home. But he had stayed there only until shortly before 11 P.M. It really *was* true that he planned to visit Tim Diener but found him asleep.

To reach his own house, Jim Groth said he cut through backyards. Now he hesitated and drew a deep breath.

"I want to tell you the real truth now," he said. "As I passed through the Petersons' yard, I stumbled across Dina's body in the dark. She was lying facedown with her arms at her side and her legs out straight. I could see the knife in her back. I think the knife belonged to Tim."

Groth recalled that he'd been "really scared," and he had nudged Dina with his foot. But she hadn't moved at all.

"What time was this?" Hergesheimer asked.

"Pushing eleven. I ran all the way to my house. I sat around smoking cigarettes at the park on the beach for a while, trying to think what to do."

It was confusing that both Tim Diener and Jim Groth had failed the first lie detector tests they took. Relieved now by "telling the truth," Groth agreed readily to another polygraph exam. This time he passed it, with no evidence of deception on questions concerning guilty knowledge in the death of Dina Peterson.

The running footprints cast at the scene had been Groth's and a bit of promising evidence was now rendered useless.

But something rankled Hergesheimer. Why hadn't Jim Groth called for help for Dina? Perhaps she was only unconscious; it seemed grotesque that the teenager would wait all through the freezing night, knowing that Dina lay outside. Alone.

Randy Hergesheimer talked with a neighbor whose home's backyard abutted the Petersons' backyard. She recalled that she'd fallen asleep at 9:30 that evening and wakened around 10:30 or 10:35 because she heard what sounded like "children's" voices in distress. It sounded like whimpering.

"By the time I was fully awake, the noises had stopped," she said. "I felt like the voices were coming from the Petersons' house. I fell back to sleep around eleven and I didn't hear anything else."

Roger Dunn and Randy Hergesheimer talked to dozens of Dina Peterson's friends at Shoreline High School. Not one of them could recall any threats on her life, or come up with anyone she was even afraid of. She had never been in any trouble and was considered a popular and perpetually cheerful girl.

Still, the rumors circulated wildly. One girl said she was afraid of Tim Diener and that she had heard he "killed animals."

Many students believed that Tim Diener was guilty of stabbing Dina.

At length, Tim was arrested, but he was soon released because the lawyers in the King County Prosecuting Attorney's Office didn't think there was enough evidence to charge him with murder.

One of Jim Groth's acquaintances had a discomfiting encounter with him in April 1975, but the homicide investigators didn't know about it because his complaint had gone to the Juvenile Unit by mistake.

"I was working at my dad's newspaper hut, and Jim showed up and started hassling me for some reason," the youth said. "When I told him to leave me alone, he said, 'I've killed a girl before—and I'm not afraid to do it again.'"

Groth might only have had a macabre sense of humor or enjoyed showing off by scaring people. Kathy Strunk, Dina's friend who gave her a ride home just before she was killed, also had a scary encounter with Jim Groth.

"It wasn't too long after Dina died," she recalled a long time later. "Jim came up behind me and put a knife close to my back. He said 'Gotcha!' when I jumped. He didn't hurt me because he slid his hand down the blade so that it wouldn't go in my back—but that was an awfully bad joke to pull on someone who had just lost her friend."

Each of the teenagers Jim had pretended to threaten believed that he was just making sick jokes at their expense. They didn't really think he was dangerous.

*   *   *

A pall fell over the neighborhood at Richmond Beach.

In his grief and rage, George Peterson walked down to the beach on Puget Sound and shouted into the wind and the roar of the tide coming in, "God! How could you do this to us?"

The Petersons suspected it was Tim Diener who killed Dina, but the investigators couldn't corroborate that.

George found himself crying at unexpected moments. "I couldn't cry," Leanne said. "If I started, I knew I could never stop."

Leanne, who was a petite and kind woman, sometimes found herself filled with a need for revenge.

"I was peeling potatoes," she said, "with this little paring knife, and I thought if I knew Tim killed our daughter, I could cut his heart out with it . . ."

Seeing their parents so desolate, the Petersons' surviving children decided they couldn't talk about the loss of Dina without making their mother and father feel even worse.

There was a miasma of fear combined with their grief. The three surviving Peterson daughters, twenty, fifteen, and ten, and their foster daughter who was Dina's age, as well as the four sons—twelve, ten, and the eight-year-old twins—were no longer free to come and go. They all had to check in and out—and none of them went anywhere alone.

"It's sad when you have to tell children they can't walk to the grocery store alone in broad daylight," Leanne Peterson commented. "But we were so afraid for them."

It was impossible to believe Dina could have been

ANN RULE

stabbed in her own yard—and that her killer was still out there somewhere. Without knowing his motivation, they didn't dare risk the lives of their other children. In fact the entire neighborhood was frightened. It had been a street of houses where families had many children, and the yards, sidewalks, and streets were always rife with youngsters. No longer. Now it was a quiet, shuttered area.

A resident who lived several blocks away reported a strange incident that occurred at his home on February 8. He'd heard a prowler at one in the morning and confronted a youth who asked to see "Dan." There was no "Dan" living there and the intruder said he was sure Dan lived on 192nd.

The teenager walked away, but fifteen minutes later, the homeowner heard noises that indicated he was back. The prowler was trying to steal his car and the owner ran out and chased him away. Another neighbor had some stereo tapes stolen from his car on the same night.

The complainant told deputies that he'd seen the same stranger later, walking what appeared to be a large yellow Lab—although he wasn't exactly sure of the dog's breed. He was positive the dog was the same animal who had attacked his own small dog a month before and ripped his tiny pet's throat open.

"The guy wasn't very old—probably in his teens," the tipster said. "White—with dark hair, about five foot six to five foot eight."

He had no idea where the teenager lived. And, realistically, car prowling was a crime far removed from murder.

On February 18, another neighbor told deputies that a

car had driven up her long driveway on Valentine's night. Her three Afghan hounds had begun barking frantically and continued to bark for two hours. But this had occurred after two in the morning and all indications were that Dina was already dead by 11 P.M. The woman said that there was a lot of foot traffic in the woods near her home—woods that extended almost to the Peterson home. Officers checked the woods and found a fire pit, liquor bottles, and signs that the area had been a gathering place for juveniles.

There were other scattered reports—from areas that were increasingly farther away from the spot where Dina died. One man reported that he'd seen an injured white male at a 7-Eleven store in the north end not too far from the Richmond Beach area. It had been late on Valentine's night.

But there were no signs that Dina's killer had been injured. Only *her* blood had been found, and the lack of defense wounds showed that she hadn't had a chance to fight her attacker.

Many of the witnesses interviewed marked the time of their activities by what they were watching on television on the night of February 14. They'd been viewing either *Murderers' Row* or *Police Woman*, the TV show starring Angie Dickinson, the episode titled "Nothing Left to Lose."

Hergesheimer's crew fit possible witness testimony into every component of time on Dina's last evening. Finally they had a matrix that made sense. It indicated that she had been killed while there were many people around.

Her friends stood on the sidewalk talking in front of her house. Neighbors were home in adjacent houses. Her own mother saw her wrestling or tussling with some faceless person.

She had entered her home at 10:30 without saying goodbye to her friends. And, almost immediately, she left by the back door. Had she planned to meet someone, someone she loved and trusted? Or had she gone to the basement to watch TV and glimpsed someone in the back-yard and gone to investigate? She was the girl who felt everyone was basically good, and fear for her own safety was simply not part of her emotional makeup.

The time charts worked, but there was still one glaring blank space. Who was Dina's murderer and why had he taken her life so brutally?

Perhaps a sexual attack had been the killer's motive, and he had been frightened away when he heard Leanne Peterson calling Dina's name.

Detectives were quite sure that Dina was killed by someone she knew, someone with whom she felt completely safe in the darkness of that February night. When she turned away from him, that someone plunged a knife deep into her back.

That person had his own conscience to live with. Only he knew "why," and the reasons for Dina's death. Perhaps those reasons seemed negligible now compared to the pangs of regret over a loving, giving, sixteen-year-old girl's murder.

And then again, it was possible he *had* no conscience.

*   *   *

As soon as they could, George and Leanne Peterson moved their family away from the house where Dina died. The memories there were too terrible to live with.

The King County Major Crimes Unit had its hands full. They had a number of "cold cases"—although they weren't called that in 1975. A serial killer called "Ted" had murdered or kidnapped seven young women in King County and around Washington and Oregon. A task force was mobilized to try to catch him before the toll grew higher. Lieutenant Dick Kraske, who oversaw the investigation of Dina's murder, was pulled off her case and transferred to the "Ted Task Force."

It wasn't that the King County sheriff's crew didn't care about Dina and her family; they had simply run out of leads. Moreover, they were racing to stop whoever Ted was from killing again. Of necessity, Dina's case was shoved to the back of their agenda. It wasn't closed; it was suspended until they had more manpower to follow up information.

Tim Diener joined the service after high school, and Jim Groth moved away, too. Although several detectives still suspected one of them might very well be guilty of killing Dina, there wasn't enough physical evidence to go further.

Hergesheimer and Kraske conferred with senior deputy prosecutors Michael Ruark and Brian Gain many times about the Peterson case, and all of them tried to construct a case that was strong enough to bring a suspect to trial.

But it was impossible. With today's forensic science advances, they might have been able to arrest someone and hope to achieve a conviction on murder charges. But there were no DNA matches in the seventies, and the hairs found on Dina's clothing could not be matched absolutely to a suspect. Those could only be found "microscopically similar in class and characteristic."

And there were no witnesses who actually saw Dina being stabbed.

Years passed. In 1985, Leanne Peterson said sadly, "They're never going to solve this." She and George decided to request Dina's belongings that the sheriff's office was still holding in evidence. They were stunned to find that the agency now called the King County Sheriff's Office had thrown out all of the evidence, keeping only the bone-handled knife.

The Petersons learned that one man—a sergeant—had made the decision to clear out the evidence room to make room for newer items that were coming in on more recent cases. Dina's clothing, the plaster moulages, hairs and fibers, Tim's trousers—all of them gone forever.

It was a few years into the twenty-first century and the detectives who had originally investigated Dina Peterson's murder had retired. But Randy Hergesheimer didn't live long enough to retire; he was still a young man when he was killed in a head-on collision with a drunk driver on a

Montana highway. By 2006, generations of lawmen had come and gone from the King County Sheriff's Office in the three decades since Dina perished.

Dina's family and her friends remembered her, and as her siblings grew older and started families of their own, they missed their sister, the aunt their children would never know. I, too, remembered her murder. It was one of the first cases I ever wrote about back in the days when I wrote for five fact-detective magazines.

She would be forever sixteen years old, a lovable and loving innocent girl. I kept my files on Dina's case, hoping without much expectation that one day her killer might be identified and arrested.

A day didn't go by when George and Leanne Peterson didn't think of the daughter they had lost so brutally, but they had to go on for the sake of the rest of their family. Dina's loss was saddest on holidays and on her birthday, in mid-July.

And, of course, on Valentine's Day.

"I could not function for a number of years after her death," her mother said. "I could not laugh *or* cry."

Only families who have lost a child to sudden violence can understand the unrelenting pain that comes with that loss. And yet, they do go on.

The King County Sherriff's Office had a new unit in 2006—the Cold Case Squad. Detective sergeant Jim Allen was assigned to investigate cases that had long gathered dust, far back in files rarely touched. Although the physical evidence was gone, Allen found that Dina Peterson's case itself still existed on paper: crime scene notes, follow-up reports, lie detector test results, photos of the crime scene.

Curious, he began to read through the file, aware that if Dina had lived she would be nearing fifty, probably a mother, quite possibly a grandmother.

Allen approached the case with fresh eyes; he was still in school when Dina died, and he had no preconceived opinions about it. As he read, he began to see inconsistencies, things that didn't add up. The original detectives had focused far more on Tim Diener than they had on Jim Groth. Both of them had initially failed lie detector tests, but Diener was the only one arrested, however briefly.

Allen's take on the two suspects was weighted on a different scale than his predecessors. Diener had apparently had no reason to want Dina dead. They were in love—at least puppy love—when she died. They got along well, and they had just spent a happy day together. Why would he have wanted to kill her?

Jim Groth, on the other hand, seemed to have been obsessed with her in vain. Dina wasn't interested in him as anything more than a neighbor kid who kept hanging around. Her younger sister Marilyn confirmed that. Groth was a misfit whom Dina tolerated because she was kind.

And then Allen found a report buried in juvenile files that fascinated him. It involved Dina, and a complaint that had come in eighteen months before her murder. A neighborhood boy had been suspected of peering into her bedroom one night. Was it possible that he'd had some kind of fixation about the pretty teenager? Quite likely.

Stalkers could be anyone, of any age. This teenager lived two houses away from the Petersons' home, and he was questioned. But he denied any knowledge of voyeurism.

That kid had been fourteen-year-old Jim Groth! *He* was the "Peeping Tom" who looked into Dina's window.

And then there was Groth's strange behavior after he found Dina's body. He hadn't told anyone—or tried to get help for her. He was the one who was afraid he might be linked to her murder. He seemed a far more likely "person of interest." But earlier detectives' interest was focused in another direction.

Jim Allen began to try to locate the teenage boys who had been part of Dina's life way back in 1975. Tim Diener wasn't hard to find. After he left the army, he had worked for The Boeing Airplane Company at the time of Dina's death when he was nineteen, and he'd stayed there for thirty-two years, until he retired at the age of forty-nine in 2005. Tim was suffering from liver cancer at a relatively young age. He had a longtime female companion, Charlotte Ressen,* and the two of them hoped to have a few more years to enjoy a home Tim owned in Mexico. There, he could live his favorite outdoor lifestyle and learn to scuba dive.

In the thirty-some years since Dina's death, Tim Diener had lived under a constant shadow; some of his peers still believed that he had killed her. He lost friends, and he half-expected to hear footsteps behind him and feel hand-cuffs encircling his wrists.

It never happened, but it blunted his life considerably.

Sergeant Allen discovered that Jim Groth had dropped out of Shoreline High School when he was seventeen and joined the army. After his service years, he had spent much of his life in Alaska, working as a fisherman or a laborer in construction.

The three decades had not been particularly kind to Groth. In 2006, Jim was forty-eight and his wild mane of "hippie hair" had vanished, leaving him bald. He had matured into a surly man who wasn't the best companion for the women in his life. Jim Allen found that in the intervening years, Jim Groth had been convicted three times for assaulting females.

In 1985, when his former wife had refused to give him a ride, he had punched her so forcefully that emergency room doctors first feared he had fractured her skull.

Groth had two children, but he was estranged from both of them.

When confronted by Jim Allen in May 2006, Groth insisted he had nothing to tell the sheriff's investigators. Yes, he had stumbled upon Dina's body, but he had nothing at all to do with her death.

Allen suggested that Jim Groth take another lie detector test. He agreed. This would be Groth's third polygraph examination in as many decades. And his responses to the examiner's questions indicated he wasn't telling the truth. He failed this lie detector test.

Groth had showed deception on the first polygraph. He passed the second. And now he failed again as he answered questions about his knowledge of what happened to Dina Peterson. Two fails out of three exams. What did it really mean?

Allen located several of the students who had gone to Shoreline High. They were now in their late forties to mid-fifties, but they remembered the night Dina Peterson was murdered. Further investigation turned up information that the teenage Jim Groth had made lewd comments about Dina behind her back. The picture of a pubescent youth who was sexually obsessed with a girl he couldn't have was emerging. Allen wasn't convinced that Groth was as innocent as he claimed to be.

In December 2007, King County investigators decided it was time to talk with Jim Groth again. Tim Diener had had several witnesses who placed him just where he said he was on February 14, 1975. The only connection Diener had with the murder was that the fatal weapon *had* belonged to him. Diener had told detectives in the seventies that the knife was stolen from his room, which had had an unlocked door leading to his backyard. Most of the teenagers in the neighborhood had known the bone-handled knife was there.

Diener had never wavered in his recall that he had gotten home in time to watch the NBC local newscast on Valentine's night. He was hoping that Dina might be able to sneak out of her house and run over to his door for a quick visit. But he was tired as he waited to watch the Johnny Carson show, and he'd fallen asleep.

The Tonight Show began at 11:30 P.M., and Dina had probably died around 10:20 to 10:40. At that time, Diener hadn't arrived home yet. He probably missed the fatal attack on her by fifteen or twenty minutes.

Tim had been very upset and grieving for his girlfriend at the time he failed the polygraph test. Emotions can affect lie detector results. Tim Diener said he would be willing to testify in any trial of a yet-unknown defendant who might have murdered Dina. He was confident that he had been leaving another county at the time she was killed, and he still had witnesses who would vouch for him regarding that.

Tim said that Jim Groth had stopped talking to him after Dina died, and that the students of Shoreline High spread theories like wildfire—theories that named Groth as the killer.

On December 21, 2007, Jim Allen decided it was time to reinterview Jim Groth. The second suspect wasn't far away; he was in jail—serving time for domestic abuse. Actually, he was three days away from being released after serving an eight-month sentence for assaulting his girlfriend.

Mary Lou Coates,* who had been dating Groth since 2003, was sorry that she had ever called the police on Groth. After he was questioned in May 2006, she said they had had a long talk.

"He told me then that he didn't kill Dina Peterson. And he felt better when he talked to the police. He thought he had finally been cleared as a suspect in her murder."

She had believed him. "He wouldn't do something like this," she offered. "He told me that they were just good friends."

Mary Lou denied that Groth had physically assaulted her, insisting that he was only verbally abusive to her, and that was what the domestic violence charges against him were about.

"I blame myself for his arrest. I never wanted him to go to jail—to be locked up," she said softly.

Even given Jim Groth's history of violence toward women, he must have said some pretty bad things to his girlfriend. That made no sense at all. It's quite possible that he threatened her. But now, as so many abused women do, Mary Lou was feeling very sorry for Jim.

"He's the nicest person in the world," she emphasized to *Seattle Times* reporter Jennifer Sullivan.

Jim Groth didn't get out of jail in December 2007. He was arrested and charged with first-degree murder in the long-fallow case of Dina Peterson.

"What will I tell my girlfriend?" Groth asked. "I'll never get out of jail."

On January 9, 2008, Groth pleaded not guilty to the murder charges.

Judge Laura Inveen's King County Superior Court room was crowded with observers, among them the Peterson family, who had not seen Groth for more than thirty-two years. Leanne Peterson looked at the stocky, bald man and realized he didn't look at all like the teenage boy who used to be their neighbor.

"I never thought this would happen," she told Sullivan of the *Seattle Times*. "We are grateful to the cold-case people."

Leanne had been hopeful that Jim Groth would plead

guilty to the charges against him, so that she and her family wouldn't have to relive the pain they had felt in 1975. That didn't happen.

Sheriff's spokesman John Urquhart told reporters that Jim Groth had been under intense scrutiny by current detectives and prosecutors for more than a year. Although Groth was a "person of interest," Urquhart acknowledged that there were no DNA matches.

The single piece of physical evidence was Tim Diener's bone-handled knife, and even forensic science of the new century could not isolate DNA or blood on it.

On May 12, 2009, after another seventeen months' delay, King County senior deputy prosecutor Carla Carlstrom was prepared to present a case based on circumstantial evidence to the jurors selected. It certainly wasn't the easiest case to prosecute. Nor was Groth an easy defendant to represent. Julie Lawry, Jim Groth's public defender, however, felt confident that she could raise enough doubt in the jury that her client would go free.

Lawry had been a public defender for sixteen years.

As the trial began, it was unlikely that Tim Diener would be able to testify. He was in the final stages of liver cancer. His testimony had been videotaped, and that would have to serve.

In her opening statement, Carla Carlstrom asked the jurors to correct the mistake that sheriff's detectives had made in 1975. She submitted that they had had tunnel vision "within days" after Dina Peterson was murdered in her own yard.

"Because of that," Carlstrom said, "they focused on the

wrong person, and her killer went unpunished for *thirty-four years*!"

Moreover, she offered, the original investigators had soon turned to the "Ted Bundy murders" and "disregarded" many factors in the "vicious and angry" attack that could be linked to Jim Groth.

Defense attorney Julie Lawry pointed out in her opening statement that there was no new evidence that might clear Tim Diener of the crime. "In this country, we don't 'guess' people guilty." She explained that the case against Groth was based "on a whole lot of rumor and speculation.

"Ms. Carlstrom doesn't know who killed Dina Peterson. Jim Groth doesn't know who killed Dina Peterson. At the end of this trial, you still won't know who killed Dina Peterson."

Jim Groth's trial took three weeks. Detectives, Dina's family, and witnesses testified. The defendant declined to testify. Tim Diener's testimony on videotape was needed as the whole case played out in the trial. He was far too ill to appear in person.

On June 2, 2009, the jury in Judge Inveen's courtroom returned with a verdict. They found James E. Groth guilty of Dina Peterson's murder, although they agreed on the lesser charge of second-degree murder.

Sentencing was set for July 24.

Tim Diener died of liver cancer on June 19, 2009. He was fifty-three. For most of his life, he had been a suspect in the murder of the girl he loved. He lived only seventeen months after he was relieved of that dark shadow when Jim Groth was arrested.

Although Jim Groth didn't take the witness stand in his own defense, he did grant a jail interview to Jennifer Sullivan. He told her that he didn't kill Dina. When asked who had committed that murder, he said he wasn't sure.

"My life is over in a sense," Groth said. "How did these people—knowing what they know—make this determination?"

Lawry said that she had never been so upset by a verdict in her sixteen years in the public defenders' office. "The evidence is so thin. There's no DNA—there's no forensic evidence. There's no confession. There's no eyewitnesses . . ."

Circumstantial evidence demands a criteria of what a reasonable man would deem a reasonable outcome when he knows the facts of the case.

Jim Groth was fixated sexually on Dina Peterson. She was seriously dating another suitor. She may have been in her backyard, headed to Tim Diener's house, when another figure approached her in the dark. Perhaps that person—Jim Groth—was so frustrated that he grabbed her and attempted to kiss, fondle, or rape her. Her natural instinct would have been to fight back, scratching him.

And a reasonable man might well conclude that he had stabbed her with the knife that belonged to the teenager that Dina really cared for.

But Dina was found with her face toward the sky. Someone undoubtedly came back and turned her over. There is little question that that was Jim Groth. As he sat smoking on the beach, he must have begun to wonder if she might still be alive. If she was, Dina would tell on him and he would be in big trouble. And so, I believe, he went back to reassure himself that she was truly dead—and that he would not be identified as the one who stabbed her.

Jim Groth lied, and his two versions of what happened on Valentine's night were bizarre. He went on to live a life marked by violence to the women in his life.

On July 24, 2009, judge Laura Inveen sentenced Jim Groth to a minimum of sixteen years in prison. His final sentence would go to the Washington State's Indeterminate Sentencing Review Board, which could sentence him to life in prison.

At Groth's sentencing, George Peterson spoke as tears ran down his face. Jim Groth stared straight ahead, his face blank of expression.

"Thirty-four years doesn't heal," Dina's father said. "There is a scar on my heart with the loss of my daughter. I have forgiven you, Jim Groth."

Julie Lawry announced her plans to appeal his sentence. Thus far, that has not been granted.

THE MAN WHO
LOVED TOO MUCH

It was Halloween night in 1977, a holiday for all things ghostlike, macabre, and frightening, and the streets of Seattle were shrouded with appropriate fog and mist. The mournful wail of the foghorns near Puget Sound added to the bleak atmosphere of the night. Lights on the ferries steaming toward the docks on Seattle's waterfront were only dim beacons. Trick-or-treaters were long since off the streets and home counting their largesse. As the rain began to fall in earnest, it was a time to be home, and anyone with a place to go had headed there.

The only traffic on that Monday night consisted of emergency vehicles. The Seattle Police Department's blue and white patrol cars crept along in the fog, and an occasional Medic One unit screeched by on an urgent run.

At the downtown police headquarters, the 911 lines had been busy with both critical and crank calls. Operators, used to frantic calls, answered in deceptively laconic voices, fielded the calls, got as much information as they could, and dispatched the cars on the street to addresses all over the city.

The call from the manager at the Rendezvous Restaurant was fairly routine. Their female bartender hadn't shown up for work that day—nor had she come in to supervise the Halloween party that she'd planned. Her fellow employees were concerned because it wasn't like Sue Ann Elizabeth Baker to let them down. They had tried to call her repeatedly, only to get a busy signal. They'd checked with an operator at the phone company and learned that Sue Ann's phone was off the hook.

The 911 operator asked a few questions and then told the manager that she would send a car to Baker's apartment on Magnolia Bluff.

Police radio communications are, of necessity, terse and to the point. The call that went out shortly after nine that Halloween night didn't sound particularly ominous.

"Three-Queen-One, copy on a call."

"Three-Queen-One by, go ahead."

"Three-Queen-One, service call. Check on the welfare of a Sue Baker, 3459 23 West. No apartment number given. Possibly husband's name 'Ron Baker' is on the mailbox. The phone is off the hook now and someone called her in sick today for work."

"Received."

"Subject is a white female about twenty-eight."

"Received."

The 911 operator returned to taking other calls. Within a few minutes, the patrolman in Three-Queen-One—Tim Dillon—was calling back in.

"911—Operator 70."

"Yeah. This is Three-Queen-One on a call to check the welfare of—"

"Uh-huh."

"I have a dead body. Get me a sergeant. Get me Homicide."

"Okay, okay. Will do."

The wheels of a murder investigation were in motion. Homicide detective sergeant Craig VandePutte's crew was working its last night shift. All the homicide crews worked the night shift every three months. On November 1, they were due to report for the day shift at 7:45 A.M.

But now they had a full night's work ahead of them. VandePutte and detectives Ted Fonis and Gary Fowler left for the scene with the homicide van. The streets were wet and it was 46 degrees out as they headed north to the upper-middle-class residential district of Magnolia Bluff, one of Seattle's lowest crime areas.

Patrol Officer Dillon met them outside the cedar-sided apartment house and explained what he had discovered. He'd quickly determined that the apartment where Sue Baker lived was on an upper level, reachable by stairs and then along a catwalk/porch. He'd knocked, and then knocked louder, but there was no response from the darkened apartment.

"I tried the front door handle and found it locked," he said. "Then I contacted the owner-manager who lives in a downstairs apartment. She came with me back upstairs, carrying her keys."

Dillon said he opened the door and used only his flashlight as he entered the apartment. He checked the living room and found nothing unusual, and preceded down the hall, calling, "Sue Ann—Sue Ann—"

There was no answer.

He opened the first door to the right of the hall and found a small bedroom—empty. Continuing on down the hall, Dillon checked the main bathroom and found it neat and clean, and also empty.

It had been very still, almost eerie, as Dillon crept quietly down the hallway playing his flashlight over the walls. The only room left was the master bedroom, where he found the door was ajar. Dillon nudged the door with his flashlight, and it swung open.

"There was a king-sized bed there," he told VandePutte and Fonis. "I could see the spread had red roses on it. She was there in the center of the bed, and the spread and blankets were drawn up under her chin. Her long dark hair spread out over the pillow.

"I said, 'Sue Ann?' but she didn't answer."

Dillon said he moved closer to the bed and shined his flashlight on the woman. Her eyes were slightly open, her chin tilted up. But she didn't move, and Dillon touched her nose and cheek. She was cold to the touch. He pulled the covers down to her waist level. A red towel had been draped over her breasts and it seemed to be stained a deeper red in spots.

"That's when I called for Homicide," Dillon finished. "While I was waiting, I checked the other rooms again to see if anyone might still be hiding in here—but it was clear."

VandePutte, Fonis, and Fowler looked at the woman on the bed. Even in death, she was beautiful. They folded the rose-dotted coverlet and blankets down to the foot of the bed. Now they could see that she was completely nude except for the red towel over her breasts.

Sue Ann Baker was a very tall woman, close to six feet, with the figure of a model. She lay in the center of the bed as if someone had positioned her there almost lovingly, her head resting on two fluffed pillows. One hand lay next to her hip, and the other was just under her body. At six feet, even though she was slender, she must have weighed 150 pounds and it would have taken a very strong individual to lift her.

The woman's legs were spread somewhat—but not in the classic position in which rape victims are often found. She might have been only sleeping. But she was dead, and had been for some time. Rigor mortis was fully established.

The homicide detectives noted a red hand towel under her left knee and a red washcloth next to her right hand. The flowered sheet beneath her body was stained dark reddish brown in spots. A large pool of coagulated blood had seeped over the right side of the mattress when it was still liquid.

Oddly, despite the profusion of blood, the victim's body was exceptionally clean. Looking closer, the investigators could see faint traceries of pink on her skin, as if someone had washed the blood off.

They removed the red towel that covered her breasts and could see the single wound over her right breast. It appeared to be a puncture wound about an inch long, its edges gaping open. That was all. No other wounds, no signs of defense wounds, no hesitation wounds—just the awful, deep wound in her chest. Because her body had been washed, there wasn't even any blood on it.

At the foot of the bed, the detectives found a pair of women's blue jeans; they were inside out, with a pair of panty hose inside. Apparently these had been stripped from the woman's body either before or after death.

Starting at the front entrance, Sergeant VandePutte photographed everything in the apartment. The living room was lavishly furnished with a gold couch and matching love seat, gold lamps, and a glass-topped coffee table. A floor-to-ceiling stone fireplace almost covered one wall. There were many plants, carefully tended, a TV set, and a stereo with the tape in a cassette still circling, although the sound was turned down.

Like all the rooms, the living room was very clean but slightly cluttered. It looked as if someone might have been sleeping on the larger couch; a pillow and two blankets were tangled on the couch. Ted Fonis pointed out a glass on the end table next to the couch. It was half-full of a yellow liquid. He sniffed it and smelled alcohol. A woman's red purse rested on the love seat. Its clasp was fastened.

The glass coffee table in front of the larger couch held an ashtray overflowing with cigarette butts. The top of the glass table seemed smudged. With a flashlight held obliquely, the detectives could make out smears of blood that had been haphazardly wiped up.

The kitchen was neat. There were no dirty dishes in the sink, but there was a brown paper bag on the counter containing an empty MacNaughton's whiskey bottle. A full bottle of the same brand was opened next to it. There was also a steak knife on the counter. When Gary Fowler and Ted Fonis looked in a drawer, they found four more knives—steak knives and a hunting knife. The latter appeared to have bloodstains near the handle. It was more than five inches long, and the blade width appeared to match the wound found in Sue Ann Baker's breast.

The smaller bedroom wasn't nearly as neat as the rest of the apartment. There were clothes strewn around on the bed and the floor. Blood spattered the pair of men's blue jeans on the bed. Peering into the closet, the detectives found a bra with its right cup saturated with blood, along with a bulky knit sweater with bloodstains over the right side.

"She had to have been wearing the sweater, the bra, and probably the jeans in the master bedroom when she was stabbed," Fowler observed. "The stains look as though they're in line. And why would anyone undress her after she was dead?"

"Maybe he was sorry. Maybe it was someone who cared about her and didn't want her found the way she was," VandePutte guessed.

It looked that way. Sue Ann Baker had been bathed and laid out on the bed like a princess lying in state. With the coverlet pulled up, she appeared to be only sleeping.

They found men's clothes hanging in closets around the apartment.

Fonis asked the manager if Sue Ann Baker lived with someone, but the woman shook her head.

"She lived alone. She was separated from her husband."

"What's his name?"

"I believe it's Ron—Ron Baker."

There was no sign of any luggage in the place to indicate a visitor.

Craig VandePutte called Lieutenant Ernie Bisset and the King County chief medical examiner, Dr. Donald Reay, at 10:45 P.M., and they responded to the scene. Reay checked the body and confirmed that Sue Ann Baker had been dead for some time. The nether side of her body was striated with the pinkish purple marks of livor mortis, which indicated that she had lain in the bed in the same position for many hours.

Moreover, the room temperature was 65 degrees, and the victim's body temperature was 65, too.

"I'd say she's been dead for about twenty-four hours," 'Doc' Reay said. "This, which seems to be the only wound, was caused by a single-edged knife."

Sue Ann Baker's fingernails were long and unbroken, perfectly manicured with silver polish. She still wore an expensive watch and rings. The investigators weren't thinking that robbery had been the motive for her death, and this tended to confirm their first impressions.

They encased her hands in bags in the unlikely event that she had attempted to scratch her killer. Some of his—or her—skin might be found under her nails.

Fowler, Fonis, and VandePutte retraced the path they

had made, entering the living room again. Lieutenant Bisset and Dr. Reay and were scrutinizing the large gold couch carefully. The top blanket appeared to have blood-stains. When both blankets were removed, a large blood-stain came into view; it had soaked deep into the couch.

"It looks like she was killed here—or at least stabbed here," Reay commented.

"That fits with the blood that was wiped off the coffee table," Fowler agreed.

Sue Ann's body was removed to await autopsy, but the detectives' night on the job was far from over. They gathered, labeled, and sealed fifty-one pieces of evidence: bloodstained clothing, bedding, the cassette that had played over and over again on the stereo, the knives, and, strangely, a pair of scissors found in a drawer, and which also appeared to bear bloodstains.

Criminalist Tim Taylor arrived from the Western Washington State Crime Lab to process various areas of the crime scene. He used swabs moistened with distilled water to lift samples of blood. It was essential to determine if they were all the victim's blood, or if someone else had bled here.

The most important piece of physical evidence would be a killer's fingerprints in blood or even on the cassette, showing that he or she had been in the apartment at the time Sue Ann was stabbed. It didn't happen often and the homicide detectives would be very lucky if any of these kinds of prints were not Sue Ann's.

*   *   *

At 4 A.M., Sergeant VandePutte's crew was finally back in the Homicide Unit's office, and talking further with Officer Dillon.

Dillon had taken in-depth statements from the couple who managed the apartments.

"The manager and her husband told me that they heard 'normal' activity in the Baker apartment all day long on Sunday—October 30—but nothing on the thirty-first," Dillon said.

Dillon taped their recall of the weekend, and on Halloween.

"I saw Ron's car—that's her husband—parked up by the Tie-Up Tavern this morning about nine thirty," the manager's husband's voice said.

"It's a dark green Buick Electra. The tavern's just down the street from us."

"So evidently Sue Ann's husband—this Ron guy—was around and with her at least part of the last couple of days," Dillon said.

The tape played on. "I think they were together yesterday," the female half of the management team added. "I saw Sue go out to the car yesterday morning—Sunday—and then go back into her apartment."

Dillon said that his information indicated that Sue Ann Baker had worked as a bartender at the Rendezvous Restaurant on Second Avenue West, a popular neighborhood spot.

"I guess she was supposed to be at work today," the woman continued. "And her husband called in this morning and told them she was ill. He said she would call in

428

later in the day—but she never did. They got concerned at the bar when her phone was busy for hours."

Detectives dumped the contents of Sue Ann's purse on a sheet of white paper, noting what was inside. Few men know exactly what the women in their lives carry in their handbags, but nothing seemed to be missing. There was the usual jumble of cosmetics, a learner's permit from the Department of Motor Vehicles that said she could drive but only with a licensed companion on board, a bottle of tranquilizers prescribed for Sue Ann on October 4, a Canadian citizen's registration card, and a card indicating a doctor's appointment on November 4.

There were pictures, too. Some of Sue Ann, and others of her and a man who was, presumably her husband. There were four letters whose envelopes bore the return address of Keith William "Ron" Baker, all postmarked Dutch Harbor, Alaska.

Ron had mailed the letters in early October. They must have meant something to the dead woman because she had kept them in her purse for almost four weeks.

In his letters, Ron Baker wrote about his "change of attitude" since he'd arrived in Alaska. He spoke of looking forward with happy expectation to the time he would return to Seattle in the first week of December. He cautioned Sue Ann about drinking too much.

If they were as estranged as the detectives had heard, their relationship was clearly still close. At least it was in Ron Baker's mind. He'd written about looking forward to their wonderful physical relationship.

The rest of the letters detailed his days as a cook on a

crab boat owned by the New England Fish Company. Any job on a crab boat in the far north in midwinter is dangerous. Storms at sea are not uncommon, and many fishermen and crew fear being tossed into the frigid sea, where they could quickly perish of hypothermia or drowning.

But the pay was good. It sounded as though Ron Baker was determined to save his marriage to Sue Ann.

And then, for some reason, Ron didn't last out the season on the crab boat. He had evidently returned to Seattle a lot sooner than either Sue Ann or he had expected. The management couple had seen his green Buick parked near the apartment and they had seen him, too.

But had they really? Was it possible that Ron Baker was still in Alaska, and the man they saw was someone else who resembled him? The homicide detectives felt they needed corroboration one way or the other on that from other sources.

If Baker had been home, he was missing now. He was certainly the main "person of interest" that they wanted to talk to. A man saying he was Sue Ann's husband had called the Rendezvous on the morning of the thirty-first saying that she was ill.

Yet Dr. Reay's determination of time of death indicated that she had likely been dead for hours then.

The investigation was less than a day old when Gary Fowler, Ted Fonis, and Craig VandePutte left the homicide office. A new day was dawning and they had had no sleep, but they would catch a few hours' nap and then return to work on the case.

On November 1, Gary Fowler sent out a teletype at

8:45 A.M. requesting that law enforcement departments in the seven western states and Alaska pick up Ron Baker for questioning if he was spotted. His photographs and neighbors' descriptions indicated that he was a big man, six feet two, and well over two hundred pounds. He had light blue eyes and brown hair. The information on the dark green Buick Electra was included.

The autumn wind blew orange and black remnants of Halloween crepe paper decorations along Seattle streets, and exhausted youngsters who had gone to bed with makeup on their faces woke up to paw through what was left of their treats from the night before.

Finding witnesses during the daytime was usually easier than in the middle of the night. Now Gary Fowler talked to the young woman who occupied the apartment directly next to Sue Ann Baker's—Gemma Lytle.* Gemma worked as a human resources coordinator in an investment firm.

Shocked that such violence had happened so close to her, Gemma said, "Our two apartments share a common wall and I can't help but overhear sounds, and sometimes even conversations coming from next door."

Because they usually worked different hours, Gemma Lytle said that she didn't know Sue Ann Baker very well. "But we recognized each other and said 'Hi' when we passed going to our apartments."

Because of the flimsy wall between their apartments, Gemma knew more about what happened there than she wanted to.

"I moved in around the first of June and I hadn't seen

Mrs. Baker for three weeks then," she told Fowler. "I knew she was married, but I haven't seen him for a month. He's a big, muscular man in his thirties."

"Did you ever hear any sounds coming from their apartment that would indicate the state of their family life?" Fowler asked.

"I couldn't help but overhear their arguments. And there were a lot of arguments, bickering, you know. But there was never any violence, at least not until recently. A couple of weeks ago, I heard arguing and crying and screaming. It sounded like they were tossing each other against the wall."

"Could you hear what she said?"

"Yes. She kept yelling that she didn't know why she'd put up with him all these years. She said he was worthless. I didn't know what to do, you know—so I didn't say anything to anyone."

"When was the last time you heard conversation in their apartment?"

"It was Friday. That was October twenty-eighth. I couldn't really hear him because it wasn't loud—so I don't know if he was there. But I could hear her crying. It was kind of sad, and I wished I didn't have to listen to it."

"When was the last time you saw Ron Baker's car? Would you recognize his car?"

"Yes—it's a green Buick. Yesterday—Halloween day—it was about seven thirty in the morning. I was surprised it was there because, when he's home, he normally drove her to work before that."

"Okay, what about the sounds coming from next door? When did you hear anyone alive there?"

"Early yesterday morning—about one thirty or two A.M., I heard footsteps coming down the walkway— I recognized his steps because I've heard them so many times, and he's a large man who walks heavy. This time, I could hear his voice—but not hers."

Gemma Lytle was a helpful witness, but she had not actually seen Ron Baker over the past few days. She'd heard a man's voice, and a man's heavy footfall.

Was it Ron—or had it been some other man in Sue Ann's life?

The apartment manager thought he'd seen Ron Baker's car outside the Tie-Up Tavern, and said it was one of his regular hangouts when he was in town. That seemed as good a place as any to find witnesses who might confirm that Baker really *was* in Seattle on Halloween. Fonis and Fowler headed there.

Business in a tavern on a weekday morning was desultory at best. A few serious beer drinkers sat at the bar, and a skeleton staff was setting up for the lunch crowd when the two detectives walked in.

The news of Sue Ann Baker's murder had already reached the rumor mill at the Tie-Up, and the two detectives were directed to a barmaid who knew Ron.

"She works here part-time," the bartender said. "I've seen her talking to Ron."

Toni Giametti* acknowledged readily that she knew Ron Baker.

"How well do you know him?" Ted Fonis asked.

"Pretty well, I guess," she said, looking down.

"Do you know if he was in town this last week—and on Halloween?"

"He was here. A long time ago, we hooked up. I kind of have a warm spot in my heart for him," she said. "Ron stayed two nights with me last week. He told me that he and Susie had broken up for good. After two nights, he moved in with a friend of his."

"When did you see Ron last?" Gary Fowler asked.

"Yesterday morning," Toni said, surprising the investigators. "About nine thirty on Halloween day. He was in the Tie-Up. I said something to him about hearing he and Sue were back together and he said that wasn't true. He told me he was leaving in three days on a Foss [Maritime Company] tug that was heading out to sea for several weeks, going to Hawaii."

Their conversation with Toni Giametti convinced the two detectives that Ron Baker *had* come back to Seattle almost two months early.

"I guess he and Susie made up," Toni said. "I saw him and her in his car on Saturday, and I figured they were back together because they were sitting real close to each other."

The man that Toni described didn't sound at all like a knife-wielding killer, but Fonis and Fowler knew well that violence and rage can be bottled up, and hidden behind a benign façade.

"Ron's a very easygoing person," Toni said. "I've

never seen him angry. He usually drank only Cokes or coffee when he came in here."

"Ever see him drunk?" Fowler asked.

"No—never."

"You don't know of any time he attacked his wife
then?" Fowler pressed. "Any time he'd been violent with
her?"

"I hate to say this. I really do—because I can't imagine
that it could be Ron who did that to her. But the night
before he came to stay with me, he told me that both of
them had gotten drunk and that he grabbed Sue around her
neck. He said he just didn't know why he'd grabbed Sue
around the neck, whether it was because he was drunk or
what was going on in his head. That's when he decided he
had to move out."

Perhaps it hadn't been Ron Baker who'd killed his
wife. Robbery detective Bud Lee had talked with a man
who called headquarters the evening of the thirty-first
to inquire if anyone had reported that Sue Ann was
hurt. This would have been well before her body was
found. The man insisted that he was concerned about her
because she hadn't shown up for the Halloween party at
the Rendezvous. He had seen her the day before and she'd
been fine.

The informant said he had only a platonic interest in
the tall brunette and didn't even know her address. He just
thought it was strange that she hadn't come to work. The
male caller's whereabouts on October 31 were checked
and he was cleared.

Detective Dick Sanford contacted the owner of the Rendezvous to see if Sue Ann Baker's personal problems had been common knowledge.

"Sue Ann talked to us some about Ron. She was trying to break off with him," Sue Ann's boss said. "And she came to work about two weeks ago with big bruises on her neck. They looked like fingerprints.

"Sue Ann was frightened; she'd thought Ron was going to kill her. I know it happened, because Ron himself came in and admitted it to me. He said, 'I just about killed my wife.' I already knew about it, and I said, 'I know Ron.' "

Baker had asked the Rendezvous owner to talk to him and they had discussed the marital problems for a while. Ron had promised he wouldn't come around Sue Ann anymore.

"I told him that was what Sue Ann wanted, and he said he guessed that was the way it had to be . . . and he left alone."

"When was the last time you saw Sue Ann?" Sanford asked.

"Friday—the twenty-eighth. She worked from eight to five. Ron had been in the day before and thanked me for talking to him and he told me he was determined not to bother Sue Ann anymore."

The manager said that Ron had called in Monday, the thirty-first, to say that Sue Ann had "female problems" and couldn't come to work.

"I just couldn't understand why she wouldn't at least call to discuss the party she planned for Halloween night, and then the phone was off the hook, so I called the police to check on her."

Sue Ann was described as "the best" as far as employees went; she drew customers with her ready smile and was very dependable. Apparently she felt compelled to work because her husband had a very spotty work record and seldom held a job for long, even though he was accomplished as a cook. He didn't have any trouble getting jobs, but he quit with a regularity that upset his wife. She'd had hopes that the job in Alaska as a cook on the crab boat would turn out to be more permanent, and she was disappointed when Ron quit after a few weeks and came home.

A friend of Sue's called the homicide office and came in to talk to detectives. She said she'd been out of town until Friday, and had occasion to call Sue and ask about chances for a job at the Rendezvous. She'd learned that the Bakers were separated, and Sue had seemed very glad to have her old friend to talk to.

Ron Baker was described as a "very deep thinker," concerned with "mind development," but also as a man who hadn't been able to hold down a job. "He was just totally dependent on Sue—emotionally as well as financially."

Sanford contacted the bartender at the Tie-Up Tavern and the woman told him that she had last seen Sue Ann and Ron on Sunday night, October 30, when Sue Ann bowled in her league game. She had seen Ron Baker in the tavern on Monday between 10:30 A.M. and 1 P.M. and he had seemed preoccupied and hadn't said much.

Other members of the bowling team were contacted

by detectives. They had seen Ron and Sue Ann together on Sunday about 10 P.M. Sue Ann had mentioned to one member of the team that she was afraid to go home with Ron.

"Then Ron asked us if we wanted to have a drink with them after, but we had to get home because of the baby-sitter. I never saw them after that." The man did say that he thought Sue Ann had filed for divorce and gave the name of her attorney.

Many people had seen Sue Ann alive—but frightened—at 10 P.M. on the night of October 30. After that, only Ron alone had appeared at their usual haunts.

Detective Sanford talked to a friend of Baker's who said that Ron had come into the Tie-Up at 11:30 on Sunday night. The two men had shot pool together until sometime after 1 A.M. He hadn't sensed Ron was particularly upset, and thought he'd been his normal self.

But Ron Baker's "normal self" had vacillated a great deal in the month preceding his wife's murder. The friend said that Ron was sometimes mellow and resigned to the fact that she was leaving him. And sometimes desperately jealous. Baker had reason to be. Cal Samuelson,* who was instrumental in getting him the Alaska job, had bragged to the witness that he and Sue Ann had "a thing going," and that he was going to try to arrange to have Ron sent to Alaska a week ahead of him. That way he could be alone with Sue Ann. Baker had evidently not been aware of his benefactor's hidden reason for getting him a job so far away. But he had found out after he'd been up on the crab boat, and come home.

The witness said that he felt Ron Baker might try to kill the man who had cuckolded him. Fonis called the Alaska State Troopers and urged them to be on the lookout for Baker and keep a protective surveillance on Cal Samuelson, who was supposed to be serving as head cook on the crab boat. "We've got a homicide down here and Baker is the chief suspect. We can't locate him," Fonis advised, "and we think he may be headed up there."

A short while later, Fonis received a call from the chief of police of Dutch Harbor, Alaska, who said he knew Cal well and that the man was presently on the boat. "We can monitor all incoming flights from the lower forty-eight and we'll be able to spot Baker if he does come up here."

Whether Sue Ann Baker had been interested in Cal Samuelson or not is a moot point. During the weeks before she died, she seemed to be agonizing over ending her marriage. She feared her husband, yet she hesitated about filing a divorce action. Friends had advised her to move out, stay with a girlfriend, and get a restraining order. And she said she would, that she'd had enough of the marriage, yet she hesitated; she had loved Baker, and maybe she still did.

She was not a chaser. Sue Ann had talked to several platonic male friends about her marital problems. One in particular, Benny Larson,* a very large man, recalled that she'd begged him twice to come home with her because she was afraid.

"She wanted me to sleep on her couch—but I told her that would just make things worse because he wouldn't understand."

Larson recalled one evening when he'd gone to Sue Ann's apartment to watch TV and to keep her company because she was frightened.

"I went over there on the twenty-fourth of October, but as soon as I got there, Ron and a friend of his showed up. He was really hot when he saw me. He came walking up when I was knocking on the door—she'd called me because she thought he was coming over. He kept pounding on the door and yelling, 'Open up the goddammed door or I'm going to bust it in!' and she finally did."

Larson agreed to stand by in case there was trouble, but to stay out of the argument so that they wouldn't provoke Baker's anger further.

"I guess he wanted to get his things out of there, and he went in and slammed the door behind him. We could hear them wrestling around, but then Ron let us in and he seemed to have cooled down a little bit. Sue was crying, and I stayed with her awhile after they left. She told me, 'I don't know what I'm going to do,' and I just told her to run—get out of there and find another place where he couldn't find her. She said he told her that if he couldn't have her, no other man would, either. I left after about an hour and she was still saying that she wasn't going to move, that she wanted to stay in her own place. . . .

"I saw her on Friday the twenty-eighth at the Rendezvous . . . and then I left to go elk hunting and I never saw her again."

Detective Fonis talked to Sue Ann's lawyer. The lawyer said that Sue Ann had come to him a week or so before she was killed and talked to him about a restraining order.

He had advised her that he'd need to know where Baker was living so that it could be served, and she had promised she would try to find an address where her estranged husband might be located.

"I saw the marks on her throat—two huge bruises, like finger marks. She was supposed to come into the office this week and start divorce proceedings," the lawyer said.

Sue Ann Baker had been walking a tragic tightrope yet, oddly, she apparently had made one last effort at reconciliation with Ron Baker. On the Saturday night before she was killed, she had invited Ron over for a steak dinner. Ron had told a close friend that he planned to go over there and act like a "reasonable person—not a jealous husband or anything. Maybe we could just get along if I can act civilized."

Apparently, the evening had gone all right because Ron told the friend the next day that they hadn't fought, that they'd just sat and talked and eaten the steaks.

At that point, Sue Ann had twenty-four hours to live.

What had gone wrong? By Sunday evening, at the bowling league game, the victim was so frightened of her husband that she'd begged friends to stay with them, claiming she feared being alone with him. Yet she had been alone with him. And by morning she was dead, her lung pierced with one deadly thrust that caused massive hemorrhaging and was so deep it extended into her liver. She might have lived three or four minutes after the attack. No more.

An odd sidelight of the autopsy exam was evidence

that Sue Ann had engaged in intercourse shortly before her death; there were still intact sperm in her vaginal vault when she was found.

Love. And then death.

The teletype on the arrest warrant of Ron Baker had thus far failed to produce any results. He had not flown to Alaska to finish off the man he blamed for the breakup of his marriage, nor had he been seen in his usual haunts. Detectives Fonis and Fowler wondered if the suspect might be dead himself, a suicide whose body had not yet been discovered.

A floor-by-floor check of the vast parking lot at Sea-Tac Airport had not turned up any sign of Baker's green Buick, indicating that he probably hadn't flown out of the area. When the investigators learned that Baker had friends in Kitsap County, just across Puget Sound from Seattle, a special alert was sent to law enforcement departments there.

On November 2, Gary Fowler and Ted Fonis received a call from deputy Pat Jones of the Kitsap County Sheriff's Department. He advised them that he and Poulsbo police chief Robert "Rick" Weatherill had arrested Ron Baker in Poulsbo. Arrangements were made for the arresting officers to meet with the Seattle detectives in the Winslow, Washington, city hall.

Shortly before noon, lieutenant Ernie Bisset, sergeant Craig VandePutte, and detective Dick Sanford boarded a ferry from Seattle headed for Winslow. Ron Baker was seated in Chief Weatherill's patrol car, his face haggard and his eyes red-rimmed from either lack of sleep or tears.

Or both. Sanford advised him of his rights. The suspect showed no surprise at his arrest. He said he didn't want to make any statements.

Their trip back to Seattle was delayed when they missed the ferry, and they waited on the dock for the next passage.

"Do you understand why you've been arrested?" VandePutte asked Baker.

"Yes, for a murder. Of my wife."

When they asked Baker if he had any questions, the big man's shoulders suddenly began to heave as sobs racked his body.

"I've got to tell you what happened," he said, crying. "That's the only way anybody will know the truth."

"You're sure you want to make a statement?"

"I have to," Baker said, haltingly, "or else nobody will know what happened. I want to tell you. I want to tell you now. What do you want me to tell you?"

"What is it that you want to tell us?" VandePutte asked quietly.

"It all happened so fast. I really don't know how it happened."

"Did you mean to murder your wife?"

"Yes, but it all happened so quickly. I don't know what the reason was. I just did it."

"Had you had a fight with your wife about the divorce?"

"No. It just happened. We weren't arguing. We were just sitting there yakking."

"Did anything trigger you to kill her?"

"No. It just happened."

VandePutte told Ron Baker that the detectives had done a good deal of investigating and had uncovered Baker's personal problems. "Did the trouble with Sue Ann began before you left for your job in Alaska?"

"Before that. My marriage was going sour. I didn't want to go up north but I felt like I had to. I knew it was all over before I went. I knew when I came back that I wouldn't have anything."

Asked about his mental state, Baker said, "I went to Alaska as one person—and I came back another. I was really completely changed. I got off the plane in Alaska and I was walking down the dock to the boat and I had the feeling I wasn't there—that the wind was blowing right through me. When I came home again, I knew everything would be over," Baker added again.

Ron Baker's recollection of the actual killing was blurry. He knew he'd stabbed Sue Ann with the knife but he continued to insist that it had happened so fast that he couldn't believe it himself. He couldn't remember what had happened just after she died.

"We were both drinking MacNaughton's whiskey during that day, but I'm not sure if I was drunk. My adrenaline was pumping so bad I don't think the liquor affected me much."

"What time was Sue Ann killed?" VandePutte asked.

"I don't know. Since I went to Alaska, time doesn't mean anything to me. I have no concept of time."

He'd remained with the body of his wife for about an hour after she died, and then he went out for a few hours, returning to sleep on the couch in the living room while Sue Ann lay dead in the master bedroom. He'd wiped up the blood from the coffee table and cleaned the apartment a little. Baker did recall that he'd gone to the Tie-Up Tavern after the murder and played pool with his friend.

On Monday morning, Halloween, he'd called in sick for Sue Ann to the Rendezvous, and then gone back to the Tie-Up for a while. Later he worked on his car, and then left the apartment.

"Did you feel any emotion about what you'd done?"

"No. I am a highly emotional person but I didn't feel anything when I killed Sue Ann. Nothing at all. I still don't have any emotions."

Ron Baker said he'd thought some of suicide after his wife died. "I did consider it for a long time, but I didn't do anything about it. I just couldn't bring myself to do it."

"Why did you kill your wife?" VandePutte asked again.

"I don't know. It just happened. It just happened—"

Baker said that he knew about the man who had been seeing his wife—the senior cook on the crab boat—but he insisted that her alleged infidelity had nothing to do with the murder.

"Where have you been since you left her place?" Ted Fonis asked.

"Just riding back and forth on the ferry. I was really tired, but I couldn't sleep. I expected to be arrested because I went back to the island where I'm well-known. I would have turned myself in eventually."

Keith William "Ron" Baker was booked into jail on homicide charges. On January 27, 1978, he pleaded guilty to second-degree murder and was sentenced to ten years minimum in prison and twenty years maximum for the murder of his wife.

And so the troubled marriage of the lovely bartender and the man who loved her beyond all reason was over. She had ignored the warnings of dozens of friends in the vain hope that she and Ron might be able to find some friendly solution, but she had gambled her life on the losing side.

Perhaps there was no way out except the deadly scene played out on the eve of Halloween.

TERROR ON A
MOUNTAIN TRAIL

Among all the violent crimes against persons, the crime of rape is proliferating faster than any other; every nine minutes, somewhere in the United States, another woman is raped. And that statistic covers only reported rapes. Crime statistic experts estimate that only one-fifth to one-third of rapes are ever reported. Embarrassment, fear of reprisal, shock, and myriad other reasons can prevent women from coming forward to give statements about what has happened to them. It takes a brave woman to file charges and agree to appear in court to testify against her sexual assailant when she has dreaded ever being in the same room with him again. But when she does, she is helping to protect other women who might be the next terrorized victims.

It is certainly wise for all women to be aware of the threat of sexual attack. It can happen anywhere: in their own homes, on the street, in a crowded shopping mall— even in a school or in the sanctuary of a church. For two Washington State women, it happened in the peaceful sylvan setting of Mount Rainier National Park.

*   *   *

Mount Rainier is much beloved by tourists and native Washingtonians alike. Fifty miles southeast of Seattle, its 14,410-foot snowy peak suddenly rises almost magically against bright blue sky. It can be seen on clear days for miles and miles in every direction, its majestic height crowned with glistening white. Locals smile as they tell each other, "The mountain is out today!"

Mount Rainier looks like the cover of a calendar, so perfect. But it can be both welcoming and cruel. Its endless swaths of sunny meadows dotted with wildflowers—daisies, rhododendrons, lupines, and columbines—end suddenly in the deep shadows of evergreen forests. Winter snow piles up and sparkles when the daylight hits the drifts, but there are also bleak, rocky stretches, covered with ice and crisscrossed with crevasses of unfathomable depth.

No one knows exactly how many climbers have fallen to their deaths when ice bridges collapsed beneath them and they plunged down into those chasms, so far that no one could save them. They rest there forever, on the mountain that drew them almost hypnotically to take a chance. Expert mountain climbers and neophytes alike have set out to experience the wonder of Mount Rainier only to have sudden storms come out of nowhere to blanket higher elevations with wind and ice. These whiteouts catch them unaware. Those who know what they are doing are equipped to wait out the storm and survive. Those who are unprepared often don't make it.

Sometimes a pervading fog envelops Mount Rainier and hikers can see no more than three feet in any direction. When the storms and fog come, the safest place is inside the rustic lodges, next to roaring fireplaces.

There are other elements to fear on a mountain as high as Mount Rainier. There, creatures often hide along the trails: bears, cougars, wolves, and, most dangerous of all, human predators.

On June 3, 1978, the bleakness and danger of winter storms when the sun sets at 3 P.M. were far away. It was a brilliant late spring day when two young women set out for a hike along the Rampart Ridge Trail. Filtered sunlight etched dappled shadows on the vegetation along the pathway. Their own voices were the only sounds.

The women had no thought of danger. They were familiar with the trail, experienced hikers who had all the gear they needed for any eventuality—or so they thought. They planned to climb the path through the woods until they came to the high meadows rampant with spring flowers. They would share a picnic lunch there, and then return to their car near the lodge long before dark. The longest day of the year was just a little over two weeks away and in the Northwest at that time of year it doesn't get dark until almost 10 P.M.

They were all alone. Yet, on a day like this was, they could expect to meet other hikers who had set out from Longmire Lodge and exchange greetings with them—the easy camaraderie of hikers.

Kit Spencer* was twenty-eight and worked as an economist in Seattle; her companion, Rose Fairless,* also twenty-eight, was a law student from Tacoma. They were highly competent, intelligent women. Neither would have walked along certain streets in Tacoma or Seattle at night—but this was Mount Rainier National Park and it was broad daylight.

They laughed and talked as they headed up the trail from Longmire Lodge to Paradise Lodge farther up the mountain, their voices cutting through the serene silence around them.

Kit and Rose heard footsteps thudding up the trail behind them and wondered momentarily at the energy of the person approaching. The recommended technique for trail hiking is based on steady walking. But the person behind them seemed to be in a tearing hurry.

Suddenly Rose let out a surprised yelp. A hand had reached out from nowhere and grabbed her arm. As both women turned to look behind them, they gasped to see a tall, apparition-like figure dressed in military camouflage clothing. They couldn't see his face because it was covered with a green ski mask, leaving only his eyes and mouth visible.

Oddly, the man wore socks over his shoes. Each of them wondered briefly if this was some kind of bad joke.

Then they saw the gun. It appeared to be a small-caliber weapon, but he was waving it at them menacingly.

"I'm going to rob you!" the man rasped. He forced them to walk in front of him into a secluded clearing about four hundred feet off the trail.

"How much money do you have?" the masked stranger asked.

"None. I don't have any," Kit answered.

"Wait. Here—I've got about thirty dollars," Rose said quietly. "Take it."

The man pocketed the cash, but he didn't leave, and he quickly blocked their way so they couldn't return to the trail.

Finally, Kit asked him the question that was burning in both women's minds. "Do you want money. Or sex?"

"Both," the hooded figure answered.

"Why? Why are you doing this?" she countered.

"For kicks," he said. "I want to find out what it's like."

Fighting panic, the women begged the man not to rape them. They urged him to take the money and let them go.

"We promise you," Rose said. "We won't report this to anyone. It would be too embarrassing for us."

He wasn't dissuaded. The robbery had been only the first part of his plan to achieve "kicks."

"Why do you have the gun, anyway?" Kit asked him.

"For safety. It's my insurance policy. But don't worry—I won't use it if you both do what I want."

They realized that they were absolutely helpless. The only sound in the woods now was the calling of birds, the scurrying of little animals, and the buzz of mosquitoes in the dank underbrush that never quite caught the sun as it sliced through the giant firs.

Kit and Rose stared at each other, trying to send small signals by tilting their heads and altering their expressions slightly. They knew each other well. They were both in good shape. Maybe together they could overcome him enough so they would have a chance to run.

But he was a very large man, with very strong hands. And he had a loaded gun.

At this point, it had come down to a matter of their living or dying. He could kill them easily, and no one would hear the gun's roar. The frightened women knew that their bodies might well lie undiscovered for days, months—perhaps forever.

"Now take off your clothes—all of them," their captor ordered.

Slowly, they complied. As their bare skin was exposed, they were suddenly assailed by mosquitoes, scores of them. The buzzing insects bit them, drawing blood out and dotting their flesh with stings.

As the gunman blindfolded the women—Kit with her own shirt, and Rose with his ski mask, which he turned around backward—they complained that they were being eaten alive by the mosquitoes.

He was well supplied for the wilderness, and in a bizarre act of concern, handed them a bottle of insect repellent and told them to rub it on their bodies. It was a considerate gesture, while he was clearly planning to hurt them more than the mosquitoes ever could.

Shivering with fear and the dank chill of the black-green forest, Kit and Rose dabbed at their bodies with the repellent.

"You can call me Joe," the man said.

They doubted that that was his real name, but they played along; they did not want to irritate him in any way.

Each had noticed that the man spoke with a New York or East Coast accent. Both Kit and Rose had lived in New York at one time and they recognized the dialect.

Now the man told them, in obscenely explicit terms, what he wanted: intercourse and fellatio. Naked, blindfolded, and remembering the gun in his hands and the six-inch knife they had spotted in a sheath at his waist, they complied.

But they were making mental notes to remember him by. If they got out of the forest alive, they would never forget him and they *would* report him to authorities as soon as they could.

As he forced each of them to kiss him, they moved their hands over his head. Unlike many young men of the seventies, he had extremely short hair—the kind of haircut required for military men. When his mouth crushed theirs in openmouthed kisses, both Kit and Rose felt the several jagged teeth in the front of his jaw.

For the moment, at least, the rapist had everything on his side, and he confidently ran his hands over their helpless bodies, fondling them. Each could hear the other shudder and gag as he forced his attentions on them.

The sexual attacks seemed to go on endlessly, but eventually he climaxed and moved away from them. They could hear his harsh breathing, and their own hearts thudding. Was he satiated? They prayed so.

He could kill them. He might kill them. Then he wouldn't have to worry that they might be able to identify him. Aching, scratched, sickened, they feared what might come next. They could hear him putting his clothes back on, and they felt around in the brush for theirs and cautiously began to get dressed.

"Now," he instructed them, "I'm leaving, but you'll be watched. Wait twenty minutes before you try to leave—or I'll have to—"

"We'll wait," they both assured him.

They could hear crashing in the brush and breaking twigs as the man dove deeper into the thickets of evergreens. Soon there was no sound but the forest noises. Rose and Kit ripped off their blindfolds. They looked around cautiously, daring to hope that he was really gone.

They couldn't see him, but that didn't mean much; there were so many places for him to hide, watching them. They held their breath, listening. But there was no sign of their attacker.

The two young women waited only ten minutes. He had appeared out of nowhere, and he might still be out there, waiting for them to make their way through the dense underbrush, perhaps planning to pick them off with his gun.

Still, they decided they had to risk it.

Once they were back on the trail, everything seemed normal, but of course it wasn't. Kit and Rose were both in deep shock. They discussed in whispers about whether they should report the man who had just raped them. Their dilemma was to be expected. They felt violated, dirty, and wanted only to forget what had happened. They feared the man who had forced them into the woods and worried that he might somehow find them and take his revenge. Had he looked through their belongings while they were blindfolded? If he had, he probably knew where they lived.

The camouflaged man had seemed in such complete control, as if he knew the forested mountainside like the back of his hand. He could be waiting for them just around the next bend in the trail, watching to see what they were going to do. He might be taking pleasure in hunting them.

Someone was coming toward them, and they froze with fear. Vastly relieved, they saw a man and woman walking down the trail from Paradise Lodge. The couple could see at once that the young women were very frightened and seemed confused.

"Are you lost?" the man asked.

"Yes. Yes—we're not sure where we are," Kit stammered.

"Follow us—we'll lead you to Longmire," he answered.

Kit and Rose followed the couple, but now shock was really taking its toll, and they shivered, feeling almost numb, as they walked down the trail that had seemed so sunny and friendly such a short time before.

The couple from the lodge were puzzled by the two women's demeanor but assumed that they were only frightened because they'd been lost on the mountain. Neither Kit nor Rose had mentioned the violent stranger to their rescuers.

At Longmire Lodge, they decided they had to do something; *they* were alive, but the next females who were alone on the wooded trail might not survive. Rose placed a call to Rape Relief in Seattle and then to one of her law school professors.

"They both said we should report him," Rose said. "I know we should."

The two women approached chief park ranger Robert Dunnagan and Ranger William Larson and told them about the masked man in the woods who had held them captive, raped them, and forced them to perform oral sodomy.

"What did he look like?" Dunnagan asked. "Tell me as much as you remember and I'll notify all of our rangers and also the law enforcement departments that are nearby."

"I wish we could describe his face," Kit said. "But we didn't really see him. He was wearing an army camouflage outfit—maybe coveralls. He had a very short crew cut—and his front teeth were kind of snaggled—broken."

"Oh," Rose added, "we couldn't look up at him, but I looked down. He wore socks over his shoes."

"That's probably because he didn't want to leave tracks—patterns from his shoes," Dunnagan said. "He must have known what he was doing."

Finding the suspect was not going to be easy. Fort Lewis, the second-largest military compound in the United States, was located nearby and soldiers camping or training in the vast mountain park area were not unusual. Any suspect who wanted to hide would have a relatively easy time, especially a suspect who knew the trails as well as the rapist seemed to.

A few hours later, Rangers Dunnagan and Larson were scouting the parking lot in a widening area around Longmire Lodge when they spotted a tall man with a crew cut. He was wearing an army camouflage jacket.

"You! Stop!" Dunnagan shouted, and shone a flashlight

into the man's face. He noted that the man was "wound up like a spring." He stopped walking away, but he refused to come any closer to the rangers.

"What are you doing around here?" Dunnagan asked.

"I'm camping up near Paradise," the man said, shrugging his shoulders. "I guess I'm lost."

Dunnagan and Larson gave him directions to the Paradise area, but they watched him closely. Suddenly he bolted and took off running into the now-dark woods in an entirely different direction. They searched for him in vain.

By the morning of June 4, Mount Rainier National Park was alive with park rangers and FBI agents—because the park was on federal land. Pierce County sheriff's deputies had also been directed to the mountain to assist in the search. Tracking dogs padded along trails and then crashed into the undergrowth.

The consensus was that the rapist was still within the park's boundaries; police vehicles had sealed off the usual exits overnight, and the widespread search began again by 4 A.M. in the first pale light of dawn.

The lawmen staked out a number of cars that bore Fort Lewis parking stickers, but none of the individuals who approached the vehicles matched the description that Kit and Rose had given.

FBI agent Richard Rudy stopped a soldier in the parking lot at Longmire Lodge and asked him his reasons for being there. The man, who gave his name as Alan Showalter,* resembled the suspect they sought. He appeared to be about the same height as the man the victims had described and he had a very short crew cut.

Showalter explained that he was a member of the army's elite Ranger unit. Agent Rudy knew that the army Rangers were trained in wilderness survival and, if need be, to kill quietly and swiftly.

"What are you doing here?" Rudy asked.

"I left my buddy up here yesterday," Showalter explained. "He was going to camp out and I'm on my way to pick him up at Narada Falls."

Alan Showalter held out his identification, and the searchers relaxed a little. Showalter said his friend and former roommate was also an army Ranger. He had come to pick up Mark Leslie Rivenburgh, twenty-six.

"He's from New York State," Showalter said.

"We'll walk you up there," Rudy said easily, signaling to Park Ranger John Wilcox to accompany them. "We'd like to talk to him. He may have seen the guy we're looking for."

The trio set out along a forested trail. If Rivenburgh had been in the park all night, he might be a good witness— or a likely suspect in the double rape. Special Agent Rudy speculated privately that a Ranger, with the specialized training he had received, would be a formidable quarry if he was the man they sought. With his knowledge of forest lore, a Ranger could easily hide himself from the massive search.

After walking awhile into the deep woods, Rudy, Wilcox, and Showalter heard footsteps approaching. Army Ranger Showalter had the code of Rangers deeply ingrained in him; Rangers protected each other reflexively. A tall man wearing camouflage apparel, a man with a crew cut and a mustache, appeared on the trail. Ranger Showalter quickly lifted one hand and drew it across his neck in a "throat-cutting" gesture, a "danger" signal to Rangers.

Rudy and Wilcox spotted the signal and dropped to a crouch, guns drawn. They could not be sure if Showalter was helping them or a danger to them. And then the man coming toward them stopped like a fox who had caught the scent of danger. In a heartbeat, he disappeared into the almost impenetrable brush along the trail.

The FBI special agent and the park ranger could hear him breaking through the trees, and then the camouflaged man appeared on the trail below them.

He shouted at them, "You stupid bastards—you could be dead now if I'd wanted to shoot you!"

"We want to talk to you!" Rudy called as he neared the man. Rudy reached out to frisk the suspect, but the man they sought instantly jerked away and was gone. One thing was certain: his actions were certainly not those of an innocent man.

Showalter admitted that the man who had once again vanished into the woods was his friend Mark Rivenburgh. Rudy chastised him for warning Rivenburgh with the Rangers' danger signal when they'd spotted him. Showalter spread his hands in apology.

"I'm sorry," he blurted. "That was just reflex. We're trained to always protect each other."

Alan Showalter positively identified the man who was playing cat-and-mouse with the Mount Rainier park rangers and the FBI special agent. They were longtime partners and friends.

"Yes," he said, sounding puzzled. "That was Mark. There's no question. But I don't know why he's acting this way."

All Showalter could figure was that, somehow, his buddy's mind had slipped a cog.

"He's acting as though he's still in the jungle in Vietnam, escaping from the enemy," Showalter suggested. "He might be having some kind of a flashback."

Maybe he was right; it was possible that Mark Rivenburgh was suffering from post-traumatic stress disorder. Honed as he was for jungle warfare, he was as comfortable in the forest as the animals who were born to it. Even the park rangers and FBI special agents' training wasn't equal to that received by the carefully picked army Ranger unit. Rivenburgh had been taught to survive—to walk on little cat feet. But if his mind had cracked under pressure, he was as dangerous as any rabid cougar on the mountain.

As the day progressed, Agent Richard Rudy again encountered the elusive suspect, this time on the Wonderland Trail. Once more, Rivenburgh screamed out obscenities. Rudy knew he and the park rangers were confronting a perilous situation. Too many law enforcement officers who have to deal with a psychotic subject don't survive. Rivenburgh appeared to be on the edge of psychosis, trigger-happy and furious. If they tried to rush him, he was likely to shoot, and the park was still alive with tourists despite all efforts to find them and warn them away. At any moment, a family might come around a bend in the path and be caught in crossfire.

Loath to risk that, Rudy watched helplessly as Rivenburgh again disappeared into the thick cluster of fir trees. This time the men who tracked him were afraid he had made a clean escape.

It seemed so. The manhunt in the park continued for a solid week without a sign of Rivenburgh.

Mark Rivenburgh was assigned to Fort Lewis, and a check with officials there brought the news that he was AWOL (absent without leave) from the sprawling base. If he had managed to slip past the park's gate stakeouts, he could be anywhere. Or he might still be somewhere on the mountain, using his physical strength and training to avoid detection. Despite the manhunt on Mount Rainier, he had escaped as easily as fog vanishes from the treetops when the sun appears.

As long as the sexual marauder remained free to wander the secluded trails, the investigators worried for the safety of other women in the park. It wasn't as if they had a public address system that could ring out warnings. Cell phones hadn't even been invented yet.

The park rangers, FBI agents, and police officers from nearby towns and counties braced for word that Mark Rivenburgh had struck again. They were relieved when the only reports of problems came from some women campers who said they'd been "annoyed" by a bunch of soldiers who were "aggressively flirting" with them.

At Fort Lewis, Mark Rivenburgh's superiors were stunned to learn that he was the prime suspect in a vicious rape attack. Colonel Wayne Downing, his commanding officer, shook his head as he described the missing Ranger.

"Mark is a good soldier," Downing said. "He has a good reputation and a bright future in the army. No one but the cream of the crop is chosen for Ranger training in the first place."

Back home in Beacon, New York, Rivenburgh's fiancée, twenty-two-year-old Francie O'Brien,* was stunned to hear that Mark had been AWOL for almost a week. The pretty, dark-haired woman caught a flight to Tacoma with Mark's sister, and the two of them waited anxiously for some word of him. Rather than doubting him, Francie was worried sick that something must have happened to him to make him behave so erratically.

Mark Rivenburgh had not come from a family where breaking the law was either expected or accepted. His father, a prison supervisor, had been killed in a boating accident ten months earlier. His mother was also a prison supervisor—at a women's facility—and he had five younger brothers and sisters. Rivenburgh had grown up with Francie in Beacon, a town on the Hudson River one hundred miles north of New York City. She was totally bewildered and had never known him to be unfaithful to her or even to lie to her.

Still, if Mark was innocent of the charges waiting for him, why hadn't he come forward?

Why indeed?

On June 10, the seventh day, Mark Rivenburgh *did*

come forward. He walked and jogged for many miles until he arrived at the Lakewood, Washington, home of his sergeant. He said he was turning himself in for being AWOL and asked to be taken to Colonel Downing. He had quite a story to tell, and seemed almost proud of his ability to evade detection for almost a week.

Although most of the lawmen searching for him believed he had slipped through their dragnet, Mark Rivenburgh said he'd remained inside the Mount Rainier Park boundaries all the time. Hidden in plain sight behind a veil of trees, he had used all of his survival skills to stay underground as he watched the men and dogs who hunted him.

For the first fourteen hours, the Ranger said, he'd hidden near a service station inside the park's boundaries. He was waiting, he claimed, to make a phone call to Fort Lewis and arrange to turn himself in. But everywhere he turned, he'd found roads blocked with police cars.

"So I headed cross-country until I came to Silver Lake and I broke into a cabin there. I changed from my Ranger camo gear into some olive-colored trousers and a blue sweatshirt I found inside.

"Food wasn't much of a problem," he bragged. "I knew which berries and roots to eat, and there were some supplies in the cabin."

"Did the dogs get close to you?" someone asked. "Were you concerned about them?"

Mark Rivenburgh shook his head. "Nope. There were enough streams I could wade through, and they lost my scent."

As Rivenburgh appeared at the army Ranger headquarters where Colonel Downing waited, he suddenly seemed extremely worried. Still he insisted that was because he'd been AWOL, and he didn't want to be brought up on charges about that—he wanted to keep on being a Ranger.

"You have much more serious charges to worry about than being AWOL," Downing informed him. "They want you for rape."

Rivenburgh appeared shocked at that. He categorically denied that he had raped anyone.

"The only thing I'm guilty of is being away from my duty here," he insisted. "I know I should have reported in."

Colonel Downing and Special Agent Rudy didn't believe him, not unless he'd suffered a psychotic blackout, and that was an excuse for committing crimes that suspects used so often that it had little merit. Moreover, there were living victims and other witnesses who placed him where Kit Spencer and Rose Fairless had been terrorized.

Rose and Kit picked Rivenburgh's picture out of a photo lay-down and they also identified him in a lineup. As much as they wanted to forget him, they had tried to remember everything they could about him. They had no doubt he was the man who raped them. They told investigators that they recognized his voice and his New York accent. He had the army crew cut and the chipped teeth that both of them felt as he forced his kisses on them.

Mark Rivenburgh was arrested and charged with two counts of rape and one of robbery. He was allowed to remain free on fifteen-thousand-dollars bail until trial.

But the story of the stalking army Ranger was far from over.

Some thirty miles north of Fort Lewis, detectives in the Port of Seattle Police Department read follow-up reports on Mark Rivenburgh with great interest.

Chief Neil Moloney's department had been investigating a series of frightening incidents involving women employees at the Sea-Tac Airport, on Old Highway 99, located halfway between Seattle and Tacoma. Between February and May, flight attendants and women who worked at the counters for a number of airlines had grown increasingly afraid. Their jobs meant that they often had to walk through parking areas at all hours of the day and night. And several of them had been accosted, molested, threatened, or sexually attacked. Although they tried to walk to their cars in pairs, that wasn't always possible.

On March 20, 1978, the investigation took on an urgency. Joyce Lee Sparks Kennedy O'Keefe, forty-five, worked as a ticket agent at the Pan Am desk and she was unfailingly on time for work. Some fellow employees reported that Joyce didn't show up at all for her 2:30 P.M. shift. Others recall that she worked that first day of spring, and *left* at 2:30. It's most likely that she ended her workday in mid-afternoon. Whichever it was, Joyce disappeared completely in the misty rain. That was less than three months before the mountain stalker attacked.

When relatives and friends became worried that she

ANN RULE

didn't answer her phone or her door, Port of Seattle police officers searched the many levels of the Sea-Tac parking garage. They located her car. Its doors were unlocked and her purse and keys were lying on the front seat. There was no sign of a struggle, and the car started immediately when they tried the key.

Joyce had red hair and bright blue eyes, and she was petite at five feet, three inches and 130 pounds. She usually wore glasses and they were not found in her car. The last coworkers to see her recalled she was wearing a red blouse and tan slacks. She had on an expensive gold ring set with diamonds and featuring the engraving "Love."

Joyce Kennedy was an attractive, well-adjusted woman who family and friends insisted would never disappear voluntarily. Although her marriage was strained, she cared too much about her family, and especially her mother, Virginia Beach Sparks, who had been widowed a decade before. And Joyce had four children: Mark, Sherry, Michele, and Matthew. She would never have left them voluntarily. Coworkers said Joyce worried about their problems a lot.

Chief Neil Moloney divided the massive airport into grids and assigned his officers to search every inch of it. All to no avail. No one they talked to recalled seeing or hearing anything unusual on March 20. It would seem that the missing woman had left the airport complex in someone else's vehicle, or that she—or her body—was hidden someplace within its confines.

And yet, from that day to this, no one has seen Joyce Kennedy. The siege at Sea-Tac continued. On April 4,

Ginger LeMay,* a slender twenty-year-old woman who worked at a catering company, Servair Incorporated, which was located on the Sea-Tac grounds, left work at about 10:45 P.M. As usual, she headed toward her parked car. She wasn't particularly afraid; the airport never really sleeps and giant jets were taking off regularly, while vehicles arrive constantly to deposit or pick up passengers. There were other people around, although their number diminished as she moved out of the brightly lit area.

Tired and eager to get home, she was lost in thought. She slowly became aware of a utility van that was keeping pace with her. The male driver suddenly pulled up alongside her and stopped.

"Miss? Miss—would you stop a moment?" The driver's voice was polite as he called to her.

She walked a little closer to the van, figuring that he needed directions.

"We've got an emergency going on here," he explained. "There's a hijacking going on right now and I've been sent to move people into a safer area. Hop in and I'll see you're taken to a spot where you'll be out of danger."

The young, dark-haired man seemed in earnest and Ginger Lemay believed him. But once she was inside the van, she realized to her horror that the hijacking story had been only a ruse to get her into the vehicle. The driver didn't seem to be taking her anywhere except to an isolated area of the airport.

She reached for the door handle, but she couldn't unlock the passenger door. Once they were in a really dark area, her abductor stopped, set the brake, and began to tear at her clothing. Ginger, filled with the adrenaline of fear, fought back with all of her strength.

Finally, she was able to break away from him. She ran as fast as she could to a lighted area. She told Port of Seattle officers that the stranger had been Caucasian, probably in his twenties, and that he had very short hair and well-developed muscles. She wasn't sure if she could identify him because the interior of his van was almost pitch-dark when he began to attack her.

The unsettling assaults on young women continued. On May 8, Bren Forsell,* a twenty-eight-year-old flight attendant, was heading for her car in the multitiered parking building adjoining the main airport structures when she heard footsteps behind her. When she got off the elevator, there were no other drivers retrieving their cars. Now she was all alone—except for the man whose footsteps behind her were growing closer and closer.

Before Bren could run, he was on her, his breath hot against her neck. She wasn't going down without a fight, and the spunky flight attendant pulled away from him and kicked her assailant hard where it would do the most damage. As he grunted, bent over with pain, Bren, too, escaped.

All the women who had been approached and/or attacked by the "Sea-Tac Stalker" had given very similar descriptions of the dangerous stranger, and when the Port of Seattle detectives learned about the double rapes in the Mount Rainier National Park, they saw a number of similarities to their cases.

Furthermore, as they checked out airline manifestoes,

they discovered that Mark Rivenburgh had passed through Sea-Tac on the very day that Ginger LeMay was abducted.

On July 31, Port of Seattle detectives arrested Mark Rivenburgh and charged him with first-degree kidnapping, second-degree assault, and second-degree attempted rape in the case of Ginger LeMay on April 4, when the would-be rapist was playing "Good Samaritan" in the fake hijack scheme. Bail was set at twenty thousand dollars and he was scheduled to go on trial on those charges in September.

But the prosecution case against Rivenburgh did not run smoothly. The day before the trial was to begin, charges were dropped against him. Army authorities said that the times didn't mesh. Although Rivenburgh flew into Sea-Tac on April 4, their records showed that he arrived at the airport a few hours *after* Ginger LeMay was assaulted. According to their records, the Ranger had been training in Georgia at a special survival school for some weeks prior to April 4.

Possibly. And possibly not.

The charges from the dual attacks on Rose Fairless and Kit Spencer on Mount Rainier remained, however. On September 25, Mark Rivenburgh went on trial in U.S. district court judge Jack E. Tanner's packed courtroom in Tacoma.

The handsome Ranger, dressed in a brown suit with a brown and orange checked shirt, clutched Francie O'Brien's hand as he entered the courtroom. Francie still believed every word Mark said, and she gave him a hug and a kiss before she found a seat in the gallery.

471

But Francie didn't stay there long. The bailiff tapped her on the shoulder and told she would have to leave. She was on the defense's witness list, and she wasn't allowed in the courtroom until after she testified. Francie sat outside her fiancé's trial, reading a paperback book and chain-smoking.

She had stuck by Mark since he was arrested, and she told reporters that she would remain loyal to him. "I have faith in my fiancé," she said proudly. "I know he is innocent."

She vowed that she would marry him as soon as he was cleared of the charges against him. She simply could not imagine that Mark would harm a woman, much less rape her. The army appeared to agree with her. Rivenburgh had remained on duty at Fort Lewis until his trial.

Kit Spencer and Rose Fairless each took the witness stand for the prosecution, although it was clear they were frightened. Their voices wavered and they kept their eyes tightly shut as they related the details of the violent sexual attack on the Rampart Ridge Trail. Mark Rivenburgh sat calmly at the defense table as they identified him as the sadist who had tormented them.

Kit told the jurors that she and Rose had submitted to his demand for bizarre sex acts only because they were convinced he would kill them if they refused.

FBI agent Richard Rudy and the park rangers testified about their encounters with the defendant after the attack. The park rangers said they had found a pair of olive, army-issue socks partially burned at the Paradise River Campgrounds after Rivenburgh's arrest. They believed that these were the socks the rapist had worn over his shoes as he crept up on his victims.

To counter that, however, Captain Richard McCreight and Colonel Downing testified that army Rangers were not trained to wear socks over their shoes.

"They don't need to do that. They can move without making a sound without taking such precautions," Downing said.

"Our men are not trained to burn their gear," McCreight added. "They are instructed to *bury* anything that might give them away."

Mark Rivenburgh's sergeant, the man he'd sought out after he escaped from the park, testified for the defense, too. Kit Spencer and Rose Fairless had identified a Gerber Mark II hunting knife as the weapon Rivenburgh used to threaten them into submission, but the sergeant disagreed.

"He didn't have that knife with him," the sergeant declared. "It was at our house all the time. He left it with us when he went to Georgia in March for training."

Was this all a case of faulty identification? Francie O'Brien thought so. "Mark is a gentle man who could never have done what he was accused of," she said passionately. "It is absolutely *impossible* that he could have done it."

Defense attorney John Henry Browne was in his early thirties at Mark Rivenburgh's trial, at the beginning of a career that would one day make him one of the most recognizable criminal defense attorneys in America. He questioned Francie gently.

"Do you and the defendant have an adequate sexual relationship?"

"Yes," she murmured, bowing her head in embarrassment.

Would the jury feel that a man with a fulfilling sex life was immune from aberrant sexual lust? A layman might. Browne hoped so. But anyone familiar with the peculiar compulsions of a rapist would find Francie's testimony unconvincing. Many rapists have enviable sex lives with willing women—and still they *do* force sexual perversions on other women. And the man who raped Kit and Rose had told them he was doing it "for kicks."

On September 28, the tall Ranger took the stand in his own defense. His version of the incidents in the park after the attacks was bizarre, to say the least. He admitted that he had come across FBI agents and park rangers on three occasions, and run from them because "their unprofessional manner" had caused him to fear for his life.

"After Alan Showalter gave me a ride to the park, I hiked cross-country," Mark Rivenburgh explained to the jurors. "And I camped in a clearing near the Paradise River Campgrounds. That night—the third night—I hiked down to the lodge at Longmire to eat, but the restaurant was closed. I stopped to look at the stars. And then these two park rangers flashed a light in my face as I was crossing the parking lot.

"I had a .25-caliber automatic pistol with me, and I was worried because I knew that guns were not allowed in the park. So I kept my hand inside my shirt so the gun wouldn't show. I asked them for directions to Paradise.

But they backed off," he testified. "It seemed like they didn't want to talk to me."

Assistant U.S. attorney Bob Westinghouse cross-examined Rivenburgh aggressively.

"Didn't you really go to the Longmire parking lot that night to see if the heat was on you?"

"Walk into the middle of the plaza like that?" the defendant replied indignantly. "Of course not!"

Mark Rivenburgh said that he'd seen his friend Alan Showalter give him the "danger" signal the next day. "He looked scared. I figured the park rangers were going to snag me for camping in a nondesignated area."

The defendant next described FBI agent Richard Rudy as being "nervous" and "out of control" when he pulled his gun. "I was afraid I was going to be shot," Rivenburgh said gravely.

"He said he was the FBI and he wanted to talk about some hikers—but not there. I called him obscenities and told him we'd discuss whatever it was right there. I told him to put that fucking gun away."

Rivenburgh said that neither the park rangers nor the FBI agent would tell him what they wanted with him. "They came on too strong, too fast, and tried to push me against a rock wall. I said, 'You guys are fucking crazy!' "

According to his testimony, the defendant was clearly the victim of police abuse. "I was threatened with being shot, and, yes, I swore at them and took off into the woods.

"I wanted to get to the park headquarters for professional help. At that point, I thought that something must have happened at the park, a murder or something."

That was a curious non sequitur. Mark Rivenburgh evidently assumed the jury would believe that he continually dodged the lawmen who wanted to talk to him because he was an innocent, rational man, a man afraid for his life.

He did not appear to sense the effect his string of obscenities and his odd story of hiding out in the woods was having on the jury. He apparently expected sympathy; he was getting just the opposite. Nor did it apparently seem strange to him that he had chosen to be a fugitive on the mountain for a week because he thought he'd be punished for camping in a nondesignated area.

If he thought he was swaying the jury panel to his side, he was wrong.

Mark Rivenburgh's two rape victims had identified him, and his testimony and actions had only accentuated that this was a man filled with lies.

The jurors deliberated only a short time before they found Rivenburgh guilty of rape and robbery. He was sentenced later to up to twenty years in federal prison.

The investigation into the mysterious disappearance of Joyce Lee Sparks Kennedy O'Keefe from Sea-Tac Airport continues to this day, more than three decades later, as does the probe into the many attempted rapes in the spring of 1978.

Joyce's parents are deceased. Her first husband, John Kennedy, died in 1990, and her estranged widower, John Thomas O'Keefe, passed away in 2010. Joyce's son Mark Kennedy died on Valentine's Day 2008, at the age of fifty-three. Her granddaughter, Tia Kennedy, posted photos of a young Joyce on the Internet a few years ago.

"Joyce Lee Kennedy is my grandmother on my Mom's side," Tia posted. "I never got to meet her because she went missing two years before I was born. Please join me as I embark on a journey into the history of my Grandmother Joyce's life, disappearance, and, hopefully, solving her case."

So Joyce Kennedy is not forgotten. Descendants she never knew still care about her and long to learn what her fate was. Was she another of Mark Rivenburgh's victims? That may well be something that can never be proved. Still, I have been able to write the conclusions of many cases of the seventies that were unsolved when I first covered them.

Perhaps Joyce's story will be one of them. I hope so. But her abductor may not turn out to be Rivenburgh. Some of those closely connected to her case believe that it was her last husband who had a motive to want her gone. They had an extremely contentious relationship. Until her remains are found, it is impossible to determine whether she died at the hands of a stranger—or someone she knew.

Army Ranger Mark Rivenburgh had everything on his side when he encountered two vulnerable victims on the densely wooded trail in Mount Rainier National Park; he was trained to stalk, to kill, and to cover up his tracks. He got his "kicks" but the diligent work of the FBI and the Mount Rainier park rangers made *him* the quarry in the end.

Mark Rivenburgh served fifteen years in federal prison

and was paroled in the mid-nineties. He returned to Ulster County, New York, where his four brothers and one sister lived. He moved in with a girlfriend, got a job, and started life as a free man.

That should have been the end of this story. But it wasn't.

On May 26, 1998, twenty years—less a week and a day—since Kit Spencer and Rose Fairless were assaulted in faraway Washington State, Rivenburgh, now forty-six, lived in Marlboro, New York, in Ulster County about half-way between New York City and Albany.

One of his neighbors, Jeffery Hurd, forty-three, was newly married, and he had a very prestigious career as a research physicist at IBM.

As usual, Hurd went for a walk in the woods shortly before eight on that Tuesday evening. It was a soft spring night, still warm, and the air was redolent of honeysuckle and roses. But he hadn't returned to his home by full sunset, or for hours afterward. His worried wife asked neighbors for help in finding him.

Sadly, they did locate Jeffery Hurd. By 11:45 P.M., New York State troopers responded to their call for help. The "man down" report listed a location at the end of Reservoir Road in a very remote area of Marlboro.

Hurd was dead. He had suffered several fatal gunshot wounds. They appeared to have come from a relatively large-caliber weapon, and ballistics experts for the New York State Police identified the projectiles removed from Hurd as being from a .38-caliber revolver.

The state police investigators spoke to nearby residents,

including Mark Rivenburgh, and asked them what they might have heard or seen during the evening, and what their own activities had been. Hurd's murder was entered in their reports as an "unwitnessed crime," except, of course, by Hurd's killer.

If they hadn't actually seen the murder happen, the investigators hoped that one or more of the victim's neighbors might have seen or heard *something* that would help them locate possible suspects.

The concerned neighbors all agreed to voluntarily accompany the detectives back to the state police barracks for further questioning.

It was shortly after 1 A.M. when Mark was led to an interview room. He was not a suspect at this point—no more than any of the residents who lived near Reservoir Road. He wasn't handcuffed, frisked, or accused of any crime. He was free to move around freely in between questioning.

When he was asked about how he'd spent the early part of the evening, Mark recalled that he'd left home to go to the store around twenty minutes after seven. When he got there, he realized that he had lost his wallet.

"I went to my mom's to look," he said, "and then to my job—but I didn't find it. I finally went back home. That's when I heard that Jeffery Hurd was missing."

It was close to 3:30 A.M. on May 27 when Rivenburgh admitted to the state police detectives that he owned several rifles. This was, of course, in violation of his parole, and he knew it. Still, he agreed to sign a written statement agreeing that he did own those rifles. As a federal parolee, he nodded as he listened to his rights under Miranda, and he stated he was quite familiar with the warnings and understood them.

With his background of violence, Mark Rivenburgh *was* a natural suspect. That was a given. However, he didn't appear nervous about being questioned. He didn't ask to leave the interview room, although he would later claim on an appeal that he had been subjected to "custodial interrogation" without ever being read his Miranda rights.

The New York police detectives questioned him off and on until 6:30 A.M. At that time they asked him if he would tell them again about his lost wallet. They had noticed that he had bulges in his pants pockets, and they wondered if one of them held his wallet.

Agreeably, Mark Rivenburgh emptied his pockets. There was no wallet, but he was carrying a pouch of .38-caliber bullets, something considerably more incriminating than a lie about his wallet.

At this point he was arrested. To be sure he understood, the interviewers once again read the Miranda warnings. He said he understood he could stop questioning, he could call an attorney, and that anything he said from this point on might be used against him in any court procedure. The New York State troopers searched him more thoroughly. As they frisked him, they felt a hard lump in the small of his back. When they lifted his shirt, they uncovered a loaded .38-caliber handgun strapped to the back of his waistband.

It was somewhat unnerving for them to realize he had

been armed and carrying about forty rounds of ammunition all the time they were questioning him.

Mark Rivenburgh admitted that he'd purchased the gun several years earlier, but he said he had no choice.

"It goes everywhere with me," he said firmly.

"How about your wallet?"

"That was a lie. I didn't lose it."

When they lifted the cuffs of his trousers, the state police interrogators saw that the onetime Ranger's socks had partially dried dark stains on them. Criminalists later identified those as blood that had the exact DNA pattern of Jeffery Hurd.

The bullets removed from Hurd's body proved to have been fired from the .38-caliber revolver that Mark Rivenburgh always carried. There was no question that Rivenburgh had shot his neighbor, probably in cold blood.

But why? What was his motivation to kill Jeffery Hurd? Whether it was true or only Rivenburgh's imagination, he had been voluble as he complained to neighbors—as he now told state police detectives—that he resented Hurd. He claimed that the physicist had taken certain items from his house without any authorization to do so.

Most physicists earn well over a hundred thousand dollars a year. It seemed unlikely that a man who had such a well-paying and respected job as Hurd would have any need or motive to steal from Rivenburgh.

This time, Mark Rivenburgh did not remain free on bail. He was held in the Ulster County Jail in Kingston, awaiting trial for the murder of Jeffery Hurd.

There were many delays. Almost a year later, on the first weekend in May 1999, Rivenburgh was three days away from his pretrial hearing. Everything seemed normal as he strolled out into "the Yard" at the county jail, just as he always did for his weekly one-hour exercise session. He carried a wooden "sit-up" board that some inmates put up against the twelve-foot concrete walls to make that exercise tougher as they worked to maintain "washboard abs."

Mark Rivenburgh was in excellent physical shape. Even though he was forty-seven, he prided himself on staying in "Ranger condition." At 10:45 that particular Saturday morning, however, he had another use for the board. Before corrections officers could stop him, he used it to get up and over the wall in less than a minute.

Even the many layers of razor wire didn't slow him down. His next hurdle was an eighteen-foot jump off a roof. He could hear guards shouting at him to stop, but he leapt anyway. Encountering two corrections officers on the ground, he fought with them briefly before he managed to break free again.

A pond lay ahead of him, and he plunged in, swimming strongly for the other side. But the officers could swim as well as he could and the water chase began. They caught up with Rivenburgh on the other side.

Finally, he gave up.

On top of the other crimes he was charged with, the former Ranger now faced charges of first-degree escape, and he was forbidden to leave his cell—except, of course, to attend his trial for murder.

Although his lawyer warned him against testifying—as

the majority of defense attorneys do—Mark Rivenburgh insisted on taking the witness stand. He told the jury that he had good reason to carry a gun because a certain underground group had threatened him and made him fear for his life. It was possible he was attempting to raise questions about his sanity under the M'Naghten Rule. If that was the case, it didn't work.

There had been a paucity of physical evidence in the crimes against Kit Spencer and Rose Fairless in 1978. There were no DNA matches then, but this time the prosecution team was armed with both DNA evidence and ballistics results that could not be explained away.

On Thursday, June 24, 1999, an Ulster County jury deliberated for only four hours before they signaled that they had reached a verdict in the murder trial of Mark Rivenburgh for the shooting of Jeffery Hurd. They found him guilty of second-degree murder, third-degree criminal possession of a weapon, and several other charges, not the least of which was first-degree escape. He was sentenced to consecutive terms of twenty-five years to life on the murder charge and seven years on the weapons charge. That meant thirty-two years in prison.

Mark Rivenburgh would be almost eighty years old before he might be considered for parole.

He appealed his conviction in 2003, and on November 13, the Supreme Court of New York, Appellate Division, concurred with the lower court. They did, however, find some merit in Rivenburgh's objection to the Ulster County Court's allowing a state police trooper to testify about a series of unsolved crimes—rapes and robberies—

in an adjacent county. Although the jury didn't know about his sexual crimes in Washington State, there was, the Supreme Court said, a possible inference by the state that Rivenburgh was a prime suspect in those more recent cases.

Perhaps he was. Perhaps there was another sexual stalker who used MOs so similar to Rivenburgh's 1978 assaults.

At any rate, his appeal of the conviction for Jeffery Hurd's murder was denied.

Mark Rivenburgh remains in prison as this is written. He is now sixty years old. One has to wonder why a young soldier, chosen among the "cream of the crop," veered so far off what he seemed to be. His superiors deemed him an outstanding army Ranger, but he threw it all away in his obsession with sexual and murderous violence.

NO ONE KNOWS
WHERE WENDY IS

I wrote another case that involved the military complex that stretches south from Tacoma, Washington. It is
very different from the Mark Rivenburgh cases, and far
more likely to break our hearts. Still, this is a cautionary
tale that every parent or caregiver should read. We don't
always know the people who live or spend time in close
proximity to us. And, too often, we trust someone we
shouldn't.

Until October 2010, Fort Lewis, McChord Air Force
Base, and Madigan Military Hospital were separate enti-
ties, but it was inevitable that they would one day merge.
They have become one of twelve joint bases in the world,
known now as JBLM (Joint Base Lewis-McChord).

This joint base is a community unto itself, the second-
largest military installation in the country, with dozens
of divisions, each with its own specifications and duties.
As with every huge military base, businesses have pro-
liferated nearby. Along Interstate 5, the freeway that runs
from the Canadian border to Tijuana, Mexico, there are
massage parlors, taverns, tawdry nightspots, dry cleaners

for uniforms, trailer parks, loan and check-cashing companies, and myriad other enterprises abounding there, all anxious to help servicemen spend their paychecks. Neon signs flash for twenty-four hours a day, luring them in.

For many service families, however, the military bases are as homey as any street in the Midwest. Family housing neighborhoods stretch out, row upon row of almost identical houses. They can be pretty basic, but residents grow gardens and add special touches that make their houses distinctive. As rank escalates, the homes become bigger, and farther apart. Majors, colonels, and up are allotted sumptuous Colonials with spreading lawns.

But there are facilities that make off-duty life better for all men and women serving our country. There are theaters, swimming pools, the BX, and other commissaries, medical facilities—everything a family needs right on the bases. The honky-tonks along the freeway are a world apart, shut off by miles of fences along the freeway.

And the joint base is almost impossible to enter for someone who has no business there. Guards man gates at all times, and visitors have to have more than adequate identification.

JBLM is "good duty," and military families who live there take advantage of the Northwest's many recreational opportunities, including camping, hiking, skiing, sledding, and deepwater fishing on the Pacific Ocean down in Grays Harbor County.

It has always been so, and on Saturday, July 10, 1976, a staff sergeant took his family out on a strawberry-picking expedition. He had spent the earlier part of the day working on a picnic table in the backyard of the duplex where they lived, a project that excited his nine-year-old step-daughter, Wendy Ann Smith, and her six-year-old brother. It seems almost impossible to realize that Wendy would be forty-five years old today. If only she hadn't trusted some-one. If only she could have seen behind his friendly smile. But nine-year-olds aren't especially skilled at detecting evil.

The sun was low in the sky at eight that evening when the berry-picking group returned to the duplex. The children were tired and dirty after their hours playing between the strawberry rows, and Wendy's mother went immediately to run a bath for the youngsters. As the water splattered into the tub, she remembered that she'd left her favorite blue sweater in the car. She asked Wendy to run out and get it.

"While you're out there, honey," she added, "get the lit-ter bag and empty it."

Wendy skipped off to the van. She retrieved her moth-er's sweater and emptied the car trash bag into a garbage can outside the duplex. Wendy's aunt, visiting from Ari-zona, was watching the beautiful blond child. But Wendy didn't come in the house. Instead, her aunt saw Wendy look up as if she recognized someone, someone just out of the aunt's range of vision.

In a moment, Wendy had dashed out of sight.

It was a normal thing, and there was nothing to be con-cerned about. Wendy would surely come in for her bath in a little while.

"It was just like she had seen someone she knew. I

ANN RULE

thought she had run off to tell the kids about the berries she'd picked," the aunt would recall later.

She could see the blue sweater on the ground between the carport and the back door of the house. It was probably going to get dirty, and she wondered why Wendy had dropped it so carelessly. She'd have to speak to her about that when she ran back in.

But Wendy didn't come in. Wendy never came back at all.

As full dark descended, her family was uneasy but still believed she must be at one of her friends' homes. They phoned all of them, and she wasn't at any of the neighboring houses. As the hours passed, Wendy's parents were frightened. Wendy was an obedient little girl, and she knew the boundaries of her play area. She knew she was always supposed to be inside the house after dark, and that, if she was ever delayed, she was to call home.

Her family members began to knock on nearby doors, but no one remembered seeing Wendy during the evening. It didn't seem possible that she could have vanished so quickly right in front of her aunt's eyes, yet she was gone.

The fact that Wendy was an exceptionally beautiful child could not be denied; they tried to fight down their fear that she had been abducted by a sexual offender whose perverted fantasies were directed toward little girls, but it wasn't easy. They had warned Wendy hundreds of times that she must never get into a stranger's car, but now they wondered if she'd forgotten. If someone had enticed her with candy or perhaps the promise of a pet, she might have gone with them. She loved animals, and she was, after all, just a little girl.

Long before midnight, Wendy's stepfather called the base's Office of Special Investigations and asked for help. OSI investigators went immediately to the family's residence. Her parents described the clothing Wendy was wearing: baby blue knit pants, and a dark flowered shirt. She was four feet tall, and weighed just sixty-five pounds, and she had long blond-brown hair and brown eyes.

Asked if she might have run away, Wendy's parents shook their heads. They stressed that she was a happy child.

"We had a wonderful day," her stepfather said. "Nothing happened that would have upset her or given her the idea to run away. She was here, she was happy, and then she was gone."

By morning, the whole base knew that a child was missing. While other mothers in the military complex kept their children within eyesight, they checked their own areas, looking for Wendy. They searched storage sheds, discarded appliances, anything that might hide a small girl.

Volunteers, under the direction of the Tacoma Explorer Scouts' Search and Rescue Unit, marked off an area within a three-mile radius of Wendy's home. After sniffing some of the clothing she'd worn the day before and her hairbrush, bloodhounds tracked Wendy's scent to a playfield near the duplex and then they lost it. That might mean she had gotten into a car.

Two hundred searchers combed every inch of the huge circle, and yet they didn't find one trace of the missing child. Although it seemed unlikely that Wendy would have wandered toward the three lakes in the region so late in the evening, scuba divers searched each one. They were thankful they didn't find her there.

Each of the nine hundred houses on the air force base was checked in a methodically coordinated plan. Yet Wendy was in none of them, and no one had seen her.

By Monday, the base commander, Colonel Robert H. Campbell, told the press that "an abduction by car has got to be pretty high in our consideration."

But who could have taken Wendy away in a car? Why hadn't she screamed for help? Had someone been watching the pretty blond child for a long time, and had that person been waiting for her to come home after the strawberry picking?

Maybe it was someone Wendy knew—or at least recognized—so that she wouldn't have been afraid to walk toward them. Her aunt said again that it seemed as though Wendy had looked up and appeared to know whoever stood too far from the window for her to see.

Or had it been a stranger, a wicked stranger, who just happened to be driving by as Wendy finished the errands her mother had asked her to do? Probably not, unless that individual had a car that Wendy thought was familiar. She had run off willingly.

Toward what?

Her mother and stepfather tried to think of anyone they knew who acted in a peculiar manner, particularly if they had seemed particularly obsessed with Wendy. But there simply wasn't anyone.

Military investigators located Wendy's birth father, who was living in a southern state. He said he hadn't seen her in years, and her mother verified that. Moreover, he was just as worried as everyone else, and he had witnesses to prove that he hadn't left Florida.

That was a blow, because finding out that her own father had taken her away would have been the only "safe" reason for Wendy to be gone. He loved her.

Although Wendy's parents knew nothing about an earlier case, the similarities chilled Pierce County sheriff's officers and Tacoma police. They remembered Anne Marie Burr. It had been a long time ago, but that case haunted them.

In the summer of 1963, Anne Marie Burr was a pretty, dependable, strawberry-blond-haired child. She lived in a home in Tacoma with her parents and younger brothers and sisters. Sometime during one summer night, Anne Marie had wakened her parents to tell them that her little sister was complaining that the cast on her broken arm itched so much that she couldn't sleep.

And that was the last time anyone ever saw Anne Marie.

When her parents woke in the morning, they found the child gone. None of her clothes, beyond her night clothing, were missing. There was no sign of a struggle, no blood, nothing. Only a window in the front of the house left slightly open.

The search for Anne Marie was just as massive as

the search for Wendy, but no one ever found her. It was the worst possible tragedy a family could endure, never knowing. Many theories were put forward. Some thought the Burr child had been kidnapped by someone who just wanted a child to raise, someone who had taken her far away and brainwashed her until she no longer remembered who she was or where she had come from.

Others pointed out the fact that nearby streets had been torn up and excavated at the time Anne Marie had vanished. They suspected that the child had been killed and hidden in one of the deep holes, her body covered with tons of dirt and pavement as the street work was completed.

And there are many who still believe that Anne Marie was the first victim of Ted Bundy, whose uncle lived close to the Burr family.

At the time Wendy disappeared, if she *were* alive, Anne Marie Burr would have been a grown woman in her twenties. *If she were alive.*

No, Wendy's family didn't know about Anne Marie, and no one wanted to tell them. They were already experiencing profound anguish.

Monday passed, and it was Tuesday with no word of Wendy. Helicopters hovered like giant dragonflies over the bases, hoping to see something from the air that they could not see on the ground. Just a glimpse of blue, or golden hair gleaming in the sunlight. Police and military police, search dogs, volunteers on foot, soldiers *and* airmen, all of them tromping through underbrush, woods, and along dirt roads from dawn until almost midnight.

They feared they were no longer trying to find a living child, although no one would admit that out loud; instead, they searched for a body. Wendy had been gone for almost four days. If she was lost, there were homes, barracks, and businesses close to where she disappeared. Unless someone was holding her captive, the chances were great that Wendy was dead. The weather was warm, but the nights were cool and she needed food and water.

Some feared that she might have been dead within minutes of the time she ran laughing out of her aunt's line of vision.

If she had been taken away in a car, as so many searchers believed, she could be anywhere, even thousands of miles away in four days. If she was still on the base at McChord or Fort Lewis, there were so many hiding places for a small girl, living or dead; acres of forest edge Fort Lewis, deliberate wilderness used for war games and to buffer the fort from nearby property.

Wendy's mother, stepfather, aunt, and little brother waited in their home on Juniper Street, unable to believe what had happened. It was as if Wendy had walked through a hole in the curtain of eternity and it had closed up behind her, leaving no trace. She had been so safe, so happy, so closely guarded and yet she was gone.

It was 10 A.M. on Wednesday, July 14, when engineer Howard Churchill, guiding a Burlington Northern train toward the little town of Rainier, glanced idly beside the tracks. He saw something there, something that looked like a store mannequin.

And then he wondered if he had actually seen a naked human body. When he reached Rainier, Churchill reported what he had seen to Garth Jones, the town marshal.

Jones called McChord with word of the report. There was a miscommunication, however, and he was told that that section of tracks ran through Fort Lewis, not McChord.

"You should call the military police at Fort Lewis," the man on the other end of the phone line said. "Your report should be made to them."

How on earth could anyone at McChord Air Force Base be unaware of the missing girl? The grim series of misunderstandings continued. The Fort Lewis police understood Jones to say that a naked man, a streaker—a popular fad in the seventies—was running beside the tracks. They drove to the area and failed to find the man, despite a thorough search of the surroundings.

It wasn't until three hours later, when a second train crew spotted the still form beside the tracks and reported it, that a clear message came through. Military police located the body of a young girl lying facedown beside the tracks.

Oddly, that area had been searched many times over, and no one had seen her before. Had someone placed her body there recently? Or was it because the undergrowth was almost impenetrable there?

"It's really thick brush in there," an army official commented to a reporter. "It would have been real easy to miss finding her."

The three hours wouldn't have mattered. The child had been dead for four or five days. Wendy's aunt sobbed as she positively identified the dead child as her niece.

Pierce County coroner Jack Davelaar announced in a breaking news flash that Wendy Ann had died of strangulation—a cord used was still tightly wound around her neck when she was found.

OSI detectives and FBI agents cordoned off the area where her body was found. Engineer Howard Churchill told them that he had made the same run the day before, and that he hadn't seen the body then.

"I guess I could have been looking in the other direction," he said. "She could have been there yesterday and I didn't see her."

The investigators couldn't find any of Wendy's clothes near the railroad tracks, but they located a sheet and a bedspread close by. The bedding was quite new and it appeared to have been in the area only a short time; it wasn't faded by the sun or mildewed by rain. Rather, it looked as if someone had wrapped the tiny victim in the bedding to transport her to the spot beside the railroad spur line. An adult body wrapped in a shroud of bedding might well have drawn notice, but a sixty-five-pound child would have made a very small bundle, and could have looked like somebody's laundry.

Special agent Ray Mathis, a spokesman for the FBI

in Seattle, announced that the federal agents were working around the clock on the case and that twenty special
agents would assist military police in tracking down clues
and leads.

Wendy's autopsy report confirmed that she had died
of strangulation by ligature. And she had been sexually
assaulted. Her time of death would have been sometime
between Saturday night or early Sunday morning.

There would be no more agonized waiting for Wendy's
family, nor was there any hope left. They had the slight comfort of knowing where she was, that she had not been held
captive or molested for very long. That wasn't much to cling
to as they wondered *who* could have killed her and *why*.

Over and over again, the FBI agents and the military
police asked about the happenings of that fatal Saturday.
There might be something, no matter how seemingly in-
consequential, that would give them a lead in a case where
there were no leads. It might not have seemed unusual at
the time, perhaps a casual encounter that would be vital
only in retrospect.

Wendy Ann's family and neighbors tried their best to
remember the moments and hours of the day. There were
so many other dependent children on base who might
be in danger; Wendy's killer had to be found fast. They
wouldn't wish their grief on any other family.

Her stepfather searched his mind, trying to remember.
Saturday morning had been taken up with building the
picnic table.

"Any visitors?" an MP asked.

The sergeant shook his head. "Well, my wife's sister,

of course. And one of our neighbor's brothers came by. He was looking after Sam's place—Sam's our next-door neighbor—and he was out on bivouac for a couple of days."

"What's his name? Sam's brother?"

"Larry—Larry Mayo. He's about twenty-three, I think. He came over and was watching me put the table together, and then he pitched in to help. He's a sheet-metal worker but he's a pretty good carpenter, too."

After they finished with the picnic table, the Smiths left for strawberry picking.

"Anyone go with you—did you talk to anyone when you were out in the fields?"

"No, nobody."

"Was Wendy afraid of anyone? Did she talk about anyone bothering her or teasing her?"

"No. I asked my wife, and she can't remember anything like that. We warned her, of course, about strangers—and she knew about that. She never said she was scared of anyone."

That made sense. Wendy had apparently seen someone she knew Saturday evening. If she had been afraid, she wouldn't have looked up and smiled and then run over to someone she apparently trusted. If that person had no part in her death, why hadn't he (or she) come forward? The news of Wendy's disappearance and finding her body was on the front page of every paper from Olympia to Seattle, on every television news broadcast.

The investigators were fielding plenty of useless leads from people who wanted to help, but they hadn't heard from anyone who might have called to her shortly before she disappeared.

Close records are kept on all armed services personnel; any man with a known history of preying on children for sexual gratification wouldn't have been able to enlist. And if child molestation occurred while they were in uniform, they would have been discharged without delay.

There was always the chance, of course, that some serviceman had sexual aberrations that none of his superiors knew about, even some dark past where he'd never been discovered.

No screening process is perfect, and the blandest smiles and most clever lies of a sociopath can form perfect masks to hide what lies within a sick mind.

There was also the chance that Wendy Ann's murderer was not service-connected at all. It wasn't wartime; civilians could come and go on the base as long as they had a reason to be there and proper identification.

But Wendy didn't know anyone off the base. Her world was inside McChord Air Force Base.

Pierce County and Tacoma police checked through their files for known sex offenders. They didn't find any with a history or MO that would link them to Wendy's killing. Pierce County detectives had arrested a pet store employee several years earlier for the murder of a young blond girl—but that man was still safely inside prison walls. To be absolutely sure, they checked and found he had not been released to any outside halfway houses or to Western State Hospital's sexual psychopaths' program, which was notorious at the time for allowing dangerous offenders out on unsupervised leaves.

Though they scoured the woods next to the tracks, investigators found no more physical evidence. Only the sheet and bedspread, and they were common brands that were sold in thousands of department stores around the country. Short of polling every one of the nine hundred homes on the base, the detectives couldn't find out where they had come from. Without probable cause, there was no way they could search every home on the base for bedding that might match. And who was to say they had come from inside the base in the first place? A stranger might have had them in his car.

Since Wendy's disappearance, her family had been flooded with calls offering help. Neighbors brought in casseroles, cakes, and pies and offered to care for Wendy's brother. Larry Mayo, who had been one of the last people to see Wendy on Saturday before she went berry picking, tried especially to help. He offered to do anything he could, but Wendy's family assured him there was nothing left to do.

Although Larry seemed earnest in his wanting to be there for them, they finally began to lose patience with him. He was always underfoot.

"He was kind of a nuisance," another neighbor said. "He seemed to be getting in the way more than helping."

Larry Mayo's connection to the case seemed odd; he would have been more help if he'd gone out with the searchers instead of camping on Wendy's family's doorstep. Maybe he felt somehow responsible because he'd been so close and hadn't seen Wendy's abduction in time to help her.

A few days after Wendy vanished, Larry had had a run-in with a Pierce County deputy sheriff over his driving. The deputy stopped Larry on a routine traffic check after he noticed he was driving erratically. Larry had identified himself and explained he was visiting the area from the Southwest. But he seemed very nervous, and the deputy found a whiskey bottle, two-thirds empty, and a .38-caliber handgun in the vehicle. Larry had a permit for the weapon, and said he didn't know that it was illegal to carry an opened liquor bottle. He got off with a warning.

The deputy asked him where he was staying, and Larry gave his brother's address on Juniper Street at McChord Air Force Base.

The address sounded familiar to the deputy, and when he checked it and found it was right next door to Wendy Smith's home, he turned the information over to army OSI agents.

The special investigators looked more closely at Larry. The tall, suntanned young man said he hadn't seen Wendy after she came home on Saturday night, and he absolutely denied having anything to do with her disappearance.

Her stepfather had told the probers that Larry Mayo was a bit of an odd duck, who had behaved somewhat strangely and made a nuisance of himself during the days after Wendy vanished. Still, he couldn't imagine that Larry would have harmed Wendy.

"We always talked," he said. "Larry and I always got along good together."

And then, Wendy's aunt remembered that she had seen Larry shortly after Wendy disappeared.

"He was putting something in the back of his brother's car," she said, with a dawning look of horror passing across her face. "At the time, it looked like laundry."

It hadn't seemed important. Not then.

Now FBI special agent John R. Kellison questioned Larry Mayo. The sheet-metal worker continued to deny any connection with Wendy's abduction, rape, and murder.

But then, suddenly, his shoulders slumped, and he looked at Kellison and said, "I wish I could borrow a gun. I'd shoot myself. I didn't mean to do it. Oh, God damn!"

Mayo finally admitted that he had seen Wendy on Saturday evening. He said that she had tagged along after him to his brother's house. She watched him clean a fish tank.

"I had been drinking beer all day," Mayo said. "I lit a cigarette and looked at Wendy, and then a funny feeling came over me."

He told Kellison that he had put down his cigarette and walked into the living room, where he obtained a piece of nylon drapery cord. When he returned to the kitchen, Wendy had her back to him, watching the fish. "I remember walking up behind her with the cord in my hand.

"I had a thousand things going on in my head," he said.

Mayo grudgingly admitted that he had made up his mind to rape Wendy minutes before he crept up behind her as she watched the fish.

From that point on, he claimed that his mind was very

503

fuzzy. He said he had blank spaces, until he recalled falling down in the hall as he was carrying Wendy to the bedroom. Once in the bedroom, he had raped her.

"I don't know where I killed her. [It might have been] in the kitchen—or the hall—or in the bedroom. I can remember hearing a 'choking sound' in the bedroom."

Later, he had wrapped Wendy Ann up in the sheets and spread and carried her to his brother's car. He drove to the spot in the woods near the railroad tracks.

There he had "abandoned her."

Mayo said he'd returned to Juniper Street and became involved in the search, and in trying to help Wendy's family.

Larry Mayo was an enigma, a pleasant-seeming man who was popular with his new neighbors. He had a good, steady job with the sheet-metal firm in Seattle. He told detectives that he had come from Texas to try to change his life. He had been a heavy drinker since he was twelve years old.

"I went from there to drugs," he said. "I had trouble with the law in Texas, and I convinced my brother to let me come up to Washington for a new start."

At first, he thought he was going to do that. He had found his job, started going to church regularly, and did chores around his brother's home.

But he'd begun to drink again.

On Saturday, July 10, while Wendy and her family were out berry picking, Mayo said, he consumed eighteen beers in six hours.

The boyishly handsome suspect said he was used to

having sex regularly when he lived in Texas, but he had no intimate girlfriends in Washington.

The outcome of his heavy drinking and having the little girl alone in his house had led to a brutal, tragic murder—even as Wendy's family watched and waited for her next door.

On July 16, Larry Allen Mayo was charged with first-degree murder with "premeditation and malice aforethought" and kidnapping and held on two hundred thousand dollars' bail in the federal section of the Pierce County Jail.

When Mayo went on trial in U.S. district judge Walter T. McGovern's federal courtroom in October, his defense didn't attempt to deny that he had killed Wendy Ann. The courtroom battle would be a battle of the psychiatrists.

Mayo's court-appointed defense attorney, Kenneth Kanev, told the jury he would prove that Mayo was mentally irresponsible when he killed Wendy to keep her from screaming.

Assistant U.S. attorney Robert Westinghouse, for the prosecution, maintained that Mayo was quite sane at the time of the murder.

Westinghouse called his witnesses: Wendy's stepfather, her aunt, and FBI agent John Kellison. Her family described how frantic they were when Wendy vanished so quickly, and their hopeless search for her. Wendy's stepfather cried as he told of how helpful Larry Mayo he had been while they were building the picnic table, and of how his family had trusted Larry. They had never suspected him of being a threat. Wendy had trusted him, too. It would have been natural for her to feel she could follow him safely into his brother's home.

FBI agent Kellison told jurors about Larry Mayo's confession, and it was entered into evidence.

Counselor Kanev said he would produce expert witnesses to testify that Mayo put the cord around Wendy's neck only to keep her from screaming, and that he had been "unable to realize that his act would result in her death."

Mayo listened impassively as Dr. Adolph Whiting, a psychiatrist, described the personality of a child killer. Whiting said that Mayo was mentally ill and not responsible for what he did at the time of the murder. He confirmed that Larry Mayo had strangled Wendy because he was afraid she would scream to summon help, but also because he feared her screams "would arouse his sympathy for her."

That made little sense and jurors as well as court watchers shook their heads, confused.

Dr. Whiting described Larry Mayo as having an immature personality, of being irresponsible and incapable of holding a job for long.

"He had engaged in a lot of antisocial acts in his past. He was lonely and under a lot of stress because he was trying to remake himself into another person."

Dr. Whiting called Mayo's mental illness "disassociation" and said that he did not have the capacity to willfully take a life. A hypnotic interview, he said, confirmed that

Mayo had "disassociated his ability to care what he did, and the ability to realize that tightening the cord around the girl's neck would kill her. He only meant to stop her screams."

Whiting attributed this to Mayo's "primitive thinking" and said he had "immature and childlike mental mechanisms in dealing with basic problems."

A second psychiatrist, Dr. Ralph Stolzheise, testified for the defense. He said that he had attempted to hypnotize Larry Mayo in an effort to let him recall why he had killed Wendy.

"I couldn't get a meaningful answer as to why he made his initial move to put down his cigarette and pick up the cord," the psychiatrist concluded.

Prosecutor Westinghouse subjected Dr. Stolzheise to a grueling cross-examination. The doctor finally allowed that hypnotism is not a universally accepted tool in psychiatric diagnosis and treatment. However, the psychiatrist said, he was confident that Mayo told the truth during the critical portions of the hypnotic interview.

A psychiatrist called by the state testified that Mayo was neither disassociated nor mentally deranged at the time of the murder.

"Mayo had to elect to walk into the living room to pick up the cord, walk back to the kitchen where the girl was, place it around her neck, and strangle her," Westinghouse told the jury. "That, ladies and gentlemen, is premeditation. That is murder in cold blood."

Defense attorney Kanev told the jurors that if they should find Mayo sane, they should find him guilty of manslaughter because he killed Wendy "without malice aforethought."

The plea of temporary insanity, diminished responsibility, is a common theme in murder defenses. The number of confessed murderers who later say they committed murder in a "dream" state is legend. Under the M'Naghten Rule, a killer has to be so deranged that he does not realize he is committing a crime, cannot tell right from wrong, *at the exact moment* of his murders.

And who can really know what the state of someone else's mind is at any precise time?

Credulity is stretched a great deal when a murderer almost immediately regains his sanity and cleverly covers his crime. Larry Mayo had enough stability to carry Wendy from his home, wrapped in sheets to make her look like a bundle of laundry. He had enough sanity to hide her body in a deserted area, enough to go to her home and offer to help in the search, enough to hang around her home and play the part of the sympathetic friend. If he was insane, he had it under perfect control.

Wendy never got a chance to tell what happened that night. Those who knew her feel it is doubtful that she would have willingly followed Larry Mayo into his brother's house. It is far more likely that he used some kind of ruse or trick to make her run after him. Once he had her captive inside, she would have been helpless as she struggled to leave and go back to her family.

Only Larry Mayo knows what really happened, and his version seems fashioned to make him look as a "victim" of his own disturbed mind.

On October 8, 1976, the federal jury rejected Larry Mayo's plea of insanity and found him guilty of murder in the first degree. They acquitted him of kidnapping, the charge that stemmed from his carrying the child into a bedroom to sexually assault her after he choked her with the drapery cord.

First-degree murder carries a maximum penalty of life imprisonment. Had he been acquitted on grounds of insanity, he would have walked out of the courtroom a free man.

Life in prison rarely means true life in prison, and that was even more true in the seventies. Even so—thirty-six years after Wendy Smith died—Larry Mayo is in prison in a state far from where he killed Wendy. Unfortunately his prison counselor has failed to respond to my requests for information about his status or parole date. He may still be serving his life sentence for Wendy's murder, or he may have re-offended and been sent behind the walls for another crime.

The departments of prisons and parole in many states are quite willing to notify interested parties when felons come up for parole. Anyone reading this who would like to be notified on the status of someone who still frightens them should contact their state's prison and parole department.

Acknowledgments

With every book I write, I am aware of how important it is that people involved—either directly or by unpredictable chance—share their stories and feelings with me. And I so appreciate that they do! Eighty-five percent of my time, I am writing a book and it can be lonely; writing has to be a solitary pastime. But not always an isolated one. So when I thank people who help me, they range from investigators, prosecutors, survivors and their families, my own family, friends, editors and agents, and unexpected tipsters who share important confidences.

Each book—and this is number thirty-three—is a microcosm of my life, opening and closing as the pages begin and end. A trial is the same. There are several people I mention in every book because, God bless them, they are always there for me.

Gerry Hay, Shirley Hickman, Donna Anders, Carol Lovall, Barb Thompson, Kate Jewell, Kathleen Huget, Cindy Wilkinson, Anne Jaeger, the courageous volunteers and staff at Family and Friends of Violent Crime Victims and Missing Persons, The Jolly Matrons—friends since college—Barbara Easton, Eilene Schultz, and all the ARFs (Ann Rule Fans).

Anne Bremner, Misty Scott, Chuck and Judy Cox, Anne Cox, Mary, Denise, and Marie Cox, Pam Cox, Laurie Nielsen and Jennifer Powell Graves. Ed Troyer, Paul Pastor, Mark Lindquist, Gary Sanders, Lynette Smith, Brad Owen, Steve Gonzales, Ben Benson, Denny Wood, and Steve Downing. Mary and Doug Loehner, Cyril and Ben Wecht, and Dawna Kaufmann.

Laura, Rebecca, Miya, Amari, and Matt Harris. Leslie and Glenn Scott, Andy Rule and Lindsey Galand, Mike, Marie, Holland, and Grey Michael Rule, Bruce, Machel, Olivia, Tyra and Logan Sherles, and Pat and new baby girl Cara Jean Kelly.

When I wrote my last book, I had Waters & Wood construction crews demolishing and rebuilding over my head and under my feet, but as long as they didn't cut off my power, I wrote. That was true of this book, too. Some talented and hardy folks built me another wing, sloshing through wind and rain to do it, and it gives me much more room to breathe—and write. In no particular order to an outstanding group effort: Mark T. Brooks, Ray Delduca, Mike Hughes, Debby Royce, Mike Aromin, Jeff Keehr, Lee Barnhart, Tim Haisch, Mark Kerkoff, Bobbie Fritcher, Ty Pendergraft, Jamie Carter, Francisco Diaz, Brian Franchini, Amy Olsen, Dave Mehl, Kristi Roberson, Eric Hamilton, Don Wilde, Michele Healy, Joy Mitchell, Tim Miller, John Edwards, Dave Myers, Kyle Carbary, Jose Perez, Christopher Timpson, Kevyn Boudreau, Jeff Cundiff, Esteban

Flores, and project manager/problem solver—always—Bryce Salzman.

I am a lucky woman indeed to have the backup of my lifetime agents, Joan and Joe Foley, *and* my publishing team at Pocket Books and Free Press, who have nudged me patiently to the finish line of thirty-three books! I have learned so much from all of them: Louise Burke and Martha Levin, my truly supportive publishers; Mitchell Ivers, my brilliant and tactful editor, and his assistant, Natasha Simons, who always comes through when we're on deadline; and my attorney Felice Javit. Production manager Hector Rodriguez Jr., production editor Christine Masters, managing editor Sally Franklin, copyeditor Tom Pitoniak, proofreaders Polly Watson and Annette Szlachta, art director Lisa Litwack, and book designer Kyle Kabel.

Seattle is a long way from New York City but it feels as though my friends at Simon & Schuster are just the next block over.

And, finally, my writing pets: Willow, the Bernese mountain dog, and Toonces, K.C., and Poppy, the very intelligent cats. They all gather around me when I work, and they're good company but somewhat intrusive as they step on the keyboard of my computer.